SHELLEY AND SCRIPTURE

The Interpreting Angel

BRYAN SHELLEY

CLARENDON PRESS · OXFORD

1994

Oxford University Press, Walton Street, Oxford OX2 6DP
Oxford New York Toronto
Delhi Bombay Calcutta Madras Karachi
Kuala Lumpur Singapore Hong Kong Tokyo
Nairobi Dar es Salaam Cape Town
Melbourne Auckland Madrid
and associated companies in
Berlin Ibadan

Oxford is a trade mark of Oxford University Press

Published in the United States
by Oxford University Press Inc., New York

© Bryan Shelley 1994

British Library Cataloguing in Publication Data
Data available

Library of Congress Cataloging in Publication Data
Shelley, Bryan.
Shelley and Scripture: the interpreting angel / Bryan Shelley.
(Oxford English monographs)
Includes bibliographical references (p.) and index.
1. Shelley, Percy Bysshe, 1792–1822—Religion.   2. Christianity
and literature—History—19th century.   3. Heresies, Christian, in
literature.   4. Gnosticism in literature.   5. Bible in literature.
I. Title.   II. Series.
PR5442.R5S48   1994
821'.7—dc20   93–32348
ISBN 0–19–812284–5

1 3 5 7 9 10 8 6 4 2

Set by Hope Services (Abingdon) Ltd.
Printed in Great Britain
on acid-free paper by
Bookcraft Ltd.
Midsomer Norton, Bath

FOR
Keith and Mildred Shelley

Preface

In his Notes on *Queen Mab* (1813) Shelley writes that 'the genius of human happiness must tear every leaf from the accursed book of God, ere man can read the inscription on his heart' (*PS*, i. 373).[1] This inscription, he continues, is consonant with 'nature'. Thus he sets nature, truth, and happiness against the artificiality, falsity, and moroseness of biblical religion. What is revealing is that even in his wish to see the utter obliteration of the Scriptures, Shelley ironically expresses himself in a way that brings to mind a passage from the Bible.[2] The great apostle writes that 'when the Gentiles, which have not the law, do by nature the things contained in the law, these, having not the law, are a law unto themselves: Which shew the work of the law written in their hearts . . .' (Rom. 2: 14–15). Both Shelley and St Paul affirm that the revelation inscribed on the heart is both good and natural. They disagree over the relationship of the biblical revelation to the natural one; for the Romantic poet denies the veracity and authority of the Bible. As is the case throughout his works, he turns biblically informed language against the biblical world-view.

According to Shelley's own ideas of literary influence, there would be nothing strange in using scriptural language.[3] More than any other single source, the Bible has influenced English literature. In his 'Speculations on Metaphysics' Shelley writes that '[o]ur whole style of expression and sentiment is infected with the tritest plagiarisms. Our words are dead, our thoughts are cold and borrowed' (Jul. vii. 62). At one level—the level at which any literary corpus may be quarried, even unwittingly, for words and phrases—Shelley's observation would explain biblical influence. But as C. S. Lewis has noted, the conception of 'the Bible as literature' is misleading; for, historically, the Holy Scriptures have been regarded not as an article of *belles-lettres*, but as a

---

[1] For miscellaneous remarks about the Bible in the correspondence of the young Shelley, see *Letters*, i. 50, 55, 100, 115, 212, 215–16, 265, 277, and 348.

[2] All citations from the two canonical Testaments and from the Apocrypha will be from the Authorized Version.

[3] The subject of biblical influence and of Shelley's own hermeneutical stance toward the Scriptures will be pursued further in the Introduction.

sacred book.[4] The force and authority of the Scriptures derive from their claim to divine inspiration. And the profoundest response one can have to them is a spiritual one. Shelley describes a deeper level of influence in his *Defence of Poetry*. Here the poet records his maxim that 'no nation or religion can supersede any other without incorporating into itself a portion of that which it supersedes' (*SPP*, 496). It is a rationale similar to the one described by Thomas Paine. Paine had argued in *The Age of Reason* that the Catholic Church, in accumulating its gallery of saints, had simply adapted the Roman pantheon.[5] That Shelley's own formulation of an alternative to the Christian creed would itself be 'biblical' is therefore not remarkable, even in terms of his own notions of literary and cultural influence.

Literary allusion—the casual but ascertainable reference to a person, place, event, or text—is a Janus-headed phenomenon. It places the reader on familiar ground, as Wolfgang Iser has observed, but it also orients him toward a new meaning. The fact that allusions are lifted from one context and placed in another indicates that they cannot simply duplicate meaning.[6] All allusion, then, is interpretive. It may rely on verbal proximity, typically in the form of a quotation or paraphrase, or it may deal with content alone.[7] But the new context determines its significance. This is all the more so in the case of Shelley's reading of the Bible, since the Romantic poet intentionally deviates from the orthodox understanding of the text.

Shelley's relation to the biblical faith was the subject of two books published in the 1930s. In his study of Shelley's use of biblical materials, Bennett Weaver claimed to have found in Shelley's essay 'On Christianity' a fundamental 'kinship with the spirit of the New Testament'.[8] His Jesus, however, was more of a social reformer than the incarnation of God. Weaver joined Shelley to the prophetic tradition

---

[4] 'The Literary Impact of the Authorised Version', in *They Asked for a Paper* (London, 1962), 27, 46–7. My practice in this study will be to indicate first references to a given source in a footnote, but to note subsequent references parenthetically in the text in most cases.

[5] *The Complete Writings of Thomas Paine*, ed. P. S. Foner (2 vols.; New York, 1945), i. 467.

[6] *The Act of Reading*, trans. D. Wilson (London, 1978), 79.

[7] An echo, as Lucy Newlyn considers the term, is 'heard within the mind as distinctly recalling or reproducing an original pattern of sound, rhythm, or language' (*Coleridge, Wordsworth, and the Language of Allusion* [Oxford, 1986], p. viii). Newlyn sensibly points out that maintaining a clear distinction between 'allusion' and 'echo' is difficult, preferring to view the latter as 'less sustained' than the former (p. ix).

[8] *Toward the Understanding of Shelley* (1932; New York, 1966), 104.

which denounced clerical corruption and demanded social justice (pp. 59–73). Ellsworth Barnard attempted in an analysis of Shelley's religion to subsume the ethical aspects of Shelley's biblical knowledge, previously conceived as either humanistic or prophetic, under the larger headings of love and imagination.[9] Both critics were well versed in Shelley's writings, and they unfailingly adduced the right primary texts. But each attempted to interpret Shelley as in some sense a Christian, either by misrepresenting the poet or by reinterpreting Christianity as a form of altruism or humanism.

In the present study, I have described Shelley's poetic career in terms of three successive phases. During the first of these periods, which lasts approximately until his departure for Italy in 1818, he is primarily concerned with the transformation of society, the biblical model for which is the period of Edenic restoration known as the millennium. The character of this transformed state is frequently defined by the biblical ideas of the Kingdom of God and by the moral teachings of both Jesus and the prophets. As Richard Cronin observes, ethical poetry is simultaneously the embodiment of the poet's character and a means of inculcating that character in others. Because the poet of ethos projects virtue from within, the attention of the reader is thus drawn to the author.[10] In the case of Shelley, there is a considerable body of lore to illustrate his character of magnanimity and compassion. It is perhaps no coincidence that the tales of Shelley's acts of charity tend to centre on the time of his residence at Marlow (1817–18). Peacock, who saw Shelley frequently during this period, records that during a walk through a village churchyard, Shelley once made an astonishing confession:

'I feel strongly inclined to enter the Church.' 'What,' I said, 'to become a clergyman, with your ideas of the faith?' 'Assent to the supernatural part of it', he said, 'is merely technical. Of the moral doctrines of Christianity I am a more decided disciple than many of its more ostentatious professors. And consider for a moment how much good a good clergyman may do.'[11]

Shelley's fondness for the Christian ethos can be seen in his major work of this period, *The Revolt of Islam*, particularly in Laon's forgiveness of the tyrant Othman (V. xxx–xxxvi). The poet never abandons his affirmation of the Bible's moral teaching about love; but two factors

---

[9] *Shelley's Religion* (Minneapolis, Minn., 1937).

[10] *Shelley's Poetic Thoughts* (London, 1981), 110.

[11] *Memoirs of Shelley* (1875), in *The Life of Percy Bysshe Shelley*, ed. H. Wolfe (London, 1933), ii. 327.

compel him to refine it. One is the problem of the self, its lusts and its
acquisitiveness, which he explores as early as *Queen Mab*. The other is
the awareness of a culturally Protestant identity resulting from his move
to Italy. What Protestant theology had long emphasized was the need
for personal regeneration of the self. Thus Shelley's second period
(1818–20) is one of defining the self, or mind ($\nu o\tilde{v}\varsigma$), and exploring its
own potential for regeneration. Analogous to this is the Christian idea
of repentance ($\mu\epsilon\tau\acute{a}\nu o\iota a$), which, by its etymology, has reference to
the operation of the mind and therefore has a bearing on the leading
work of this period, *Prometheus Unbound*.

The ultimate effect of this tendency toward introspection is the
unveiling of the spiritual (pneumatic) self. In Shelley's final period
(1820–2), this self may be metaphorized as the God-like power which
'creates' the world. Yet the spiritual self increasingly realizes that its
kingdom is not of this world and longs to transcend it. Ross Woodman
has observed of Shelley's visionary works that 'his desire to reform the
world is always crossed by a desire to transcend it'.[12] The statement
seems especially relevant to the poetry of Shelley's third period. As we
shall see, it is the yearning to escape the cosmic dungeon that triumphs
in the poems of his final year. The alteration in perspective from the
temporally oriented progressivism in his first phase to the movement of
transcendence in the latter is marked by a generic shift from the model
of prophetic literature—with its vision of a millennium and its ethical
concern for social justice—to that of apocalyptic, with its visions of an
obliterated temporal order giving way to an eternal realm.

The mode of apocalypse as an unveiling of the spiritual self and of
that self's ultimate estrangement from the mundane world thus arises
from the tendency of the mind to arrogate to itself all objective reality.
As in the book of Revelation, Shelley's renovated social order is ulti-
mately realized in an ideal, eternal sphere. My plan in the present study
is to analyse this three-stage development in Shelley's career as poet and
theoretician. The outline should not obscure the fact that my general
method is to provide readings of Shelley's poems in the light of their
biblical content. For this reason, many of the other literary and philo-
sophical influences on Shelley are either omitted from the discussion or
given a more or less attenuated treatment. My goal is to assess the bibli-
cal element in terms of the poet's own religious outlook. Because
Shelley could simultaneously reject Christianity and yet affirm many of

---

[12] *The Apocalyptic Vision in the Poetry of Shelley* (Toronto, 1964), 189.

its ideals, I have concluded that it is essential to establish a hermeneuti-
cal basis for his reading of the Bible. In the introductory chapter, I have
attempted to do so by presenting Gnosticism as a revisionist impulse;
for Shelley informs us at the outset of his fragment 'The Assassins' that
Christianity, purified of its cultural and doctrinal accretions, is similar to
the creed of the Gnostics.[13]

The question of 'influence' therefore involves both a hermeneutical
posture and a guiding theology. I acknowledge with C. S. Lewis that
choices in diction, imagery, the use of embedded quotations, and sen-
tence rhythms may all be valid gauges of what is known as biblical
influence (pp. 38–41). But I am not primarily concerned with specula-
tion into the relative significance of such terms as 'allusion', 'echo',
'quotation', or 'paraphrase'. Nor does this study feature, as have similar
studies, any system of classifying such items or tabulating the frequency
of their occurrence.[14] Since such schemes of classification invariably
entail an element of arbitrariness, I have avoided making one up, and
have simply appended to this book a list of biblical glosses on Shelley's
poetry for the student or scholar who is interested in pursuing the sub-
ject further. Many of these are discussed in the text. I should add that
since my interest in Shelley's use of the Bible has more to do with the
literary adaptation of biblical images and ideas than with the prose criti-
cism of the Bible which occurs sporadically in his works, I do not deal
extensively with this commentary. Since the content of Shelley's bibli-
cal criticism is largely derivative, it is discussed in the context of either
the sources from which it appears to have been drawn or the poetry
itself.

That Shelley was an eclectic reader will be evident in the pages that
follow. That he was a syncretist fabricator of myth, uniting biblical and
classical elements, is borne out by analysis. The syncretist mythology of
the eighteenth and nineteenth centuries revealed a range of speculative
possibilities for the creative application of learning. One of its most
influential representatives, Jacob Bryant, claimed that by looking at
Gentile histories of 'the infancy of the world' beside the Pentateuch, he

---

[13] A Gnosis is a scheme of knowledge which emancipates the spirit from the corrup-
tion of the world. 'Gnosticism' refers to the syncretist heresies of late antiquity derived
from the various schools of Gnosis. The Gnostic perspective on the Scriptures and its rel-
evance to the study of Romantic literature will be considered in the Introduction.

[14] See Bennett Weaver, 'Shelley's *Biblical Extracts*', *Papers of the Michigan Academy of
Sciences, Arts, and Letters*, 20 (1934), 523–38; and Travis Looper, *Byron and the Bible*
(Metuchen, NJ, 1978).

could vindicate the 'sacred penman'.[15] But what he in fact revealed was an ingenious capacity for making associations on the basis of features which resembled each other. Noah, for example, was Zeus. Bryant arrived at this conclusion by synthesizing various Middle Eastern traditions of the great flood. *Xuthus* (the flood-survivor in one such legend) was transmuted into *Theuth, Zuth, Zeuth,* and finally *Zeus* (ii. 198–9). But Noah was also Dionysus, since both could be associated with the origins of wine (ibid.). The glory of syncretism, as Thomas Blackwell explained it, was that 'Mythology confines you to no Creed, nor pins you down to a Set of Principles'.[16] Such a perspective is especially relevant to Shelley. The new mythology could be used either to validate the biblical record or to reduce it to the level of an archetypal pattern, as Albert Kuhn has shown. Bryant, Kuhn observes, used it to show that primitive myths were derived from biblical sources, while a sceptic like Sir William Drummond employed the same method to level Christianity to the stature of other religions.[17] Shelley was an admirer of Drummond's philosophy, and Donald Reiman has recently shown that his formulations of myth are in fact an outgrowth of his own sceptical impulses.[18] This scepticism, however, does not in the least diminish Shelley's admiration for the book most frequently denigrated as 'mythical' by the *philosophes*—the Bible.

[15] *A New System, or, an Analysis of Ancient Mythology,* 2nd edn. (3 vols.; London, 1775–6), i. p. v.

[16] *Letters concerning Mythology* (London, 1748), 120.

[17] 'English Deism and the Development of Romantic Mythological Syncretism', *PMLA,* 71 (1956), 1095. Marilyn Butler, on the other hand, emphasizes the revolutionary aspect of the mode, viewing it as an attempt to equate all religions, and thus to belittle orthodox Christianity. See 'Myth and Mythmaking in the Shelley Circle', *Journal of English Literary History,* 49 (1982), 56.

[18] *Intervals of Inspiration* (Greenwood, Fla., 1988), 260–1. The synthesis of biblical elements with esoteric and classical myths is discussed in a consideration of Gnostic uses of Scripture in the Introduction.

Acknowledgements

I am deeply indebted to a variety of friends and scholars on both sides of the Atlantic in the preparation of this study. Its inception owes something to the influence of my undergraduate mentor, R. M. Cornelius. For information on the Shelley family Bibles I thank the staff of the Carl H. Pforzheimer Collection in the New York Public Library. I am also grateful to Bruce Barker-Benfield and the staff of the Bodleian Library of Oxford University for courteous assistance over a period of several years. Carlene Adamson has graciously allowed me to consult her transcription of Shelley's notes on the gospel of Luke (Bodleian MS Shelley adds. e. 9). Tatsuo Tokoo provided me with copies of his helpful summary and index of the contents of Shelley's Bodleian notebooks. Caroline Dalton, Assistant Archivist of New College, Oxford, helped ascertain some data pertaining to the poet's distant kinsman Thomas Shelley, Fellow of New College. Timothy Webb kindly directed me to the little-known fragment of Shelley's on the subject of Zionism, and made numerous suggestions for the improvement of this study in its conversion from a doctoral thesis to a published book. For translation assistance from Japanese I acknowledge Koji Fusa. Both Stephen Gill and Neil Fraistat read portions of the work in its early stages.

Despite my criticism of the pioneer studies by Bennett Weaver and Ellsworth Barnard on Shelley's relation to the biblical tradition, I have none the less profited from their insights. Furthermore, I have been deeply influenced by the seminal research on the nature of Gnosticism by Hans Jonas and Eric Voegelin, and on its application to literary study by Harold Bloom, James Rieger, and Paul Cantor. To Terry Barker of Magdalen College, Oxford, I am indebted for hours of informal tutoring on the subject. I am also indebted to Lucy Hartley of the Campbell University Law School Library staff for technical and editorial assistance in preparing the final version of this manuscript. I would also like to thank the editors of *The Wordsworth Circle* and *The Review of English Studies* for granting permission to use material from articles which I had published in those journals. For moral and material support, without which this research could not have been completed, I owe an incalculable debt of gratitude to my parents, Keith and Mildred Shelley. And for years of invaluable supervision, I am thankful to Roy Park of University College, Oxford. Finally, I am especially grateful to Donald H. Reiman, who read several of the chapters in their original form and who took time from a busy schedule to read this manuscript and make a number of suggestions for improving it.

Hendersonville, North Carolina

Contents

Abbreviations

BSM   *The Bodleian Shelley Manuscripts*, gen. ed. Donald H. Reiman (13 vols. to date; New York and London: Garland, 1986–92).

JMS   *The Journals of Mary Shelley: 1814–1844*, ed. Paula R. Feldman and Diana Scott-Kilvert (2 vols.; Oxford: Clarendon Press, 1987).

Jul.   *The Complete Works of Percy Bysshe Shelley*, The Julian Edition, ed. Roger Ingpen and Walter Edwin Peck (10 vols.; London: Benn, 1926–30).

K–SJ   *Keats–Shelley Journal*

K–SMB   *Keats–Shelley Memorial Bulletin*

K–SR   *Keats–Shelley Review*

Letters   *The Letters of Percy Bysshe Shelley*, ed. Frederick L. Jones (2 vols.; Oxford: Clarendon Press, 1964).

Plat.   James A. Notopoulos, *The Platonism of Shelley: A Study of Platonism and the Poetic Mind* (Durham, NC: Duke University Press, 1949).

PMLA   Publications of the Modern Language Association of America

PS   *The Poems of Shelley*, ed. Geoffrey Matthews and Kelvin Everest (1 vol. to date; London and New York: Longman, 1989).

PW   *The Prose Works of Percy Bysshe Shelley*, ed. E. B. Murray (1 vol. to date; Oxford: Oxford University Press, 1993).

SHC   *Shelley and his Circle, 1773–1822*, The Carl H. Pforzheimer Library, ed. Kenneth Neill Cameron (vols. i–iv) and Donald H. Reiman (vols. v–viii) (8 vols.; Cambridge, Mass.: Harvard University Press, 1961–86).

SPP   *Shelley's Poetry and Prose*, ed. Donald H. Reiman and Sharon B. Powers (New York: Norton, 1977).

SPW   *Shelley: Poetical Works*, ed. Thomas Hutchinson, 2nd edn. rev. G. M. Matthews (Oxford: Oxford University Press, 1970).

Given the current availability of a number of partially complete editions of Shelley's poetry and prose, it has been necessary to cite a number of texts in this study. Primarily, I quote from the Longman edition of Shelley's poetry (*PS*) in the case of the early poems and the Norton edition (*SPP*) for the later works. For works not included in either of these editions, I cite the Oxford Standard Author's edition (*SPW*). The sources for prose citations will be indicated parenthetically. For Shelley's earlier prose works, I quote from the available volume of the Oxford edition (*PW*). The text for the later prose is that of the Norton edition and *SHC*. In the case of some of the minor works not included in the above sources, I cite the Julian edition. Further reference is made to Shelley's manuscript notebook materials published in *BSM* and in the *Manuscripts of the Younger Romantics* by Garland Publishing Company. For Shelley's translations of Plato, I quote from the texts provided by James A. Notopoulos in *Plat*. And for all Shelley's letters, I cite the two-volume Oxford edition (*Letters*).

Introduction: Shelley's 'Gnostic' Assassins and the Reinterpretation of Christianity

Shelley's observation that no nation or religion can supersede another without borrowing heavily from it suggests a rationale for his own appropriation of biblical phraseology, imagery, and symbols. The fragmentary romance 'The Assassins' (c.1814) provides a major insight into the working of this rationale; for in this story, Shelley delineates the character of a Christianity which, in the pristine form he imagines, is free of the supernaturalist dogmas with which it came to be encumbered. He effects this revision of Christianity in a remarkably ingenuous way. In the first place, he confuses a community of primitive Christians with a radical Islamic sect. The Assassins were a branch of Ismaili Shiite Muslims—a group which, although regarded as heretical in the Middle Ages, was none the less able to survive into the twentieth century. In 1814, when Shelley began writing his story, it was reported that leaders of the Ismaili sect (which was then frequently identified as the Assassins) had been students of astrology and magic, and that Ismaili doctrine included belief in the transmigration of the soul, which was thought to be confined in the body as in a prison.[1] As we know from the main source which Shelley cites, the historical Assassins believed in blind obedience to their Imam, on whom they believed the Holy Spirit had descended.[2] Shelley's Assassins are quite different, for they subscribe to the liberty of individual reason.

In the second place, Shelley's misapprehension is compounded by his statement that the views of these Christian Assassins resembled those of the Gnostics (*PW*, i. 124). It must be noted that the similarity of Gnosticism to the religion of the Assassins was great, but not to that of

---

[1] Etienne-Marc Quatremère, 'Notice historique sur les Ismaëliens', *Mines de l'Orient*, 4 (1814), 341, 368. According to E. B. Murray, the story was probably written between Aug. 1814 and Apr. 1815. See 'The Dating and Composition of Shelley's *The Assassins*', *K–SJ*, 34 (1985), 14–17.

[2] See M. Falconet, 'Dissertation sur les Assassins, peuple d'Asie', *Mémoires de littérature tirés des registres de l'Académie royale des inscriptions et belles-lettres*, 17 (1751), 149–50. Under Mary Shelley's journal entry for 8 Apr. 1815, Shelley acknowledges Falconet's article (*JMS*, i. 73).

the Assassins described by Shelley. The poet's 'Gnostic' Assassins are pacific, egalitarian, philanthropic, benevolent, just, and inquisitive. They are contemptuous of the masses and their institutions, and believe human understanding to be the arbiter of morality. They are worshippers of the god of Nature and opponents of falsehood and vice. In short, they are disciples of Jesus along the lines established in Shelley's essay 'On Christianity'. What is interesting is that the poet sees such traits as 'Gnostic'. Implicitly, he sees Gnosticism as synonymous with a Christianity that has been purified of its cultural accretions and misinterpretations. Shelley's incidental reference to the Gnostics thus provides a clue not only to the heterodox way that he himself read the Bible, but also to the religious sensibility behind such a reinterpretation.

In his influential study of ancient Gnostic systems, Hans Jonas defines a Gnosis as a way of knowledge which either leads to salvation or constitutes 'the form of salvation itself'.[3] Primarily, it is arcane knowledge shared by an inner circle of the elect; for Gnosticism is pre-eminently an élitist religion (p. 46). As such, it is a spiritual discipline by which one may psychologically transcend the ordinary world. Secondarily, Gnosis becomes the means of evading the demonic hierarchies which surround the world and which strive to prevent the soul from escaping it after death (pp. 45, 167–8). In Gnosticism, the cosmos is perceived as defective and hopelessly corrupt, for matter is inherently fallen. The universe becomes analogous to a prison from which one must escape (p. 43). In Gnostic anthropology, the individual spirit ($\pi\nu\epsilon\hat{v}\mu\alpha$) which is infected by this world order lies in a state of ignorant torpor. 'Knowledge', or illumination, is the means of emancipating it from the bondage of worldliness and leading it back to the realm of light from which it had fallen (p. 44).

As a syncretist religion of late antiquity, the philosophy of Gnosticism was similar in many respects to Platonism and Neoplatonism. But what Gnosticism had and its rival systems lacked was a comprehensive revisionist stance toward the Jewish and Christian Scriptures. It is therefore potentially of great use in understanding Shelley's religious thought, and contemporary critics have introduced it as a means of understanding the poet's unique spirituality. Shelley has been considered recently in the light of Ophite, Valentinian, Hermetic, and Manichaean schools of Gnosticism.[4] However, these arguments for Shelley's affinity to

---

[3] *The Gnostic Religion*, 2nd edn. (1963; Boston, 1970), 32. See also Giovanni Filoramo, *A History of Gnosticism*, trans. A. Alcock (Oxford, 1990), 142–7.

[4] See resp. James Rieger, *The Mutiny Within* (New York, 1967), 129–62; Harold

Gnosticism are not new. Long ago, Ernst Sieper interpreted 'The Assassins' and the first canto of *The Revolt of Islam*—both of which feature the image of a linguistically proficient serpent—as narratives dealing with the matter of Ophite Gnosticism, a school which employed the serpent in its celebration of the Eucharist. Sieper isolated two Shelleyan principles which he associated with the larger Gnostic movement: belief in the nobility of free thought and the defiance of human laws and conventions.[5] He argued that there was a general agreement between Shelley's views and those of the Gnostics. Yet Shelley was not in fact an adherent of any particular Gnostic system. And it is worth asking how he could be thus identified with the Gnostics. So far as we know, the elaborate mythologies of Valentinus and Basilides were unknown to him. Yet behind the complex systems of the Gnostics lay a sensibility of estrangement, a fundamental disposition to regard the world and its established creeds as hostile to the man of enlightenment. It is in this sense that a 'Gnostic' Shelley may be discerned. And it is this sense of alienation from society and its orthodoxy which informs both his idealization of Gnostic sectarian experience and his impulse to reinterpret Scripture.

The general mood of Gnosticism is consistent with the élitist strain in Shelley which develops from the sense of being an outsider. As enlightened ones, the Gnostics saw themselves as a privileged élite, distinct from the masses who remain in ignorance. Thus they resemble some of the more radical intellectuals of the eighteenth century. Such expressions as 'the common herd', 'the masses', and 'the vulgar' are frequent in the Enlightenment thinkers Shelley had read.[6] And all his life, the poet maintained the distinction between 'the vulgar' and 'the enlightened'. Correspondingly, the Gnostics partitioned humanity into two camps, one consisting of the vast herd of mankind who walk in carnality and darkness, the other comprised of the brethren who possess the

Bloom, *Poetry and Repression* (New Haven, Conn., and London, 1976), 105–6; Ernest Lee Tuveson, *The Avatars of Thrice Great Hermes* (Lewisburg, Pa., London, and Toronto, 1982), 163; and Stuart Curran, *Shelley's Annus Mirabilis* (San Marino, Calif., 1975), 127–8.

[5] 'Spuren ophitisch-gnostischer Einflüsse in den Dichtungen Shelleys', *Archiv für das Studium der neueren Sprachen und Literaturen* [*Herrigs Archiv*], 62 (1908), 315. Sieper further argues that Ophitic Gnosticism was a direct influence on some of Shelley's work. In *Mutiny Within*, Rieger refers to several critics who have discussed this question (258 n. 10).

[6] See e.g. William Godwin, *Enquiry concerning Political Justice* (1798), 3rd edn., ed. F. E. L. Priestley (3 vols.; facs. repr. Toronto, 1946), ii. 264; and David Hume, *Enquiries concerning Human Understanding and concerning the Principles of Morals* (1777), ed. L. A. Selby-Bigge (1975; Oxford, 1979), 86.

light. As Thomas Medwin testifies, there is a strong sense of this dualism in Shelley:

So sensitive was he of external impressions, so magnetic, that I have seen him, after threading the carnival crowd in the Lung' Arno Corsos, throw himself half fainting into a chair, overpowered by the atmosphere of evil passions, as he used to say, in that sensual and unintellectual crowd. Perhaps also there contributed to this feeling of despondency the thought that he also was incapable of enjoying the Carnival, that whilst all around him were busy—happy—he had nothing in common with his fellow men, that Life was meted out to him in a different measure from that of others—that he alone was the Pariah, the Outcast.[7]

Like the Gnostic separation from those uninitiated into the sectarian mysteries—itself reflecting a corruption of the biblical admonition to 'come out from among them, and be ye separate' (2 Cor. 6: 17)—the alienation of the enlightened reformer from 'the vulgar' was the inevitable consequence of being true to his inner light.[8] Thus Shelley's Assassins live in moral separation from corrupted civilization even when forced to live in its midst (PW, i. 131).

Since Shelley identifies Gnosticism with his revision of Christianity, the hermeneutical perspective of the Gnostics on the Bible ought in turn to shed some light on the poet's own use of Scripture. Jonas points out that the Gnostic imagination was pre-eminently nonconformist and speculative (p. 42). As such, it was particularly interested in the formulation of alternatives to the religion based on the sacred books of Israel and the Church. Biblical influence in the case of the Gnostics thus has reference to the Gnostic refraction of the canonical writings. The instinctive bent of the Gnostics was to read between the lines of the Bible, to discern hidden truths, and to supply mythic material not included in the Scriptures. As Paul Cantor points out, this was especially true in the case of the biblical account of creation. Cantor says that 'it is characteristically in the blank pages before the opening of Genesis that the Gnostics found the clean slate they needed for creating their new myths'.[9] Gnostic creation myths therefore have much to say about the spiritual hierarchies and events preceding creation. In the Valentinian speculation, for

---

[7] The Life of Percy Bysshe Shelley (1847), ed. H. B. Forman, rev. edn. (London, 1913), 268.

[8] Cf. the advice of Hermes Trismegistus to his pupil Tat in Hermetic lore: 'Avoyd all Conversation with the multitude or common People; for I would not have thee subject to envy, much lesse to be ridiculous unto the Many.' See the Divine Pymander, trans. J. Everard (1650; London, 1657), 12.

[9] Creature and Creator: Myth-making and English Romanticism (Cambridge, 1984), p. xii.

example, there are fifteen masculine aeons, with corresponding feminine emanations, which constitute the fullness of the godhead ($\pi\lambda\acute{\eta}\rho\omega\mu\alpha$). And disruption in the fullness culminates in the emergence of matter as fallen spiritual substance. According to Gnostic reasoning, the creation is tantamount to the Fall in the book of Genesis, simply because it is material creation. And the first step toward salvation, as Cantor says, is the acquisition of forbidden knowledge in the Garden of Eden—the traditional Fall (p. x). The principle at work here is one of inversion, of turning the orthodox account on its head, and thus allowing the Devil (or serpent) to emerge as the heroic agent of Gnosis. To illustrate this point, we may refer to the account given by the Church Father Hippolytus concerning the Gnostic sect of the Peratae.

By superimposing diverse passages dealing with the serpent motif on one another, the Peratae established a new exegesis of the Fall. For them, the rod of Moses, which was transformed into a serpent at Pharaoh's court in Exodus 4: 2–4, was a manifestation of the benign 'universal serpent'.[10] Another such epiphany was the brazen serpent held up by Moses in the wilderness (Num. 21: 9), the sight of which caused those who had been bitten by poisonous snakes to be healed (V. xi; v. 62). But the universal serpent was originally manifest in 'the wise discourse of Eve' (V. xi; v. 62). When Jesus says, 'as Moses lifted up the serpent in the wilderness, so also must the Son of man be lifted up' (John 3: 14), he thus identifies himself with the wisdom of the serpent in Eden (V. xi; v. 62–3). Peratic theology therefore conflates the Christian Logos incarnate in the man Jesus with the $\lambda\acute{o}\gamma o\varsigma$ of the serpent in Eden. Shelley would have relished such an ironic twist. Edward Trelawny noted that one of the poet's nicknames was 'the Snake'.[11] And Shelley once referred to a man tried for sacrilege at Lucca as 'my fellow serpent'.[12] In The Revolt of Islam, the morning star (Venus or Lucifer) is the astronomical portent of the Spirit of Good which becomes incarnate in the serpent (I. xxvi–xxvii).[13] But in the New

[10] Hippolytus, The Refutation of all Heresies, trans. J. H. McMahon, in The Ante-Nicene Fathers, ed. A. Roberts and J. Donaldson, rev. A. C. Coxe (10 vols., 1885–96; Grand Rapids, Mich., 1971–8), v. xi; v. 62. Referencing is by book and chapter of the original, then volume and page number of the modern edition.

[11] Recollections of the Last Days of Shelley and Byron (1858), in The Life of Percy Bysshe Shelley, ed. H. Wolfe (2 vols.; London, 1933), ii. 180–1, 187. The editors of the Norton edition of Shelley state that the nickname was 'probably a pun on the name "Bysshe Shelley" and the Italian bischelli, a small snake' (SPP, 447 n. 2).

[12] Letter to Lord Byron, 13 Dec. 1821, Letters, ii. 368.

[13] Shelley's alterations in converting Laon and Cythna, with its depiction of incest and its hostility to the Church, into The Revolt of Islam are listed in Jul. i. 421–7.

Testament, Jesus is said to be the morning star (Rev. 22: 16). Both Shelley and the Peratae reverse the traditional associations of the serpent. Hippolytus says that the Peratae saw yet another representation of the universal serpent in Cain. The god of this world (Yahweh of the Old Testament) refused to accept Cain's vegetable sacrifice because he rejoices in sacrifices of blood (V. xi; v. 62–3). In *The Revolt of Islam*, Shelley's serpentine Spirit of Good comes in his wanderings to be cursed 'among / The nations of mankind' (I. xxviii. 4–5), as was Cain. The triumph of the tyrannous fiend, who becomes the god of this world, causes brother to slay brother, as Cain slew Abel (I. xxvi. 9). The God of the Old Testament thus becomes Shelley's devil, and the poet names him Legion after the Gadarene maniac who was possessed by demons (I. xxix. 1).[14]

Because of this common tendency to reverse the roles of the serpent and Cain in Genesis, it is tempting to imagine the direct influence of either the Peratae or a similar Gnostic sect on the poet. Given Shelley's breadth of reading, such an influence is conceivable, particularly as he speaks affirmatively of the serpent in 'The Assassins' and in the essay 'On the Devil, and Devils' (*PW*, i. 137–9; Jul. vii. 103). Many of the Church Fathers had written about the Gnostics, and such friends of Shelley's as Peacock and John Frank Newton were fascinated by the esoteric philosophies of antiquity.[15] But it is not necessary to postulate a direct influence. The Gnostic way of reinterpreting the Scriptures is a recurring tendency in history. One might see it as akin to the impulse behind such a work as *The Book of Mormon*, the impulse which perceives the existing canon as inadequate or defective and which sets out either to supplement or to correct it.[16] The nascent text results from the determination to reinterpret the two Testaments with authority and to bring them into a correct alignment with the final, definitive revelation. This insistence that the orthodox understanding of the Scriptures is a misinterpretation and the compulsion to present the true meaning is equally characteristic of Shelley, particularly in the essay 'On Christianity'. It is true that the Romantic poet bequeaths to us no third

---

[14] See Mark 5: 9. Shelley would later link Cain with Christ in *Adonais* (l. 306). Both Cain and Prometheus were celebrated as heroes in Gnostic tradition.

[15] Shelley could not have read Hippolytus's account of the Peratae, as the relevant portion of the manuscript was not discovered until 1842.

[16] Significantly, the revelation of Joseph Smith occurs through the agency of a visiting angel, a circumstance which suggests the Gnostic theme of the angelic emissary from the spiritual world. Shelley himself was deeply interested in the daimonic realm of angels and spirits.

testament. Yet both the impulse to revise and the elements of a reinter-
pretation are present in his works.

It is clear that the hermeneutics of Gnosticism accounted for some
radically new readings of the canonical Scriptures. Writing in the second
half of the second century, St Irenaeus discussed many of the methods
used by the Gnostics to effect these reinterpretations. One such
approach was to 'disregard the order and the connection of the
Scriptures . . . transferring passages, and dressing them up anew, and
making one thing out of another'.[17] Hippolytus's account of the
Peratae may be taken as an illustration of this method. A second strategy
was to appeal to an unwritten oral tradition through which the truth
was communicated and against which the written Word could have no
argument (III. ii. 1; i. 415). A third means of revising the Bible was to
integrate mythical elements with the biblical record. For example, the
Samaritan Simon Magus identified his mistress Helena, a former prosti-
tute, both with Helen of Troy and with the lost sheep spoken of by
Jesus (I. xxiii. 2; i. 348).[18]

Other Gnostic approaches to Scripture involved the question of the
text itself. One could simply regard as uncanonical certain passages or
whole books of the Bible. For example, Tertullian states that the heretic
Marcion, who had rejected all of the Old Testament and much of the
New, 'used the knife, not the pen, since he made such an excision of
the Scriptures as suited his own subject-matter'.[19] On the other hand,
one could add to the existing Scriptures such material as would support
Gnostic teaching. The ascription of new sayings ($\lambda \acute{o} \gamma \iota \alpha$) to Jesus was an
ideal means of accomplishing this end. In *The Book of Thomas the
Contender*, the Saviour tells Judas Thomas that 'he who has not known
himself has known nothing, but he who has known himself has at the
same time already achieved knowledge about the depth of the all'.[20]

---

[17] *Irenaeus Against Heresies*, trans. A. Roberts and W. H. Rambaut, in *The Ante-Nicene
Fathers*, I. viii. 1; i. 326. Referencing is by book, chapter, and paragraph in the original,
then volume and page number in the modern edition. See also the discussion of
Gnosticism and hermeneutics in Frank Kermode, *The Genesis of Secrecy* (Cambridge,
Mass., 1979), 55–9.

[18] See Matt. 18: 12. The Simon Magus of Gnostic history is sometimes presented as
the Samaritan sorcerer of Acts 8: 9–25.

[19] Tertullian, *The Prescription against Heretics*, trans. P. Holmes, in *The Ante-Nicene
Fathers*, xxxviii; iii. 262. Referencing is by chapter number in the original text, then vol-
ume and page number of the modern edition.

[20] In *The Nag Hammadi Library*, trans. members of the Coptic Gnostic Library Project
of the Institute for Antiquity and Christianity, ed. James Robinson, 3rd edn. (San
Francisco, 1988), 201.

The imperative of knowing oneself, which appears throughout Gnostic literature, is in effect one of realizing the nature of the spiritual self, its divine origin, and its destiny of reunion with the divine substance. As Irenaeus says, however, the Gnostics would more typically impugn the Scriptures for being either incorrect, ambiguous, or lacking in authority (III. ii. 1; i. 415). Furthermore, they could assert that the teaching of the apostles was framed 'according to the capacity of their hearers' (III. v. 1; i. 418). In these views, there is a special affinity with Shelley, who in the essay 'On Christianity' states that the gospel record was 'imperfect and obscure', and that Jesus 'accommodated his doctrines to the opinions of his auditors' (*PW*, i. 260).

Such assumptions raise difficulties in the area of hermeneutics, for this branch of biblical studies is concerned with the problem of establishing the meaning of the text. It strives to surmount the obstacle of that text's existence as an artefact belonging to a different time period, language, and culture. To suppose that Jesus adjusted his message to the predilections of his listeners or that the apostles delivered only a partial gospel complicates the analytical procedure. Biblical hermeneutics aims at a more comprehensive exegesis of the Scriptures; that is, it seeks to derive meaning 'out of' the text. The Gnostic approach is to some degree eisegetical; that is, it reads meaning *into* the text, between the lines as it were, projecting a private reality into the public domain of the scriptural passage in question.

The great authority on Gnosticism in the eighteenth century, John Lawrence Mosheim, claimed that the Gnostics 'had recourse to wild fictions and romantic fables, in order to give an account of the formation of the world, and the origin of mankind'.[21] Mosheim alleged that the 'fictitious writings' of Abraham, Zoroaster, Christ, and others provided a form of scriptural authority for Gnostic teachings (i. 138). Harold Bloom, the seminal critic of Gnosticism as a revisionist impulse, has written extensively on the process of substitution whereby a document attains this status. According to Bloom, 'we are nurtured by distortion, and not by apostolic succession'.[22] Although he is speaking of literary influence, rather than the Gnostic reconstruction of biblical texts, it is nevertheless the Gnostic response to the canonical writings which underlies his theory of poetic tradition and inspires his conception of 'misreading'. The first of Bloom's revisionary ratios, or movements, is therefore the *clinamen*, by which an aspiring poet, or ephebe,

---

[21] *An Ecclesiastical History, Antient and Modern* (*c.*1755), trans. A. MacLaine (6 vols.; *c.*1765; London, 1803), i. 87.   [22] *Kabbalah and Criticism* (New York, 1975), 103.

'swerves away from his precursor'.[23] The ephebe thus deviates from the anterior text in this initial stage of revision. One form comes to substitute for another in this process whereby the reader becomes an Overman, or as Bloom calls him, the *Überleser*.[24] This fictive reader effects the destruction of the precursor text that is necessary to allow room for the reconstructed text to come into being. When applied to the Gnostic revision of Scripture, rather than to literary 'misreading', this process reveals what Bloom calls the 'Gnostic struggle to the death with the Hebrew Bible'.[25] Regardless of whether one accepts all aspects of this theory of influence, Bloom's account of the Gnostic posture toward the canonical Scriptures is in many cases no exaggeration.

Surprisingly, Shelley seldom refers to Gnosticism, despite the fact that he shares its instinct to revise the sacred writings. This instinct is equally apparent in the poet's fascination with the Devil. Clearly, he sees a kinship between Gnostic dualism and the adversarial status of the Devil in the Bible. He begins his essay 'On the Devil, and Devils' by placing the idea of the diabolical in the context of the Gnostic philosophy of Manichaeism (Jul. vii. 87). Shelley does not endorse this philosophy, for he equates its dualism with that of orthodox Christianity. And true Gnosis, like the Devil of orthodox faith, is aligned against the popular Church. The poet elsewhere explores the nature of the diabolical in *Peter Bell the Third*, in the preface to *Prometheus Unbound*, and in his translations of Goethe and Calderón. This interest is not irrelevant to the study of Gnosticism. In his treatise against the heretical sects of his time, Irenaeus correlated Gnostic and Satanic uses of Scripture (V. xxvi. 2; i. 555). To be sure, he was not an unbiased commentator. But more recently, Paul Cantor has not only reaffirmed this correlation, but applied it to some major Romantic works which he feels are characterized by a 'sympathy for the devil' (p. ix).

Shelley's admiration for the character of Milton's Satan in 'On the Devil, and Devils' leads him to present Milton's Devil as the adversary of God (Jul. vii. 91). This antithesis may be attributed to Shelley's view of Christianity as a dualistic system. Significantly, it is the Devil's perception as well. But in the metaphysical combat of book VI of *Paradise Lost*, Satan's adversary is the archangel St Michael.[26] The belief that he

---

[23] *The Anxiety of Influence* (New York, 1973), 14.

[24] *A Map of Misreading* (1975; Oxford, 1980), 5.

[25] *Agon* (1982; New York and Oxford, 1983), 50.

[26] *Paradise Lost*, VI. 296–353, 690. All references to Milton's poetry are to *The Poems of John Milton*, ed. J. Carey and A. Fowler (1968; London and New York, 1980).

can rival God leads Satan to a fundamental denial of the created order, a denial which culminates in the pronouncement that he is a self-begotten entity (V. 857–66). The rejection of the Yahwistic creation yields a reinterpretation of the order of being. In Milton's universe, the reinterpretation is a parody. Satan constructs a palace, '[a]ffecting all equality with God' (V. 763), and what begins as an attempt to 'cast off this yoke' of submission ends in a quest for '[h]onour, dominion, glory, and renown' (V. 786; VI. 422).[27]

Shelley properly recognized in this enterprise the 'taints of ambition, envy, revenge, and a desire for personal aggrandisement', as he writes in the preface to *Prometheus Unbound* (*SPP*, 133). What is not so readily understood is Shelley's reference in the next sentence to Satan's 'wrongs' which 'exceed all measure'; for in the course of the events related, Satan is the victim of no violence or oppression. As C. S. Lewis implies in his discussion of Shelley's remark, the only 'wrong' that Satan suffers is that he must endure his rightful place in the created order.[28] The sense of having been treated unjustly is essentially a product of his own imagination.

The appeal of Satan to Shelley may indeed be traceable to Milton's having incorporated Promethean elements in his character, as R. J. Z. Werblowski has asserted.[29] However this may be, the poet was clearly fascinated by the Satanic element in literature, as is revealed in the selections from Goethe and Calderón which he chose to translate. There are several aspects of the diabolical character in these works, as well as in *Paradise Lost*, which reveal the working of the Satanic imagination. One such feature is the 'human' motive of having been slighted, the 'sense of injured merit' mentioned by Satan (I. 98). It is a motive for which Shelley would have had great sympathy as a result of his expulsion from college. As with Shakespeare's Iago, however, the emphasis is on the feeling itself, rather than on any substantial offence. And this feeling arises spontaneously in the Satanic mind.

The theme of the offended Lucifer recurs in Calderón's *El Magico Prodigioso*, though in a different manner. In the second scene of the drama which Shelley translated, the disguised demon relates to Cyprian the story of his fall. The King of kings had

---

[27] See Gal. 5: 1. Satan twists the biblical meaning of the word 'yoke' (bondage to legalism) to mean obedience to God.

[28] *A Preface to* Paradise Lost (1942; Oxford, 1979), 96.

[29] *Lucifer and Prometheus* (London, 1952), p. xvii.

Named me His counsellor. But the high praise
Stung me with pride and envy, and I rose
In mighty competition, to ascend
His seat and place my foot triumphantly
Upon His subject thrones. Chastised, I know
The depth to which ambition falls; too mad
Was the attempt, and yet more mad were now
Repentance of the irrevocable deed . . .

$$(SPW, 741)^{30}$$

Describing his expulsion as a form of exile from a far-away court, the demon brings to mind the Devil of *Paradise Lost*, particularly in his attitude of defiance. But whereas Milton's Satan voyages far to subvert an entire world, Calderón's demon claims to have journeyed through the world to find but a single adept who might be seduced to magic (*SPW*, 742).[31]

Deception, particularly as it is manifest in a disguise, is another important element of the Satanic. After his fall, Milton's Satan frequently disguises his increasingly disfigured form. And his various appearances as a youthful cherub (his initial ruse), cormorant, lion, tiger, and toad chart his descent through the hierarchy of creation, and graphically illustrate the extent of his spiritual fall.[32] Correspondingly, Calderón's devil first appears disguised in festive courtly dress, while Mephistopheles in the first part of *Faust* initially confronts Goethe's protagonist attired as a travelling scholar.[33] But costumes and protean transformations are not the only means of deception. In both Milton and Calderón, the Devil poses as a lost traveller asking directions, a fraud which is all the more effective for its ingenuous appearance.[34]

The most significant aspect of the Satanic, of course, is its ultimate goal of establishing a counterfeit reality, an order of being antithetical to

[30] Sc. ii. 118–25 in *SPW*. See Pedro Calderón de la Barca, *El Magico Prodigioso*, 2nd edn. (Zaragoza, 1966), Act II. 276–85. This posture of defiance characterizes Ahasuerus in *Queen Mab*, VII. 196–201, as well as Prometheus in *Prometheus Unbound*, I. 262–301.

[31] Sc. ii. 150–2 in *SPW*. (Act II. 312–15 in original text.) Calderón's perspective is that of a devout Catholic.

[32] Milton, *Paradise Lost*, III. 636 and IV. 196, 402, 403, and 800.

[33] *SPW*, 733; Sc. i. 57; or Act I. 88 of *El Magico Prodigioso*; and *Goethe's Faust*, trans. W. Kaufmann (Garden City, NY, 1961), l. 1321. In Shelley's translation, Mephistopheles confesses that 'In truth, I generally go about / In strict incognito' (*SPW*, 758; Sc. ii. 261–2; l. 4062).

[34] See *Paradise Lost*, II. 975–6; III. 667–74; and Shelley's translation of Calderón, *SPW*, 733; Sc. i. 61; Act I. 95 in the original text. See also the stimulating discussion of this circumstance in A. A. Parker, *The Theology of the Devil in the Drama of Calderón* (London, 1958), 14–20.

that of the Yahwistic universe. Milton's Satan thus arrogates to himself
the functions of God the Father. And after the fall from heaven, he
assumes the role of messianic deliverer. When he encounters his daugh-
ter Sin, with their son Death, he addresses her as a liberator:

> I come no enemy, but to set free
> From out this dark and dismal house of pain,
> Both him and thee, and all the heavenly host
> Of spirits that in our just pretences armed
> Fell with us from on high . . .
>
> (II. 822–6)

The proclamation suggests the occasion on which Jesus read from Isaiah
(ch. 61) in the synagogue at Nazareth: 'The Spirit of the Lord is upon
me, because he hath anointed me . . . to preach deliverance to the cap-
tives . . . to set at liberty them that are bruised' (Luke 4: 18). By claim-
ing fulfilment of this prophecy that day, Jesus aroused great controversy.
Satan, by contrast, elicits praise; for he is overturning the divine judge-
ment on the fallen angels. Parodying the Nicene Creed, Sin congratu-
lates Satan, now envisaged as the first person of a new trinity:

> . . . I shall reign
> At thy right hand voluptuous, as beseems
> Thy daughter and thy darling, without end.
>
> (II. 868–70)

Divine Providence, which will not allow the ultimate realization of
such a fantasy, and which indeed is the theme of Milton's poem, is dis-
missed by Satan, who repeatedly presents Fate, Chance, or Necessity as
possible substitutes for it.

In tempting mortals, Satan communicates this same heady prospect of
becoming like God. The biblical text for this temptation (Gen. 3: 5) is
repeated in *Paradise Lost*: '. . . ye shall be as gods, / Knowing both good
and evil as they know' (IX. 708–9). When asked to write in a student's
album in *Faust* (Part I), the disguised Mephistopheles inscribes the Latin
form of the same verse (l. 2048). Milton's Eve, upon eating the forbid-
den fruit, speaks of 'growing up to godhead' (IX. 877). The attempt to
change the order of being by its nature leads to pursuits which mimic
divine power. The fallen Adam and Eve, for example, imagine that
they will be able to fly (IX. 1010–11). Faust, who imagines himself to
be the image of the godhead (l. 614), proceeds to revise the creative
Logos of John 1: 1 into the creative act (l. 1237). And in the second
part of Goethe's drama, the divine prerogative in creation is usurped in

the alchemical generation of a homunculus, a little man, and in Faust's 'creation' of land through the reclamation project.[35] Similarly, Calderón's Cyprian moves a mountain, effecting through magic what Christ said one might accomplish through faith in God (Matt. 17: 20).[36] Milton, Goethe, and Calderón all deal with the mere creature who would become like the Creator.

These elements of the Satanic—the sense of having been deprived, the resort to disguise, and the establishment of an alternative reality—all have a bearing on the Gnostic relation to Scripture. The Gnostic's vision has been denied canonical status; its syncretist theology is often expressed in biblical language; and it is presented as an alternative to the orthodox revelation. Ultimately, this alternative revelation allows for the divinization of the self, the merging of the spirit with the divine nature. But perhaps the most significant similarity is the mutual identification with the serpent. Both Mephistopheles and Satan are associated with the snake.[37] And just as some Gnostic sects reversed the usual biblical associations of the serpent with evil, Shelley redeems the creature in 'The Assassins'. The poet's fragmentary narrative abounds with references to snakes.[38] The most prominent of these reveals the heterodox twist that Shelley often gave to biblical sources. Near the end of the fragment, the children of Albedir and Khaled play freely with a snake who understands their language (PW, i. 138). Ostensibly, Shelley is presenting his own rendering of Isaiah's idyllic vision, in which the child plays fearlessly with the serpent (Isa. 11: 8). For the biblical prophet, however, this state was to arise from the establishment of the messianic kingdom, or in Christian terms, the millennial reign of Christ. In Shelley's story, the restoration of this Edenic state is a consequence of the communal life of a sect which maintains its unique claim to a true understanding of that messianic faith.

The representations of the serpent in 'The Assassins' are integrally related to the larger question of the relation between biblical language and Shelley's adaptations of biblical language. As a man of letters, the poet uses Scripture in a variety of ways; and certainly not all of these

---

[35] Shelley could not have read Faust: Part II since it was not published until 1832.

[36] El Magico Prodigioso, II. 903–4.

[37] Faust, l. 2049; Paradise Lost, IX. 182–90; X. 511–21.

[38] In A New System, Jacob Bryant devotes an entire section to a discussion of Ophitic groups in the ancient world (i. 473–90). Curiously, the name of Albedir, the central character in 'The Assassins', is similar to Bryant's Ophite deity Abadir, who 'seems to be a variation of Ob-Adur, and signifies the serpent God Orus' (i. 476). According to Bryant, 'Abadir' is a cognate of Abaddon, the 'angel of the bottomless pit' in Rev. 9: 11 (i. 477).

have a specifically interpretive significance. When the stranger in 'The
Assassins' tells Albedir that he does not 'mean to eat the bread of idle-
ness' (*PW*, i. 137), he both alludes to and reaffirms the ethos of a bibli-
cal text (Prov. 31: 27). But this use of the Bible tells us little about the
poet's general stance toward the canon. Though far less easily detected,
the fainter biblical echo—by its suggestiveness—is often more illumi-
nating. The Assassins of Jerusalem described by Shelley are noted for
their benevolence, their adherence to the teachings of Christ, and their
'singleness and sincere self apprehension to the slavery of pagan customs
and the gross delusions of antiquated superstition' (*PW*, i. 124).
Correspondingly, the members of the Jerusalem Church in the New
Testament shared their possessions and 'did eat their meat with gladness
and singleness of heart' (Acts 2: 46). Shelley's use of the word 'single-
ness' in particular suggests that his Assassins are modelled on the early
Church (Acts 2: 42–7, 4: 32–7). Yet Shelley's sectarians stand in the
same relation to the orthodox Church that this early Church stood *vis-
à-vis* the Jewish religion. Both Judaism and orthodox Christianity are
from his perspective manifestations of 'antiquated superstition'. The
faint biblical echo in this case is more informative than the obvious
allusion.

Living in transport as 'disembodied spirits' (*PW*, i. 129), Shelley's
Assassins share with the Gnostics a fundamental delight in the life of the
spirit, which distinguishes them from the carnal masses. But, more
significantly, they share with the Gnostics the belief that they have per-
ceived the original truth of Christ's message, the truth that the popular
Church through custom had failed to see. Shelley amplifies this notion
in his essay on Christianity. Yet, if the 'Gnostic' component of Shelley's
sensibility informed his reading of the Bible, the actual content of his
views on Scripture was more typically informed by the Enlightenment
and by some of the contemporary controversies surrounding the scrip-
tural texts themselves.

PART ONE

1810–1818

I

Young Bysshe and the Bible

There are, ironically, two opposed misconceptions about Shelley's religious beliefs which have persisted since his death. One is that his diverse speculations on the idea of God may be safely subsumed in the term 'atheism'; the other is that he was in some sense a Christian. Those who hold the former view take Shelley's early pronouncements on the subject of atheism at face value. Shaw, for example, says that 'In religion, Shelley was an Atheist. There is nothing uncommon in that; but he actually called himself one, and urged others to follow his example. He never trifled with the word God. . . . He lived and died professedly, almost boastfully, godless.'[1] Such a statement is an oversimplification. At each stage of his life, Shelley maintained a conception of divine Being. Even in his Notes on *Queen Mab* (1813), the epitome of his early anti-christian radicalism, he appends to his denial of God's existence as Creator an almost dogmatic assertion that there exists 'a pervading Spirit coeternal with the universe' (*PS*, i. 381). This deity he conceives as 'the mass of infinite intelligence';[2] it is an idea that he never rejects. In the essay 'On Christianity' it recurs as an 'omnipresent Power' which overwhelms the individual much as the Spirit of God descended upon individuals in the Old Testament (*PW*, i. 252). Thus, in his correspondence he was careful to state that he was an atheist only 'in the popular sense of the word "God"'.[3] When Trelawny asked him years later why he called himself an atheist, he admitted that he used the term for its effect: 'It is a word of abuse to stop discussion, a painted devil to frighten the foolish.'[4]

Shelley, then, was not an atheist by any strict definition of the word. Allowance may be made for the Etonian definition presented by his biographer Thomas Jefferson Hogg of an 'Antitheist' as one who is 'an

---

[1] 'Shaming the Devil about Shelley', *Albemarle*, 2/3 (1892), 91, 92. The view has been restated more recently by Paul Foot in *Red Shelley* (London, 1980), 79.
[2] Letter to Elizabeth Hitchener, 2 Jan. 1812, *Letters*, i. 215.
[3] Letter to William Godwin, 10 Jan. 1812, *Letters*, i. 228.
[4] *Recollections*, ii. 190.

opposer and contemner of the gods'.[5] But he was not an atheist accord-
ing to Shaw's understanding, for Shaw limits the definition of God to 'a
personal First Cause' (p. 91), something that Shelley does not do. It is
true that Shelley rejects the presupposition of a creative God, and that
he never disowns the appellation of atheist.[6] However, his *Necessity of
Atheism* did not dogmatically deny the existence of the Judaeo-Christian
God, but rather asserted the inadequacy of existing theistic arguments.
As Newman Ivey White observes, its conclusions are sceptical, or
agnostic.[7] That the young Shelley believed scepticism to lead invariably
to atheism and Hunt's deism to be tantamount to atheism highlights the
lack of philosophical precision in his early use of the word.[8] And it is
noteworthy that in referring to his grandfather on one occasion, he
used the word pejoratively.[9]

   The second misconception, the tendency to baptize Shelley either for
his good deeds or for the sublimity of his character, is, like the first one,
maintained by partisans; it succeeds at the expense of dealing only par-
tially with his beliefs or with those of Christianity itself. The basis for
this view was established by Shelley's own circle. Those who knew him
most intimately were compelled to make 'the atheist' more palatable to
the Victorian reading public. His personal integrity and purity are
affirmed by his wife Mary in her note on *The Revolt of Islam* (*SPW*,
157); Hunt speaks of his 'natural piety';[10] and Hogg, characteristically
overstating the case, writes that 'I was of the earth, earthy. . . . He was a
pure spirit, in the divine likeness of the Archangel Gabriel . . .' (ii.
17–18). Correspondingly, all refer to Shelley's frequent acts of charity.[11]
Hunt takes this matter further by discussing Shelley's benevolent dispo-
sition in relation to the ethical aspects of the Bible: 'For his Christianity,
in the proper sense of the word, he went to the gospel of St James [*sic*],
and to the Sermon on the Mount by Christ himself, for whose truly
divine spirit he entertained the greatest reverence' (i. 323–4). The

   [5] *The Life of Percy Bysshe Shelley* (1858), in *The Life of Percy Bysshe Shelley*, ed. H.
Wolfe (2 vols.; London, 1933), i. 92.
   [6] In a fragment written in Italy, Shelley defines an atheist as 'a person who denies
certain opinions concerning the cause of the Universe' (Bodleian MS Shelley adds. c. 4,
fo. 7ᵛ). The fragment has been published recently by Timothy Webb, who dates it
*c.*1818–19, in 'The Avalanche of Ages', *K–SMB*, no. 35 (1984), 3, 10–13.
   [7] *Shelley* (2 vols.; 1940; New York, 1947), i. 112.
   [8] See resp. Shelley's letters to T. J. Hogg, 28 Apr. and 8 May 1811, *Letters*, i. 72, 77.
   [9] Letter to Elizabeth Hitchener, 26 Jan. 1812, *Letters*, i. 239.
   [10] 'Mr Shelley', in *Lord Byron and Some of his Contemporaries*, 2nd edn. (2 vols.;
London, 1828), i. 296.
   [11] See ibid. i. 316 n.–318 n.; Hogg, *Life*, i. 141–3, 152; and Medwin, *Life*, 30, 119, 192.

mellifluous language is beguiling. One must remember that Hunt's Jesus (like Shelley's) is primarily a social reformer (i. 324).[12] And Hunt's Shelley could qualify as a Christian only if Christianity is interpreted as an ethical philosophy divorced from the historic, credal Christian faith. Medwin is a little more realistic in stating that Shelley tended to 'reduce Christianity to a code of morals' (p. 271). Nevertheless, ground was established for the Victorian fantasy of a penitent Shelley. Browning wistfully imagined that if Shelley had lived long enough, he would have become a Christian.[13] And the Revd George Gilfillan speculated that if the poet's preceptors had dealt with him less reproachfully, they might have exorcized the young Gadarene: 'they might have weaned him, ere long, from the dry dugs of atheism, to the milky breast of the faith and "worship of sorrows;" and the touching spectacle had been renewed, of the demoniac sitting "clothed, and in his right mind," at the feet of Jesus'.[14]

Yet, however tempting it may be to see the poet as the severed branch 'that might have growne full straight', it is unlikely that Shelley would have fulfilled Browning's prophecy. The same poet who wrote in 1811 that 'I can scarcely set bounds to my hatred of Xtianity' lamented in 1822 that Byron remained prey to 'the delusions of Christianity'.[15] The adamantly anti-Christian Trelawny furthermore records that in later life Shelley indicted the religion for its narrowness: 'The delusions of Christianity are fatal to genius and originality: they limit thought' (ii. 190). Like the portrait of Shelley as an atheist, then, that of the 'Christian' Shelley is not convincing. Yet if Shelley defies labelling because of the apparent inconsistency of his views, he was nevertheless obstinate in maintaining them. This general intractability was prompted in part by his father's resistance to change in outward religious forms and in part by a dogged persistence in matters of the heart that seems to have been typical of his family.

Contumacy in religious affairs was a characteristic trait of the Sussex Shelleys. Newman Ivey White notes in his biography of Shelley that

---

[12] Hunt discusses Jesus in a chapter entitled 'Of the Great Benefactors of the World', in *The Religion of the Heart* (London, 1853), 83–4.

[13] 'Essay on Shelley' (1852), ed. D. Smalley, in *The Complete Works of Robert Browning*, ed. Roma King and Jack Herring (8 vols.; Athens, Oh., and Waco, Tex., 1969–89), v. 147.

[14] 'Percy Bysshe Shelley', in *A Gallery of Literary Portraits*, 1st ser. (Edinburgh, 1845), 73.

[15] Letter to T. J. Hogg, 28 Apr. 1811, *Letters*, i. 71; letter to Horace Smith, 11 Apr. 1822, *Letters*, ii. 412.

Sussex had been the last Saxon kingdom to accept Christianity and the most reluctant of counties to acknowledge the reformed Church of England (i. 4). The Shelleys of western Sussex and eastern Hampshire exemplified this tendency, and remained throughout most of the sixteenth century a Catholic family. One, Edward Shelley, a distant kinsman of the poet, officially became an English martyr of the Catholic Church, having been hanged at Tyburn Hill in 1588 for receiving and assisting a Catholic priest.[16] Refusal to accept the reformed Anglican communion incurred the designation of 'recusant'. And in what is a curious foreshadowing of the poet's expulsion from Oxford in 1811, one Thomas Shelley of Michelgrove, Sussex, was forced to resign his fellowship at New College, Oxford, in 1567 on the ground of recusancy. College archives reveal that he resigned after refusing to take communion in chapel, and that he immediately went abroad.[17] Apparently he reappeared in the Vatican three years later. When Queen Elizabeth was formally arraigned for heresy at the papal court of Pius V in 1570, two of the twelve English exiles who appeared in Rome to testify against her were Shelleys. Church historian Richard Dixon identifies one as Sir Richard Shelley, former Prior of the Knights of St John of Jerusalem, and the other as 'Richard Shelley [sic], a former Fellow of New College, Oxford'.[18]

Despite these zealous precedents in the Shelley family history, the orthodoxy of the poet's father was qualified not only by the Reformation, but also by the Enlightenment. Unlike his fervent Tudor ancestors and his wife's devout kinsmen, the Groves, Timothy Shelley of Field Place was essentially a nominal Christian. If his wife could impress their contentious son with her latitudinarian belief that all good men would ultimately find a place in heaven regardless of creed, Timothy could agree with him in denying the idea of an actively intervening Providence.[19] Both parents failed to see what their son saw very clearly, that such views were incompatible with an intellectually consistent profession of Christian faith. In this light, Medwin's reference to the poet's 'want of religious education at home' is understandable (p. 442).

[16] E. H. Burton and J. H. Pollen (eds.), 'Venerable Edward Shelley, Layman', in *Lives of the English Martyrs*, 2nd ser. (London, 1914), i. 419.

[17] James Sewell, 'Registrum Custodum, Sociorum, et Scholarium, Collegii Nov.', Archives of New College, Oxford, 1850–8, fo. 134.

[18] *History of the Church of England* (6 vols.; Oxford, 1902), vi. 252, 258. As there is no record of a fellow named Richard Shelley in the New College archives, it seems certain that Dixon must be referring to Thomas Shelley.

[19] Letters to T. J. Hogg, 14 May and 11 Jan. 1811, *Letters*, i. 85, 42.

Timothy's favourite theologian was William Paley. When the squire met his expelled son along with Hogg in London for dinner on 7 April 1811, he brought along a prepared apology for 'the existence of a Deity' which he proceeded to read aloud. When Hogg, who records the anecdote, whispered to Shelley that its substance was derived from Paley, Timothy paused, and in one of his queer attempts at conviviality pronounced, 'Yes! . . . they are Palley's [sic] arguments; I copied them out of Palley's book this morning myself: but Palley had them originally from me . . .' (i. 184). The book in question was probably Paley's *Natural Theology* (1802), which likened the cosmos to an intricately made watch from which one might infer the existence of a cosmic Watchmaker. But Paley had also issued a defence of the biblical texts themselves in *A View of the Evidences of Christianity* (1794). If the *Natural Theology* presented a universal revelation accessible to all, the *Evidences* deals with particular revelation. And such a revelation presupposes the miraculous.[20] Thus Paley devotes a portion of the *Evidences* to a refutation of the well-known argument against miracles presented in *An Enquiry concerning Human Understanding* by David Hume, whose sceptical philosophy was to have a profound influence on Timothy Shelley's son.

It is clear from his few comments on the theologian that Shelley greatly disliked Paley.[21] But this distaste for the Anglican divine did not extend to the Bible. And however little exposure Shelley may have had to an authentic form of Christianity at home, he would have had access to its main text. The family library included the Scriptures in several different forms. Primarily, there was an old family Bible: a folio volume of the Old and New Testaments published in 1639 and bound with the *Book of Common Prayer*, a concordance, and the Psalter.[22] Secondly, the library contained two of the three folio volumes which comprised *An Illustration of the Holy Scriptures* (6th edn., 1759), which had been given by Sir Timothy to his second son John in 1828. Thirdly, there was William Burkitt's *Expository Notes on the New Testament* (12th edn., 1749), a gift from a Revd Dr Hutchinson to Timothy's grandfather (also Timothy Shelley) in 1753.[23] Both the *Illustration* and Burkitt's *Expository*

[20] *A View of the Evidences of Christianity* (2 vols.; 1794; London, 1807), i. 3.

[21] See letter to Elizabeth Hitchener, 10 Dec. 1811, *Letters*, i. 200; *A Refutation of Deism* (*PW*, i. 107 n.); and the preface to *Prometheus Unbound* (*SPP*, 135).

[22] This volume, signed by Sir Timothy, was acquired in 1984 by Columbia University Library in New York.

[23] Both the *Illustration of the Holy Scriptures* and Burkitt's *Expository Notes* are in the Carl H. Pforzheimer Collection of the New York Public Library. Further reference to Burkitt's *Expository Notes* will be to the 11th edn. of 1739.

Notes integrated explanatory apparatus with the biblical text, generally providing commentary after each verse or passage.

Regardless of whether the poet made use of these resources, his addiction to reading the Bible is a commonplace among his early biographers. Hogg claims that Shelley often read the Old Testament in the Septuagint Greek (i. 86; ii. 154). And in his portrayal of Shelley as a virtuous hermit, Hunt says that '[h]is book was generally Plato, or Homer, or one of the Greek tragedians, or the Bible, in which last he took a great, though peculiar, and often admiring interest' (i. 323). He goes on to speak of Shelley's love for the book of Job and his preference for Jesus over St Paul. In similar terms, Medwin recalls that Shelley concluded the brief list of books he felt necessary to comprise a 'good library' with the statement: 'and last, yet first, the Bible' (p. 255). Furthermore, Mary Shelley's journals provide daily information on Shelley's reading of specific books of the Bible, particularly at the outset of 1820 (*JMS*, i. 304–14). Her lists reveal that Shelley read the New Testament in 1815 and virtually all the Bible (excepting Daniel and the minor prophets) in 1820 (i. 90, 345).

This interest in the Scriptures does not mean that Shelley was becoming more sympathetic to Christianity. Neither does his rejection of the Church as an institution mean that the Bible was irrelevant to his spiritual impulses. It was, in fact, susceptible to reinterpretation, as the revisionist Gnostics had so well illustrated. Shelley's reading of the Bible was coloured to a large degree by the more radical criticism of the Bible that began to emerge in the Enlightenment. This radical critique was characterized by two essential traits: a resolute anti-supernaturalism and a preoccupation with the ethical content of the Scriptures. Both features are characteristic of Spinoza's *Theologico-Political Treatise* (1670), a work which made a lasting impression on the young poet.

The outstanding assumption of Spinoza's system is that God and nature are inextricable. In a passage of the *Theologico-Political Treatise* quoted by Shelley in the Notes on *Queen Mab* (*PS*, i. 391), he says that 'Nature herself is the power of God under another name'.[24] Spinoza goes on to distinguish the law of 'natural necessity' from laws of 'human decree' (p. 57). The important thing to bear in mind in this contrast is the idea of universality attributed to the former. For Spinoza, the teachings of Jesus, which were universal, were an attempt to surmount the

---

[24] *A Theologico-Political Treatise*, trans. R. H. M. Elwes (1883; New York, 1951), 25. Shelley's annotations in his personal copy of Spinoza's treatise are reproduced in *SHC*, viii. 732–6.

obstacle of the 'particular' Mosaic Decalogue, which had been presented as a preceptual code reflecting the needs of a given culture (pp. 63–4).

Since the concept of a particular supernatural revelation is alien to Spinoza, his biblical hermeneutics is grounded on naturalistic criteria. He claims to have studied the Scriptures with a Cartesian openness of mind: 'I determined to examine the Bible afresh in a careful, impartial, and unfettered spirit, making no assumptions concerning it, and attributing to it no doctrines, which I do not find clearly therein set down' (p. 8). Spinoza's biblical hermeneutics is in the end thoroughly anti-supernaturalist. The operations of nature, man, and society comprise a plenitude that excludes the transcendent aspect of revelation. On the question of prophecy, Spinoza sounds much like his English contemporary Thomas Hobbes, for he relegates the content of specific revelation to the imagination and psychological state of the prophet (pp. 15–16).[25] Whereas the biblical view of prophecy involves both divine and human operations (2 Pet. 1: 21), Spinoza deals only with the latter. Thus he establishes the assumptions necessary for a purely ethical interpretation. The prophets, he says, have authority only in 'matters of morality' (p. 8).

These principles of biblical interpretation could not have escaped the attention of Shelley, who refers to Spinoza's treatise in *A Refutation of Deism* (*PW*, i. 122) and in the extensive Notes on *Queen Mab* (*PS*, i. 391). Although the seventeenth-century philosopher maintains the appearance of orthodoxy by his reverent tone and frequent allusion to the Scriptures, his interpretation of the Bible is essentially heterodox. Shelley would eventually undertake a translation of Spinoza's treatise.[26] And in his essay 'On Christianity' he would employ the principle used by Spinoza and others of denying the transmundane origin of the sacred writings while respecting the ethical teaching of Jesus and the prophets.

Among the *philosophes* there was no need to cloak the radical interpretation of the Bible in traditionally Christian language. The writings of Holbach, for example, are overtly anti-Christian. And it was reported that to enter his house in Paris, members of his esoteric coterie were required to trample on the Cross.[27] At the heart of Holbach's

---

[25] *Leviathan*, in *The English Works of Thomas Hobbes*, ed. W. Molesworth (11 vols.; 1839–45; London, 1962), iii. 361, 418.

[26] According to White, he apparently began the project in 1817, returning to it periodically. See *Shelley*, i. 527, and ii. 171, 188, 336. Donald H. Reiman presents evidence that Shelley left behind a completed translation of the work in *SHC*, viii. 741–2.

[27] Abbé Augustin Barruel, *Memoirs Illustrating the History of Jacobinism*, trans. anon. [R. Clifford] (4 vols.; London, 1797–8), i. 334.

Système de la nature, dutifully read by Shelley as a pupil of the Godwinian school in 1812, lay a reductionism similar to the anti-super-naturalism of Spinoza.[28] And he adduces the author of the *Theologico-Political Treatise* to support the idea that there can be no God apart from the material universe (ii. 109, 140). Since he accepts the Spinozist demand for a universal revelation, the idea of God revealing himself to a chosen people—'quelques êtres favorisés', as he calls them in *Le Christianisme dévoilé*—is unthinkable.[29] In this work, the Israelite claim to chosenness incurs guilt. The people of God 'détruisirent les nations Chananéennes avec une barbarie qui révolte tout homme en qui la superstition n'a pas totalement anéanti la raison' (p. 34). The Canaanites are thus cast as innocent primitives overcome by the unenlightened monotheistic Israelites. The emphasis is on atrocious moral conduct claiming divine sanction.

The biblical concept of divine disclosure as revelation is unacceptable to Holbach. In the *Système* he writes that the Jews created a God who was in effect an idol of 'leur propre ouvrage', and that their sacred writings were comprised of fable, oracle, and enigma.[30] The New Testament is equally fantastic in Holbach's view. In his *Histoire critique de Jésus-Christ* he claims that the gospel records 'dictée par le Saint Esprit' are far less accurate than pagan histories.[31] Moreover, the life they record was not irreproachable. Holbach's Jesus is a reformer with a weakness for the company of women, particularly those of questionable character (pp. 98, 130 n. 172). And one major reason why he does not try to usurp the throne of Judaea is that his royal genealogy is not well established (p. 223). This is essentially the picture of Jesus that Shelley would give in the Notes on *Queen Mab* a generation later (*PS*, i. 396–7, 397 n.). But it was a view that he would later abandon for a more affirmative view of Jesus.

The reinterpretation of Jesus as a benign moral teacher, a general trend of the Enlightenment, can be found even in Voltaire. But in his commentary on the Bible, Voltaire retains the *philosophes'* disdain for the character of the Israelites. He laments the 'simplicité grossière & barbare de la horde juive', and refers to them as Arab plunderers ('voleurs Arabes').[32] Apart from his conviction that the Old Testament

---

[28] Letter to William Godwin, 3 June 1812, *Letters*, i. 303.

[29] *Le Christianisme dévoilé* (London, 1767), 60.

[30] *Système de la nature* (2 pts.; London, 1770), ii. 87, 82–3.

[31] *Histoire critique de Jésus-Christ* (Amsterdam, c.1770), 96.

[32] *La Bible enfin expliquée* (Geneva, 1776), 71, 159. The title-page states that the book was authored by a group of chaplains ('plusieurs aumoniers'). This may be the work

is morally repugnant, a feeling shared by Holbach, Voltaire is simply sceptical about the accuracy and authority of Scripture. He plays on the contrast between faith and reason, pretending to support religion, which is erected on faith, while denying that it has any intellectual integrity. The following excerpts in his discussion of Genesis illustrate the point:

Ce n'est pas avec les yeux de la raison qu'il faut lire ce livre, mais avec ceux de la foi. . . . la bible ne nous a pas été donnée pour nous enseigner la géométrie & la physique. . . . Ce sont toujours des obscurités à chaque page. Ces nuages ne peuvent être dissipés que par une soumission parfaite à la Bible & à l'Eglise. (pp. 23, 25, 27)

In placing religious experience beyond the province of the rational, Voltaire echoes Hume, who in the *Enquiry concerning Human Understanding* had written that '[o]ur most holy religion is founded on *Faith*, not on reason' (p. 130). Much like his French counterpart, Hume preferred to view the Pentateuch

not as the word or testimony of God himself, but as the production of a mere human writer and historian. Here then we are first to consider a book, presented to us by a barbarous and ignorant people, written in an age when they were still more barbarous, and in all probability long after the facts which it relates. (p. 130)

But there is in Voltaire's commentary an equally strong resonance with Spinoza, who is discussed in some remarks on Genesis (p. 26). In the same manner as Spinoza, Voltaire severs God from the world of mundane experience: 'Plusieurs savants ont soutenu que ces phrases Hébraïques, *Dieu les frappa, Dieu les fit mourir de mort, Dieu les arma, Dieu les conduisit,* signifient simplement, *ils moururent, ils s'armèrent, ils allèrent*' (p. 286). Spinoza had expressed essentially the same thought in his treatise (p. 95). Again, the hypothesis of an actively intervening Providence is denied by recourse to a view of the world which has occluded the transcendent. And just as Spinoza had asserted in his treatise that the sole concern of Jesus was to teach moral doctrines (p. 71), so Voltaire concludes his commentary with a brief tribute to the founder of Christianity: 'Jésus a dit à toutes les sectes: AIMEZ DIEU, ET VOTRE PROCHAIN COMME VOUS-MÊME; CAR C'EST LA TOUT L'HOMME' (p. 524).

Shelley read in 1811 which Hogg in his biography refers to as a book of 'unfair criticism on the Old Testament, some work of Voltaire's if I mistake not' (i. 182). The book was cited in Mary's reading list for 1815 (*JMS*, i. 90).

Denied any supernatural status, Jesus survives in the Enlightenment by being reinterpreted as a great moral teacher.

The belligerence which Voltaire and Holbach had ascribed to the Old Testament Israelites could with dexterity be made to apply to the eighteenth-century ecclesiastical hierarchy. During the revolutionary period, Count Volney makes this application in *The Ruins*. He portrays a bigoted Catholic divine who rises to defend Christianity with Bible in hand.[33] Although Volney feels that such passages as the Genesis account of creation are ridiculous (pp. 105–6), he freely exploits some biblical motifs. For example, the prophetic view of the millennium (based in part on Isa. 11) helps to colour his description of the future world as a vast global family (pp. 65, 85). A similar portrait is drawn by the revolutionary Condorcet, who speculates that in the perfected future state, the human life-span would eventually increase so as to have no definite limit. Death itself might be conquered in post-capitalist society.[34]

The biblical colouring of the radicals' vision of a future world is unmistakable. As the revolutionaries saw it, mankind was standing at the threshold of a dynamic new epoch in world history, an era in which free men would be governed by reason. A standard biblical image for the destruction of the old religious and political order and the imminence of the new was taken from the words of John the Baptist to the Pharisees and Sadducees: 'And now also the axe is laid unto the root of the trees: therefore every tree which bringeth not forth good fruit is hewn down, and cast into the fire' (Matt. 3: 10). The image of striking at the root of the tree was used by Voltaire in *Le Dîner du comte de Boulainvilliers* for radical purposes.[35] It was also used in a revolutionary way by Holbach in the *Système* (ii. 411), by Condorcet in the *Outlines* (p. 248), and by Thomas Paine in *The Age of Reason* (i. 476–7). By the time it surfaces in *Queen Mab* (IV. 82–9), it is a stale revolutionist metaphor.

The more philosophical biblical analogue was the prophetic forecast of doomed monarchies (as illustrated in Jer. 45–51), a subgenre used by

[33] *The Ruins*, trans. anon., 5th edn. (London, 1811), 105. Read by Shelley in 1812, according to White, *Shelley*, i. 277. Volney's work, published in 1791 as *Les Ruins, ou Méditations sur les révolutions des empires*, quickly became available in translation.

[34] *Outlines of an Historical View of the Progress of the Human Mind*, trans. anon. (London, 1795), 327–69.

[35] Cited in Peter Gay, *The Enlightenment: An Interpretation*, i. *The Rise of Modern Paganism* (New York, 1966), 132. The image was also employed by Frederick II, the Prussian king, who used it with reference to the suppression of the Jesuits in a letter to Voltaire (5 May 1767), noted in Barruel's *Memoirs*, i. 92.

Volney at the outset of his reverie and by Shelley in the second canto of *Queen Mab*. Related to this is the image of the ruined palace, found, for example, in Isaiah 13: 22, which metonymically expresses the demise of the monarch. Volney writes that the royal palaces of antiquity had become the dwelling places of deer (p. 5); Shelley refers to 'Palmyra's ruined palaces' in *Queen Mab* (II. 110).[36] It was not difficult to use select scriptural passages to support the abolition of monarchy. The assassination of Eglon, king of Moab, in Judges (3: 22), formed part of a rumination on the subject of regicide in Voltaire's commentary (pp. 232–3). But it was equally effective to project the vision of a future in which the processes of history had rendered kingship obsolete.

Finally, Volney's presentation of *The Law of Nature* appended to *The Ruins* reveals in its format a derivation from the faith based on the Bible. Significantly, it is written in the form of a catechism, a means of instructing the novice in a new post-Christian faith. As if to mimic the Decalogue of Moses, Volney lists ten characteristics of the law of nature, the new law which substitutes for the religion derived from the patriarchal Ten Commandments (p. 8).

Shelley came to reject the materialistic French philosophy;[37] but his early biblical comments in *Queen Mab* and in *A Refutation of Deism* are indebted to the *philosophes* and the later revolutionaries. Another major influence on Shelley's view of the Bible was Paine, who had likewise learned from the French radicals. Apart from the occasional intrusion of a reverential English deism in *The Age of Reason*, there is little to distinguish Paine's biblical criticism from that of the French. His biblical hermeneutics may be summarized in his own words: 'I have now gone through the Bible, as a man would go through a wood with an axe on his shoulder, and fell trees. Here they lie' (i. 570). It would be difficult to imagine a more clearly defined hermeneutical method. Denying the existence of miracles (i. 507), Paine sets out to explode the sacred writings, asserting that all revelation which does not come directly from God is hearsay. Since the Scriptures are mediated through culture, the

---

[36] Volney begins his *Ruins* by describing the desolation of the ruins of Palmyra, an ancient city of Syria (pp. 2–3). Thomas Love Peacock also deals with the city in his poem *Palmyra* (1806) in *The Works of Thomas Love Peacock*, ed. H. F. B. Brett-Smith and C. E. Jones (10 vols.; London, 1924–34), vi. 1–31. Donald H. Reiman has pointed out that while Volney's work is optimistic about the future of post-Revolutionary society, Peacock's poem stems from an Enlightenment tradition which featured as its theme the vanity of human endeavours—itself a lament subversive of existing regimes. See Reiman's *Intervals of Inspiration*, 216–17.

[37] See the essay 'On Life', *SPP*, 476, and letter to Horace Smith, 11 Apr. 1822, *Letters*, ii. 412.

Bible is not to be trusted as revelation (i. 466). The two Testaments are essentially 'impositions and forgeries' (i. 604). But the weight of Paine's indictment falls, as it did in the case of the *philosophes*, on the morality of the Israelites, which was perceived as defective and inegalitarian. If Paine's Jesus is that Enlightenment conception of a mere mortal man who 'preached most excellent morality' and who exemplified the virtuous character of philanthropy, his Old Testament Jews are the now familiar barbarians noted for their cruelty, debauchery, and brutality (i. 469, 478, 474). That God would expressly command them to annihilate women and children in the process of subduing the Promised Land violates every norm of morality: '. . . wherein could crying or smiling infants offend?' (i. 518–19).

The best-known response to Paine's assault on the Bible came from Bishop Richard Watson. In *An Apology for the Bible*, specifically addressed to Paine, Watson claims that the Israelites were justified in their annihilation of particular cities. His strategy is to subsume Paine's sense of moral rectitude under a larger moral imperative. Thus he says of the Canaanites that 'it is needless to enter into any proof of the depraved state of their morals. . . . In the time of Moses, they were idolaters, sacrificers of their own crying or smiling infants.'[38] And he answers Paine's charge that their destruction was executed by 'the express command of God' by saying that if one grants that God is sovereign, then there is no difference between his using the Hebrews to judge the Canaanites or a natural disaster such as an earthquake (p. 6). He refuses to believe, as Shelley later would, that the Midianite maidens spared in the Pentateuch (Num. 31) were retained for sexual purposes (pp. 32–3; *PW*, i. 102, 102–3 n.).

Watson's apology, written in the form of a series of letters to Paine, begins on the most infelicitous note possible: 'it would have been fortunate for the christian world, had your life been terminated before you had fulfilled your intention' (p. 2). This posture of contempt provoked Blake to write in his annotations of Watson's book that the bishop was a 'State trickster' guilty of 'Priestly Impudence'.[39] Although no deist, Blake shared with Paine the Enlightenment rejection of the Bible as the 'Peculiar Word of God', preferring the internalized Bible of the Conscience or 'Word of God Universal' (p. 389). He agreed with Paine regarding the wickedness of the Israelites, and praised his energy (pp. 386–7).

[38] *An Apology for the Bible* (Dublin, 1796), 7.
[39] *Blake: Complete Writings*, ed. G. Keynes (1966; London, 1971), 384.

Shelley's own reaction to the Paine controversy was to see the prose-cuted publishers of *The Age of Reason*, Daniel Isaac Eaton in 1812 and Richard Carlile in 1819, as martyrs.[40] Eaton before his judge, Lord Ellenborough, is in Shelley's mind similar to the apostle Paul before the Roman procurator in Acts 24, with the notable difference that it is now the Christian who is on the prosecution's side of the bench. The London bookseller was arraigned on 6 March 1812, brought for judge-ment on 30 April, and sentenced to eighteen months in Newgate prison on 15 May. In making the charge, the Attorney-General said that in *The Age of Reason* Paine 'states, that the holy scriptures are, from begin-ning to end, mere fables', asserting that 'this blasphemous book' had as its object the destruction of Christianity.[41] In his defence, Eaton said that as a young man sent away to study at St Omer's in France, he was advised by his grandfather to study the Bible as a safeguard against becoming a Catholic:

And, above all things, I was desired to examine their doctrine by the Bible; for, if what they taught was not in the Bible, it was not true. I therefore made it my study to examine the Bible with their accounts of the saints; in doing which, I found the Bible so full of contradictions, and so full of wonderful things, that it induced me to examine this said Bible itself. (p. 23)

Although interrupted several times during his defence by Lord Ellenborough, Eaton remained firm, pleading the radicals' case (an ethi-cal argument) against the biblical representation of God: 'It appeared to me, and does so still, that Abraham chose the god *Mars*—the *god of bat-tles*' (p. 27). Jesus, on the other hand, was 'an exceedingly virtuous good man, but nothing supernatural or divine' (p. 36).

Shelley's written response to Eaton's situation in *A Letter to Lord Ellenborough* (1812) reveals that he was intimately familiar with the bookseller's trial (*PW*, i. 66–7). Eaton had referred to the popular ethic of Jesus by printing 'Why judge ye not of yourselves that which is right.—*Jesus*' [Luke 12: 57] on the title-page of the trial record. And just as Eaton's Jesus, according to this account, was 'so meek and so humble, so detached from all temporal interests' (p. 55), Shelley pre-sents in his *Letter* a 'meek reformer Jesus' (*PW*, i. 69). The outrage of Eaton's trial in Shelley's eyes lay in its ironic violation of the Galilean's own moral teaching. How could 'he, the regenerator of the world, the

---

[40] Shelley mentions the dispute between Paine and Watson in his dialogue *A Refutation of Deism*, 1814 (*PW*, i. 107 n.).

[41] *Trial of Mr Daniel Isaac Eaton* (London, 1812), 6, 8.

meek reformer, authorize one man to rise against another, and because
lictors are at his beck, to chain and torture him as an Infidel' (*PW*, i.
66)? Shelley becomes increasingly dogmatic about the supernatural
events surrounding the life of Christ (*PW*, i. 66–7). They typify a bar-
barous era, and are incredible in 'an enlightened age' (*PW*, i. 71). The
poet's rejection of them anticipates a time when Christianity 'shall have
faded from the earth' (*PW*, i. 71), just as European polytheism was
beginning to disappear at the time of St Paul's message. For just as the
Examiner had reported that 'the Christian faith itself is on the decline
and has been so these hundred and fifty years past', so Shelley believed
that its extinction was a corollary of enlightenment.[42]

A Letter to Lord Ellenborough is Shelley's areopagitica, a protest against
the imprimatur of a nominal Christianity and a demonstration of sup-
port for the controversial Paine. It reveals his fundamental inclination to
interpret the religious disagreement of his time in terms of an inquisito-
rial orthodoxy on the one hand and martyred heterodoxy on the other.
This picture of the martyr, enhanced in Shelley's mind by his own
expulsion from Oxford, recurs in the scene of the atheist's execution in
Queen Mab (VII. 1–13).

In spite of his post-Christian view of the Bible, the young Shelley
revealed a surprising degree of 'Christian' discernment regarding one of
the more arcane approaches to the Bible that began to emerge in his
time, the approach involving the use of syncretist mythology by Sir
William Drummond. In the *Oedipus Judaicus*, Drummond argued that
the Old Testament books are allegorical representations of astronomical
phenomena. The standards of the twelve tribes of Israel in their exodus
encampments, for example, were said to be based on the zodiac.[43] In
1813, Shelley wrote that the *Oedipus Judaicus* 'has completely failed in
making me a convert'.[44] Thus he relegates the argument that the Bible
could be 'collated' with Hindu writings and seen as allegorical of
ancient sun worship to a speech of the deist Theosophus in *A Refutation
of Deism* (*PW*, i. 109).

Another approach to the Bible that Shelley refused to adopt, at least
to any significant degree, was the analysis based on literary and rhetori-
cal features. The exponent of this method was Bishop Robert Lowth,
whose Latin lectures on Hebrew poetry, published in 1753, were even-

---

[42] *The Examiner*, no. 227 (3 May 1812), 275.
[43] *The Oedipus Judaicus* (London, 1811), 4–5.
[44] Letter to Thomas Hookham, 26 Jan. 1813, *Letters*, i. 350.

tually translated into English.[45] Lowth affirmed the 'imagery borrowed from common life' in Hebrew poetry, and emphasized its effusiveness (i. 123; ii. 123). Furthermore, he identified parallel structuring as the most evident rhetorical feature of Old Testament poetry (i. 58; ii. 34). Portions of the Lowthian critique would resurface in the *Biographia Literaria* of Coleridge, the literary figure the young Shelley seems to have admired most.[46] Although the young poet would occasionally refer to the scriptural writings in a belletristic sense,[47] he never became overly preoccupied with the view of the Bible as literature.

Like Coleridge, Shelley would eventually adapt biblical ideas in constructing a theological poetics. But he was deeply influenced by the tradition extending from Spinoza to the reason-mongers of the eighteenth century, the impact of which is particularly evident in *A Refutation of Deism* (1814). In this contrived debate between a deist and a Christian, Shelley presents several criticisms of the Bible which recall the antagonism of the *philosophes*. In the first place, the scriptural account of the Fall in Genesis and of salvation through Christ is simply beyond belief; it defies reason (*PW*, i. 100–1). Shelley's treatment brings to mind Volney's satirical summary of the Genesis Fall and the role of Christ in the *Ruins* (pp. 105–6). Secondly, Shelley recognizes the problem of clarity in revelation. Theosophus notes that the biblical prophecies have had a history of controversy within the Church (*PW*, i. 107). It seems that 'the God of Christianity spoke to mankind in parables, that seeing they might not see, and hearing they might not understand' (*PW*, i. 108). The question which arises had been raised by Holbach in the *Système*, and was quoted by Shelley in the Notes on *Queen Mab*: '"S'IL A PARLÉ, POURQUOI L'UNIVERS N'EST-IL PAS CONVAINCU?"' (*PS*, i. 390). Revelation that is ambiguous could only with difficulty be seen as revelation at all.

The heart of Shelley's criticism of the Bible, however, was ethical, and, like his Enlightenment forebears, he weighs the meekness of the Christian ethos against the militance of the Old Testament Hebrews. In his opening address, the Christian Eusebes praises the morality taught

---

[45] *Lectures on the Sacred Poetry of the Hebrews*, trans. G. Gregory (2 vols.; London, 1787). Ordered by Shelley in 1815 (*Letters*, i. 437).

[46] See *Biographia Literaria*, ed. J. Engell and W. J. Bate (2 vols.; Princeton, NJ, and London, 1984), i. 201–2, ii. 14–15, 44, 57. Read by Shelley in 1817 (*JMS*, i. 186). The poet's high regard for Coleridge is expressed in a letter to Peacock, 17 July 1816, *Letters*, i. 490.

[47] See e.g. the essay 'On Christianity' (*PW*, i. 249–50), the *Defence of Poetry* (*SPP*, 495, 502), and Medwin's *Life*, 255, 419.

by Christ for its ideals of humility and acquiescence (*PW*, i. 96–7). Thus he advocates an ethic established 'not by the ephemeral systems of vain philosophy, but by the word of God, which shall endure for ever' (*PW*, i. 98). He employs a biblically styled contrast by juxtaposing the Pauline warning against 'philosophy and vain deceit' (Col. 2: 8) and Isaiah's belief that 'the word of our God shall stand for ever' (Isa. 40: 8). Later in the dialogue, he accuses deistic rationalism of undermining morality, for true morality is derived from the biblical revelation (*PW*, i. 110).

Theosophus responds by impugning the Christian faith with a sustained assault on the sacred writings. While he concedes that some of the Christian virtues cited by Eusebes are meritorious, he views them mostly as props for tyranny and exploitation (*PW*, i. 105–6). But the chief argument of Theosophus against the Bible is that the Old Testament embodies a morally inferior ethos. He cites as examples the invasion of Canaan under the leadership of Moses and the sanguinary record of King David (*PW*, i. 102–3). Thus he impeaches the 'conduct of the Deity' (*PW*, i. 103). If the ethos of the Israelites was for Shelley abominable, that of the Christians—as revealed in history—was hardly an improvement. Theosophus sees the Christians to be as militant as the Hebrews: 'I will admit that one prediction of Jesus Christ has been indisputably fulfilled. *I come not to bring peace upon earth, but a sword*' (*PW*, i. 104).[48] In effect, the spirit of the crusades and the Inquisition is the spirit of conquering the land of Canaan. Thus Shelley's understanding of both the Israelites and the Christian Church differs little from the standard portrait presented by the *philosophes*.

In the immanentist philosophy of Spinoza, the Bible was examined psychologically and sociologically; it became an artefact sealed off from the transcendent. Extending the implications of this critique, the *philosophes*—who anticipated some of the developments in biblical criticism of the nineteenth century—wrote of the Bible as the tarnished mirror of a barbarous people. Nevertheless, there remained an interest in the ethos of the New Testament, that aspect of Christian teaching which demanded no supernaturalist assumptions and which could easily be detached from the main body of Christian belief. Interpreted as a preceptual code, the ethics of the gospels, particularly those of the Sermon on the Mount, could be seen to reflect the moral character of a reformed society. According to Shelley's essay 'On Christianity', the

---

[48] Shelley misquotes from Matt. 10: 34.

egalitarian order established by the primitive community of early Christians failed because it falsely assumed that the system could be established prior to inner reform. Such a state 'must result from, rather than precede the moral improvement of human kind' (*PW*, i. 270). As the young poet saw it, the ethos of the gospels typified the just society in proportion to its degree of moral improvement. The biblical model for this perfected order is the primary theme of the preaching of Jesus, the Kingdom of God.

2

The Kingdom and the Power

In his *Theologico-Political Treatise*, Spinoza rejected the metaphor of God as a monarch; for such a comparison challenged his own view, in which the universe is governed by the immanent determination of necessity (pp. 64–5). However, the anthropomorphism has proved indispensable to many theologians. C. H. Dodd, for example, has said that the significance of the metaphor lies in its expression of 'God's sovereign power becoming manifestly effective in the world of human experience'.[1] Hence his Kingdom is properly understood as an extension of his power. 'Kingdom' is the meaning of the Aramaic word *malkuth*, the term which would have been familiar to Jesus. But, as Gustaf Dalman observes, the Aramaic word does not refer to a territory but rather suggests the 'kingly rule' of God.[2] As such, it is a transcendent principle. But in that this lordship of God is acknowledged by an individual or society, it is manifest in the world. The immanence of the Kingdom is thus reflected in one's adherence to the ethical norms enjoined in the covenant with God.

The phrase 'Kingdom of God' originates with the gospels. But there are essentially two different understandings of it. Primarily Jesus has in mind a *malkuth* that is 'within', or 'in the midst of' humanity (Luke 17: 21). Secondarily, he speaks of it in a more remote, eschatological sense as the ultimate state of believers (Matt. 5: 19). But the emphasis in his teaching, as Dodd reminds us, is invariably on the Kingdom of God as a present reality (p. 36). And that present reality is manifest in Christian morality. In subsuming all of the Law under the precepts of loving God above all and one's neighbour *as oneself*, Jesus implies that the ethic of love presupposes self-esteem (Matt. 22: 37–9). Shelley's belief in self-knowledge as the corrective of 'self-contempt' approximates this principle.[3]

Like Spinoza, Shelley rejects the anthropomorphism of God as King

---

[1] *The Parables of the Kingdom*, rev. edn. (1961; Glasgow, 1980), 32.
[2] Cited in Norman Perrin, *The Kingdom of God in the Teaching of Jesus* (London, 1963), 24.
[3] See *The Revolt of Islam*, VIII. xxi–xxii.

(*PS*, i. 379). But the characterization of a sovereign necessity in his youthful writings reveals a derivation from the biblical model of the King and his Kingdom. Similarly, the ethos of these early works stems to a remarkable degree from the Old Testament prophets and from the moral teaching of Jesus. In 'The Assassins', Shelley portrays a utopian community of idealists who attempt to live by 'the doctrines of the Messiah concerning benevolence and justice for the regulation of their actions' (*PW*, i. 125). Nevertheless, these sectarians are not dogmatic on moral questions, and have a healthy regard for the spirit of inquiry (*PW*, i. 125).[4] To the extent that Shelley affirmed Christianity, he reinterpreted it. And when he employs the morality of the New Testament, he severs it from the contexts and doctrines which define it. *Queen Mab* is the outstanding instance of this tendency in Shelley's early poetry. However, the transmutation of biblical morality occurs in his early prose as well.

The ethic of the Kingdom of God is present in *An Address, to the Irish People* and *Proposals for an Association*, both of which were published in 1812; but it is pervasive in the former work, which was intended for the 'vulgar'. What Shelley could not have overlooked is that the biblical nuances of his address, like his latitudinarian posture, would have gone largely unappreciated by a Catholic audience. In fact, he appears to be frankly equivocal in insisting simultaneously that 'all religions are good which make men good', including the Catholic faith (*PW*, i. 10), and that the Roman church had a history of corruption, immorality, and persecution (*PW*, i. 10–13).

In the *Address*, Shelley promotes 'the introduction of the millennium of virtue', when 'Ireland will be an earthly Paradise', and when 'men will not then be wicked and miserable' (*PW*, i. 35, 18, 25). The biblical basis for this vision is found chiefly in the book of Isaiah. But Shelley borrows details from the accounts of the life of Jesus. One feature of the gospels found in the *Address* is the use of Jesus's Middle Eastern imagery in describing the amelioration of society. In asserting that the acquiring of riches generally hardens the heart, Shelley quotes Jesus: 'A Camel shall as soon pass through the eye of a needle, as a rich man enter the Kingdom of Heaven' (*PW*, i. 26). Good habits, on the other hand, 'contain a seed, which in future times will spring up into the tree of liberty, and bear the fruit of happiness' (*PW*, i. 24). In reaffirming the need for good habits, he again refers to an illustration used by Jesus:

---

[4] Some of the more revolutionary aspects of the Assassins of history are discussed by Walter Edwin Peck in *Shelley* (2 vols.; London, 1927), i. 386–8.

'You have built on sand. Secure a good foundation, and you may erect a fabric to stand for ever—the glory and the envy of the world!' (*PW*, i. 34). These parables of the Kingdom—the analogues of camel, seed, and sand—each express an aspect of Shelley's millennial vision for the Irish.[5]

Ostensibly, Shelley's wish is to unite Protestants and Catholics under the banner of a secularized Christian ethic. He invokes the teaching of Jesus to support the ideals of charity and meekness (*PW*, i. 15, 33). But Jesus had said that the gate which leads to eternal life is narrow, found only by a few (Matt. 7: 14). As his mother did, Shelley believes that 'the gates of Heaven are open to people of every religion, provided they are good' (*PW*, i. 11). Catholics and Protestants alike may be 'worthy of the Kingdom of Heaven' (*PW*, i. 12). However, Shelley is not really concerned with an other-worldly realm in the *Address*. The emphasis is on freedom of thought in this world. The poet writes, 'Evil designing men will spring up who will prevent your thinking as you please. . . . Take care then of smooth-faced impostors, who talk indeed of freedom, but who will cheat you into slavery' (*PW*, i. 13). The resonance is distinctively biblical, for Jesus had cautioned his followers in similar terms to beware of false prophets (Matt. 7: 15).

The general tone of the Irish address, however, brings to mind the prophet Isaiah. In saying that 'goodness of heart and purity of life are things of more value in the eye of the Spirit of Goodness, than idle earthly ceremonies', Shelley echoes the prophetic call to righteousness (*PW*, i. 16). Isaiah writes:

To what purpose *is* the multitude of your sacrifices unto me? saith the LORD. . . . Bring no more vain oblations . . . the new moons and sabbaths, the calling of assemblies, I cannot away with; *it is* iniquity, even the solemn meeting. . . . Learn to do well; seek judgment, relieve the oppressed, judge the fatherless, plead for the widow. (Isa. 1: 11, 13, 17)

This ethic of social justice precedes Isaiah's vision of the last days, when men will beat swords into plowshares and acknowledge the lordship of God (Isa. 2: 3–4). The vision of the millennium as a future state, with important social implications for the present, anticipates Christ's teaching on the Kingdom. In *Queen Mab*, undertaken later in the year and completed early in 1813, Shelley assumes a more radical posture by directing the biblical ethos against the social, political, and ecclesiastical institutions that he saw.

In his letters to Elizabeth Hitchener (1811–12), Shelley often refers to

[5] See resp. Matt. 19: 24, Mark 4: 26, Matt. 7: 24–7.

the idea of a golden age, either in the form of a millennium, a paradise, a reformed society, or a time when pain and vice will have disappeared.[6] These speculations would eventually find a focus in *Queen Mab*. The millennial character of this vision is implicit in Shelley's initial conception of the work. In 1811, he reveals his inclination to write a poem about 'a perfect state of society; tho still earthly',[7] or as Mary Shelley called it in her note on *Queen Mab*, a 'sort of millennium of freedom and brotherhood' (*SPW*, 837). On 18 August 1812, he sent samples of this poem to his publisher Thomas Hookham. And on 15 February 1813, he wrote to Hookham again to say that the poem had been finished and a fair copy made. During the time that Shelley was composing *Queen Mab*, he was also writing *Biblical Extracts*, a pamphlet apparently comprised of selected 'moral sayings of Jesus Christ'.[8] Unfortunately, no copy of this tract, in manuscript or printed form, is extant.[9] But in this light, it is not surprising to discover biblical models at many points in the poem.

Queen Mab is structured around the framework device of a dream-vision conducted by the fairy Mab, who reveals to the ascended spirit of Ianthe a vision of the past, present, and future. In the description of each of these periods, there is a prophetic element. The vision of the past is a brief survey of ancient empires modelled on Volney's *Ruins* and on the prophetic literature of doom-saying, of pronouncing woe on the rival monarchies of the ancient Near East. Mab describes the present as a time of social abuses (monarchy, war, capitalism, and religion) in the style of prophetic declamation against injustice and corrupt religious practice. And finally, the future is presented as an idyllic state analogous to the millennium of Isaiah.

The fact that history of necessity will culminate in this peaceful agrarian state does not mean that the poem is without an apocalyptic element. The present is a time of warfare, according to Ahasuerus, as men are 'Drunk from the winepress of the Almighty's wrath' (VII. 218).[10] In canto iv, Shelley presents war in all its apocalyptic horror:

---

[6] See *Letters*, i. 125, 127, 152, 215, 252, 271.

[7] Letter to Elizabeth Hitchener, 10 Dec. 1811, *Letters*, i. 201.

[8] Letter to Elizabeth Hitchener, 27 Feb. 1812, *Letters*, i. 265.

[9] David Lee Clark thinks that the undated essay on Christianity published by Lady Shelley in 1859 is 'an early draft of the *Biblical Extracts*'; see his article 'Shelley's Biblical Extracts', *Modern Language Notes*, 66 (1951), 435. Scholarly consensus, however, is that the essay on Christianity was probably written at a later date, most likely in 1817. See A. H. Koszul (ed.), *Shelley's Prose in the Bodleian Manuscripts* (London, 1910), 11; Donald Reiman, *Percy Bysshe Shelley* (New York, 1969), 60; and P. M. S. Dawson, *BSM*, iii, p. xvi.

[10] Rev. 19: 15.

> The torn deep yawns,—the vessel finds a grave
> Beneath its jagged gulf.
>   Ah! whence yon glare
> That fires the arch of heaven?—that dark red smoke
> Blotting the silver moon? The stars are quenched
> In darkness . . .

$$(\text{IV. } 32–6)$$

This passage borrows heavily from biblical apocalyptic.[11] At the open-
ing of the sixth seal in the book of Revelation, there is cosmic anarchy:
the earth shakes, the sun becomes black, the moon turns into blood,
and the stars fall (Rev. 6: 12–13). These characteristically apocalyptic
phenomena are manifestations of the Lamb's wrath. Shelley continues:

> The discord grows; till pale death shuts the scene,
> And o'er the conqueror and the conquered draws
> His cold and bloody shroud . . .

$$(\text{IV. } 46–8)$$

This image, drawn from the description of the four horsemen of the
Patmos vision (Rev. 6: 2, 8), indicates not only that warfare culminates
in death, but that the present era is one of death. But the apocalyptic
scenes of mass slaughter that Shelley presents do not govern the poem's
eschatology; for, not far from Mab's account of war, is her description
of the Edenic state that will supersede the time of bloodshed (IV. 89).

   In the first canto of *Queen Mab*, in which the fairy queen arrives in a
chariot to summon the soul of Ianthe from her body, Shelley presents
an overture of disruptive symbols which not only herald the new reve-
lation of the poem but also proclaim the advent of a dynamic new era.
The first of these is the 'rushing sound' which preludes the arrival of
Queen Mab's chariot and which Shelley describes in terms of wind (I.
45, 50). The visitation brings to mind the commission of the prophet
Ezekiel, who, caught up in the spirit, heard the noise of a 'great rush-
ing' amid the sounds of wings and wheels (Ezek. 3: 12, 13). Related
to this is the inception of the Church in the New Testament. On the
day of Pentecost, the early Christians received the Holy Spirit as they
heard 'a sound from heaven as of a rushing mighty wind' (Acts 2: 2).
In both cases, the ethereal rushing sound introduces a new spiritual
experience.[12]

---

[11] Cf. the opening of Southey's *The Curse of Kehama* (I. ii. 14–27) in *The Poems of
Robert Southey*, ed. M. Fitzgerald (London, 1909), 118.

[12] The significance of the wind as a symbol of change and renewal in Romantic litera-

The chariot itself constitutes a powerful second symbol in this series. Its 'burning wheels' link it with the theophany of Daniel in the Old Testament (I. 215). In this vision, Daniel describes the Ancient of days, whose 'throne *was like* the fiery flame, *and* his wheels *as* burning fire' (7: 9). Shelley of course is not describing a throne. But commentary on the Bible even in his time recognized that the chariot was in effect a movable throne.[13] Thus it appears as the 'chariot of paternal deity' in *Paradise Lost* (VI. 750 ff.). It is clear from Milton's allusion to the chariot's 'wheel within wheel' and to the 'four cherubic shapes' (VI. 751, 753) that the first chapter of Ezekiel, with its description of wheels within wheels, lies behind the description. But the fact that Milton's chariot has 'burning wheels' (VI. 832) suggests the vision of Daniel, as it suggests that Shelley borrowed from both Miltonic and biblical sources in describing the chariot of Mab. In all these sources available to Shelley, the chariot (or throne) is involved in a revelatory process, as it is in his own poem.[14]

A third key biblical element is the 'annunciation' in which the fairy pronounces Ianthe to be

> Judged alone worthy of the envied boon[15]
> That waits the good and the sincere; that waits
> Those who have struggled, and with resolute will
> Vanquished earth's pride and meanness, burst the chains,
> The icy chains of custom . . .
>
> (I. 123–7)

The biblical passage which parallels this declaration is the speech of the archangel Gabriel to the Virgin, who is pronounced 'blessed' in that the everlasting Kingdom is to be initiated by the child she will bear (Luke

ture is discussed by Maud Bodkin, *Archetypal Patterns in Poetry* (1934; London, 1963), 30–6, and by M. H. Abrams, 'The Correspondent Breeze', in *Kenyon Review*, 19 (1957), 113–30; rev. repr. in *English Romantic Poets*, ed. M. H. Abrams (1960; New York, 1973), 37–54.

[13] See *An Illustration of the Holy Scriptures*, ii. 1664.

[14] See the discussion of Shelley and the image of the chariot in Harold Bloom's *Poetry and Repression*, 87–98.

[15] The line suggests a kinship between Shelley's visionary guide and Godwin. On 8 Mar. 1812, Shelley wrote to Godwin: 'to you, I owe the inestimable boon of granted power, of arising from the state of intellectual sickliness and lethargy into which I was plunged two years ago' (*Letters*, i. 266). On 14 Mar. 1812, Godwin wrote back: 'Oh, that I could place you on the pinnacle of ages, from which these twenty years would shrink to an invisible point!' (Shelley's *Letters*, i. 269 n.). Thus Ianthe's spirit in *Queen Mab* is placed 'High on an isolated pinnacle; / The flood of ages combating below' (II. 253–4).

1: 28–33). In either case, a chosen maid is approved by a supernatural visitant.[16]

Mab's annunciation includes a reference to a fourth biblical symbol, the day-star which announces the dawning of a new era. The young Shelley's fondness for this image is clear from his frequent references to it.[17] In *Queen Mab*, the 'day-stars of their age' are those who have defied custom (I. 127–8). The phrase alludes to 2 Peter 1: 19: '. . . take heed, as unto a light that shineth in a dark place, until the day dawn, and the day star arise in your hearts.' Since this image accords with the metaphor of Christ as a morning star (Rev. 22: 16), Shelley appears to be humanizing the messianic emblem by applying it to a select group of people of which Ianthe is a representative. This revelation of the divine within the human is a pattern that is characteristic of Shelley. The astronomical sign is both a harbinger of the revolutionary new *malkuth* and a metaphor of this epoch's spiritual humanity.

A fifth scriptural symbol is expressed in Mab's rending the 'veil of mortal frailty' (I. 181), an act which permits the visionary experience.[18] The rending of the veil in the temple was one of the remarkable events accompanying the death of Christ on the cross (Matt. 27: 51). This veil had been prescribed by Moses to separate the chamber containing the ark, the most holy place, from the rest of the tabernacle (Exod. 26: 30–5). Annually on the Day of Atonement, the high priest would enter this veiled inner sanctum to cover the sins of Israel by sprinkling the blood of the sacrifice on the mercy seat in the most holy place (Lev. 16: 15–16). Christ's death, however, signified the end of this system of animal sacrifice, according to the New Testament. Hebrews 10: 20 speaks of Christ's broken flesh as the veil of the new covenant, just as Mab speaks of her power over the 'veil of mortal frailty'. She speaks of course only about the temporal limitations of bodily existence. But her hierophantic function is a dim echo of Christ's entering the most holy place of intimacy with God to act as high priest for eternity (Heb. 6: 19– 20). St Paul asserts that there exists a veil obstructing a clear perception of the Pentateuch and that the Judaic mind is blinded by this veil, which is removed when one acknowledges Christ as the focal point of the Mosaic system (2 Cor. 3: 13–16). Consequently, the veil as biblical

[16] Cf. the similar statement in one of Shelley's sources for the poem, Sir William Jones's 'The Palace of Fortune' in *The Poetical Works*, (2 vols.; London, 1810), ii. 149.

[17] See the 'Esdaile' poems 'The Crisis' (l. 19) and 'To the Republicans of North America' (l. 41) and the lines beginning 'Why is it said thou canst but live' (l. 12).

[18] Cf. Blake's use of the image in *Jerusalem*, 20: 36, 23: 31, 30: 40, 55: 16, 65: 61, 67: 16, 68: 42, and 69: 38–44.

symbol in *Queen Mab* does not contradict its Platonic sense. In either case, the veil stands between mortality, with its limitations, and the light of the ultimate Truth. And its removal signifies a clear apprehension of that truth.

The significance of these elements—the rushing wind-like sound, the epiphany of the chariot, the annunciation, the dawning day-star, and the rending of the veil—is therefore twofold. They announce both the vision itself and the advent of a perfected state. But before Mab can present this new spiritual epoch to the spirit of Ianthe, she must cause her pupil to recognize the vanity of building earthly kingdoms, the error of the past.

Shelley begins by presenting a composite portrait of ruined empires inspired in part by Volney's *Ruins* and by the biblical prophets. As with Volney, the tone is Ozymandian:

> Behold, the Fairy cried,
> Palmyra's ruined palaces!—
> Behold! where grandeur frowned;
> Behold! where pleasure smiled;
> What now remains? . . .
>
> (II. 109–13)

The Bible attributes such desolation to the retribution of God.[19] For Shelley, the overturning of empires occurs of necessity. But apart from this notable difference, the poet is remarkably consistent with the prophetic strain of Scripture. Mab's prediction that the pyramids of Egypt will fall (II. 129) echoes the biblical prophecy concerning the wall of Babylon, which likewise will fall (Jer. 51: 44). The successive denunciations of ancient empires proceeds in the spirit of Ezekiel's prophecies against the kingdoms of Ammon, Moab, Edom, Philistia, Phoenicia, Tyre, Zidon, and Egypt (chs. 25–32). In a spirit of irony, Mab includes the collapsed empire of the Israelites in her declamation:

> Behold yon sterile spot;
> Where now the wandering Arab's tent
> Flaps in the desert-blast.
> There once old Salem's haughty fane
> Reared high to heaven its thousand golden domes . . .
>
> (II. 134–8)

Again Shelley alludes to a prophecy against Babylon, which would become so desolate that even the nomadic Arabs would not pitch their

---

[19] See Isa. 13: 19–22, 25: 2, 32: 14, and 34: 13.

tents there (Isa. 13: 20). What Babylon was to Isaiah, Jerusalem is to
Shelley. The poet implies that the Hebrews built their temple at the
expense of social justice, for the reference to the curses of widows and
orphans (II. 141) recalls the familiar prophetic injunctions to aid such
people. The ensuing characterization of the ancient Jews as barbarians
who practised a sanguinary religion is a typically Enlightenment touch
(II. 149–61). The fairy concludes her visionary tour of these ruined
empires in canto II with a meditation on pride, a subject treated at sev-
eral points in the book of Isaiah (e.g. 14: 13, 25: 11).

The present, according to Shelley, is an era of many social evils
which may be traced to a common source. In the fifth canto he ascribes
to the principle of self the abuses of religion (l. 22), tyranny (l. 31),
commerce (l. 53), and war (ll. 256–7). In the previous canto he had dis-
missed the idea of evil as inherent in human nature, and the related
view that sin is inherited from Adam, as taught in St Paul's epistle to
the Romans (IV. 76, 117–18). But in canto V, he discourses in what can
only be described as Christian terms on 'suicidal selfishness' (v. 16).
Jeremiah writes that the heart is deceitful and inherently wicked (17: 9).
So the fairy Mab speaks of the 'mean lust' which binds most of human-
ity (v. 166–7). Shelley's view of 'the sordid lust of self' (v. 90) thus chal-
lenges his earlier denial of 'Man's evil nature' (IV. 76). He agrees with
the biblical observation that there is something desperately wrong with
the human condition.[20] But he disagrees with the biblical account of its
origin, and he presents an alternative view of redemption from that
state. In the New Testament it is virtue obtained through Christ which
frees the Christian from the corruption which subsists in the world
through lust (2 Pet. 1: 3–5). Shelley, on the other hand, believes that
virtue effects one's own self-reformation, for 'perfection's germ' exists
within every human heart (v. 147). He furthermore believes that the
virtuous constitute a kind of church which exists eschatologically in
anticipation of the universal *malkuth* of love. The effects of the 'fallen'
state of self-aggrandizement are undone in this millennial amelioration
of society:

> But hoary-headed selfishness has felt
> Its death-blow, and is tottering to the grave:
> A brighter morn awaits the human day . . .
>
> (v. 249–51)

[20] The ideas of self, self-love, and selfishness were mentioned often in Shelley's letters
to Elizabeth Hitchener during the time of *Queen Mab*'s conception and composition. See
Letters, i. 101, 151, 161, 173, 188, 191, 192, 207, 208, 244, 252, and 257.

While canto V thus deals with the subject of selfishness, it describes the inevitability of change, as represented in the motif of the renovating wind (v. 5).

The political manifestation of the selfish principle is the institution of monarchy. Pervading Shelley's description of the king in canto III is the tone of Ecclesiastes. According to the poet, there exists a natural cycle in the world:

> The golden harvests spring; the unfailing sun
> Sheds light and life; the fruits, the flowers, the trees,
> Arise in due succession . . .
>
> (III. 193–5)

These lines are essentially an amplification of Ecclesiastes 1: 4–7, which Shelley quotes in the Notes on *Queen Mab* (*PS*, i. 363). His point in the third canto is that the monarch stands outside this natural order (III. 170). He squanders his life in revelry (l. 39), becomes intemperate (l. 44), hoards gold (l. 46), builds a great palace (l. 71), and yet cannot enjoy a good night's sleep (l. 67). These activities are all confessed to be 'vanity' by the nameless king over Israel who is the 'Preacher' of Ecclesiastes and who concludes that the sleepless night is generally their reward.[21]

The major grievance against the monarch is that he accumulates wealth unjustly (III. 46–53, 118–38). Shelley may have in mind the biblical objections to monarchy raised in 1 Samuel 8: 10–18. Here the writer says that a king 'will take the tenth of your sheep: and ye shall be his servants' (1 Sam. 8: 17). Nevertheless, the Israelites insisted on having a king, largely out of a desire for conformity to the customs of other nations (1 Sam. 8: 5). 'Custom' of any sort was anathema to Shelley. But monarchy as he saw it was hardly distinguishable from tyranny. It was tyranny that spawned war (v. 64–8). And tyranny was closely associated with the origins of commerce, the system of economic selfishness that 'grinds [man] to the dust of misery' (v. 60).[22] Furthermore, tyranny led to corruption:

> Those too the tyrant serve, who, skilled to snare
> The feet of justice in the toils of law,
> Stand, ready to oppress the weaker still;
> And, right or wrong, will vindicate for gold . . .
>
> (IV. 196–9)

---

[21] See Eccles. 2: 1, 3, 4, 8, and 23.

[22] Cf. Isa. 3: 15: 'What mean ye *that* ye beat my people to pieces, and grind the faces of the poor?'

In a similar way, the prophet Micah laments that princes and judges ask for bribes (7: 3). Zephaniah includes the priesthood in his prophecy concerning Jerusalem: 'Her princes within her *are* roaring lions; her judges *are* evening wolves . . . her priests have polluted the sanctuary' (3: 3, 4). Shelley too includes the priesthood in his invective (IV. 80, 168, 237). From his point of view, organized religion simply serves the ends of the monarch.

The abuses of religion are the theme of canto VII, in which Shelley conjures up as his chief witness against the Christian faith the form of the Wandering Jew Ahasuerus. The Jew is condemned by Christ to wander eternally without dying. The irony of this circumstance is that Christ violates his own ethical teaching. In his preface to *The Wandering Jew* (1811), Shelley had quoted the 'golden rule' (Luke 6: 31). But obviously, the poet could conceive of a Christ who would abrogate his own teaching by condemning the Jew. His identification with Ahasuerus springs from his own experience of rejection by Christ.[23] Much like Shelley, Ahasuerus in *Queen Mab* persists in defying God. Like Milton's Satan, he prefers 'Hell's freedom to the servitude of heaven' (VII. 195). This similarity to Milton's Devil is not accidental; Shelley had prefaced cantos I and III of *The Wandering Jew* with quotations from *Paradise Lost* having to do with the character of Satan.

As a personification of thought, or of knowledge, the Jew is summoned by the fairy's invocation of 'Ahasuerus, rise!' (VII. 67). The phrase echoes the command of Christ, who in raising his friend from the dead says, 'Lazarus, come forth' (John 11: 43). But it also brings to mind the visit of Saul to the witch of Endor. The spirit of Samuel, much like the spectre of Ahasuerus, is summoned by the witch so that Saul may best judge what course of action to take regarding an imminent Philistine attack. He appears as an old man 'covered with a mantle' (1 Sam. 28: 14). Likewise, Ahasuerus appears as one of 'untold ancient-ness' (VII. 74).[24] Samuel speaks mainly of the future, Ahasuerus of the past, but both are oracular. The one gives voice to the will of God (foretelling Saul's death), while the other defies that will.

Essentially, Ahasuerus vindicates the attitude toward Christianity expressed by Mab. The fairy had asserted that 'Earth groans beneath religion's iron age' (VII. 43). Her lament parallels that of St Paul on the subject of the Fall: '. . . the whole creation groaneth and travaileth in

---

[23] See *Letters*, i. 29, 35, 45, 66, 71.

[24] Cf. the personified abstraction of knowledge, also mantled, in Jones's 'The Palace of Fortune', in *Poetical Works*, ii. 159.

pain' (Rom. 8: 22). But the apostle attributes this world agony to sin; Shelley attributes it to religion, which in his view arbitrarily creates the category of sin. In this 'iron age', the Church acts in violation of its own ethical standard. Mab continues:

> And priests dare babble of a God of peace,
> Even whilst their hands are red with guiltless blood,
> Murdering the while . . .
>
> (VII. 44–6)

The prophet Hosea also presents the image of a sanguinary priesthood: 'Gilead is . . . polluted with blood. And as troops of robbers wait for a man, so the company of priests murder in the way by consent' (6: 8–9). While there is therefore a biblical precedent for Shelley's tirade against priests, it must be remembered that the biblical context is the prophetic call to repentance; the Shelleyan message is that clerical corruption, like the Yahwistic tradition, is slipping into history.

Ahasuerus presents a concise summary of biblical history, from Eden to the Incarnation, beginning in the satirical tone of the *philosophes*:

> From an eternity of idleness
> I, God, awoke; in seven days' toil made earth
> From nothing; rested, and created man:
> I placed him in a paradise, and there
> Planted the tree of evil, so that he
> Might eat and perish . . .
>
> (VII. 106–11)[25]

Shelley's use of anthropomorphism renders the Judaeo-Christian system incredible to the European mind. Surely the notion of a God who is idle, who sleeps, and who wilfully rigs the scheme whereby man can only fail is an absurdity. One of the special targets of Ahasuerus's discourse is the doctrine of election, the bane of the *philosophes*. In a universe governed by a universal necessity, the idea of a particular people can stand only for bigotry, whether in the Old Testament or the New (VII. 114–15, 139–40, 156). The phenomenon of the chosen few, with its corollary of the unchosen many, violated the Enlightenment spirit of universalism and toleration, as did the militance of the Hebrews in taking the Promised Land and of the Church in its inquisitorial moments (VII. 117–20, 225–30).

In dealing with Christ's nature, Ahasuerus seems divided. On the one

---

[25] Cf. Volney's *Ruins*, 105–6.

hand, he presents a Docetic Christology by describing a Jesus whose mortal flesh was merely a veil for divinity and whose 'unterrestrial sense' prevented him from suffering on the cross (VII. 164–75). On the other, he presents a rabble-rousing demagogue who 'blessed the sword' (VII. 170). Christ, of course, had said, 'I came not to send peace, but a sword' (Matt. 10: 34). But he spoke of domestic, rather than military, conflict; the sword is that which divides. However, Shelley takes the figure of speech quite literally to mean that Christ sanctioned the many atrocities that would be committed by European armies in his name.

Behind the Christian religion, of course, lay the God of Israel, whom Shelley could never conceive of as more than a personification of the ultimate cause (VI. 93–102). But the poet particularly disdained the image of God reigning in heaven 'like an earthly king' (VI. 104–7).[26] In the sixth canto, Shelley elaborates his alternative to the sovereign Lord of the Old Testament. What is remarkable is the extent to which the poet's sovereign necessity (or nature) is patterned on the biblical Deity.

Nature is a spirit of truth, busily 'recreating' truth from collapsed falsehood (VI. 56). According to Shelley, it will 'blot in mercy from the book of earth' the woes of intransigent monotheism (VI. 57). Shelley here appropriates the prerogative of God to blot out sins forever, inverting the meaning of the biblical writer (Isa. 43: 25). Although his faith is in the natural order governed by necessity, this necessity 'reigns' much like Yahweh, for it controls the various aspects of nature. When the poet says that it governs the whirlwind and the tempest (VI. 157), the waves (VI. 165), the clouds (VI. 166), and the lightning (VI. 167), it becomes clear that necessity is simply taking over from God, for the God of the Old Testament directly controlled each of these natural operations.[27] But necessity is also like the God of the New Testament. It 'Fulfils its destined, though invisible work' (VI. 176) as the God of St Paul predestines all things according to his own purposes (Eph. 1: 11). And it regards all 'with an impartial eye' (VI. 216) as God is 'no respecter of persons' (Acts 10: 34). Yet Shelley clearly distinguishes his doctrine from that of the Judaeo-Christian God:

[26] See Shelley's later fragment 'Pater Omnipotens' (SPW, 634). The metaphor of God as a king recurs throughout the Jewish Scriptures. See 1 Sam. 12: 12, Ps. 10: 16, and Jer. 10: 10.

[27] See Nahum 1: 3, Ps. 93: 4, 78: 23, and Job 37: 3. Jerrold Hogle discusses the image and analogy of the biblical God in Shelley's Process (New York and Oxford, 1988), 6–12, 28–9, 103–12.

> Spirit of Nature! all-sufficing Power,
> Necessity! thou mother of the world!
> Unlike the God of human error, thou
> Requirest no prayers or praises . . .
>
> (VI. 197–200)

The sufficiency of God taught in the Bible (2 Cor. 3: 5) is here ascribed to necessity. But as critics have noted, Shelley's necessity in *Queen Mab* is not entirely benevolent, for the natural order contains evil as well as good (III. 81, VI. 32).[28] For this reason, Shelley's adoration of an admittedly sullied necessity is surprising. As was the case in his thinking on selfishness, it suggests that his theory required further refinement. Nevertheless, the sublime character of necessity appeared clear to him. As if to enhance the difference between necessity and the biblical God, Shelley makes his sovereign power feminine, rather than masculine, as did Holbach in the *Système* (i. 55 n.). Thus she becomes the force behind beneficial change, and this gradual amelioration promises to culminate in a future millennial state.

In his preface to *The Wandering Jew*, Shelley had expressed contempt for the 'superstitions of the battle of Armageddon, the personal reign of J——— C———, &c' (*PS*, i. 42). The Christian eschatology inevitably clashed with his own view of coming events. Thus the eighth canto of *Queen Mab* deals with the poet's alternative to the chiliasm of the Church. The chief inspiration for Shelley's description in this section is the book of Isaiah.[29] The young radical forecasts a time of 'universal peace' attained in part by Ianthe's serving as a 'lighthouse' to others (VIII. 54, 57). The book of Isaiah correspondingly speaks of a time when all nations will turn toward Zion because Israel will become a 'light to the Gentiles' (Isa. 49: 6). Shelley thus lapses into a montage of golden age vignettes drawn from the prophet. The desert will 'teem with countless rills and shady woods' (VIII. 75), as Isaiah had said it would (35: 1). All nature will be transformed. The tiger will cease to devour the lamb (VIII. 79).[30] The basilisk will lick the feet of the infant (VIII.

---

[28] See e.g. Solomon F. Gingerich, 'Shelley's Doctrine of Necessity *versus* Christianity', *PMLA*, 33 (1918), 467–8; and Joseph Barrell, *Shelley and the Thought of His Time* (New Haven, Conn., 1947), 73, 79. Stuart Sperry has more recently argued that Shelley, at least until the end of 1819, paradoxically maintained a belief in the freedom of the will as well as a 'benign conception of Necessity [which] was qualified by his deepening involvement in the problem of evil'. See 'Necessity and the Role of the Hero in Shelley's *Prometheus Unbound*', *PMLA*, 96 (1981), 248.

[29] Lowth had written in his *Lectures* that the book of Isaiah 'may be properly said to afford the most perfect model of the prophetic poetry' (ii. 84–5).   [30] Cf. Isa. 11: 6.

84–7).[31] Like Isaiah, Shelley envisions an idyllic, paradisiacal state. But unlike the prophet, the poet attributes the emergence of this utopia to the working of an impersonal necessity.

As the vision of the future fades in the ninth canto, the fairy admonishes the spirit of Ianthe to become actively involved in the struggle that will lead to the kingdom she has described, a new spiritual realm governed by nature, or necessity (IX. 146). The tone is Pauline; both Mab and St Paul portray the spiritual struggle in terms of a course to which one must faithfully adhere (2 Tim. 4: 7). The fairy urges Ianthe to 'fearlessly bear on' toward the 'happy regions of eternal hope' (IX. 164, 163).[32] Finally, St Paul writes: 'For we wrestle not against flesh and blood, but against principalities, against powers, against the rulers of the darkness of this world, against spiritual wickedness in high *places*' (Eph. 6: 12). Shelley adopts this language for his own purpose, to redefine the nature of this wickedness which keeps one from obtaining an enlightened frame of mind. Mab finally commissions her pupil:

> . . . bravely bearing on, thy will
> Is destined an eternal war to wage
> With tyranny and falsehood . . .
>
> (IX. 189–91)

The description of spiritual conflict with the powers that govern this darkened aeon raises a problem which is central in Shelley's thought. If necessity is indeed sovereign in her universe, then one may legitimately question the prophetic vocation of railing against tyrants, for they too are ordained by this Spirit of nature. And if the millennium is to arise in the course of predetermined events, then the struggle to hasten its advent equally seems of little use. The problem has a precedent in the eighteenth-century progressivist thought of David Hartley, whose *Observations on Man* Shelley ordered in the summer of 1812. Hartley encouraged his readers to co-operate with the force of determinism. The mechanism of necessity, as he puts it, 'has a Tendency to make us labour more earnestly with ourselves and others, particularly Children, from the greater Certainty attending all Endeavours that operate in a mechanical Way'.[33] Thus the individual may assist the course of necessity, which by its associational alchemy transforms pains into pleasures

---

[31] Cf. Isa. 11: 8.   [32] Cf. 1 Tim. 6: 12.

[33] *Observations on Man, His Frame, His Duty, and His Expectations*, ed. T. L. Huguelet (2 vols.; London, 1749; facsimile repr. Gainesville, Fla., 1966), i. 510. The first volume of Shelley's copy of Hartley's *Observations on Man*, with annotations in his own hand, is in the Carl H. Pforzheimer Collection of the New York Public Library.

and restores the paradisiacal state (i. 83). While the millennium thus arises through deterministic perfectibilist means, one may voluntarily participate in the process.

Although Hartley was a relatively orthodox Christian, the programme of spiritual improvement that he advocates in the second volume of the *Observations on Man* is consonant with that presented in *Queen Mab*, particularly in the notes. Hartley recommends abstaining from distilled liquors and from meat (ii. 220, 222). He enjoins the pursuit of 'Self-annihilation' and decries the irresolution of serving both God and Mammon (ii. 282, 316, 344). Certainly, there are biblical bases for this ethos.[34] But there is a radical strain in Hartley that Shelley could hardly have overlooked. The eighteenth-century physician declares that the existing political institutions must be dissolved (ii. 366–7). And he believes that Church authorities 'must incur the prophetical Censures in the highest Degree' (ii. 371). Hartley was not alone in voicing Christian concern about the social problems of his time. One can find 'prophetic' rhetoric directed against social and political ills in William Cowper as well, for the concern for social justice and reform at the heart of Old Testament prophecy was shared by many evangelical Christians in the eighteenth century.[35] Shelley too is concerned with the prophetic ethos in *Queen Mab*. But his faith is in the 'virtuous' as the chosen people by which that moral character will be legislated, and in the necessity which, acting in the place of Providence, sanctions the full flowering of that character in a millennial kingdom which *is* of this world.

Power, which was synonymous with necessity in Hume's philosophy, is essentially scrutable by its visible effects in *Queen Mab*. However, it is remote and unknowable in Shelley's chief productions of 1816, the 'Hymn to Intellectual Beauty' and 'Mont Blanc'. And whereas it demands neither prayer nor worship in *Queen Mab* (vi. 199–200), Shelley offers it praise in the 'Hymn'. The power is once more described in terms of Yahwistic analogy, but it becomes more personally involved with man. The Hebrews could simultaneously view God as the monarch of creation and allow his descent from the throne realm of Isaiah's initial vision into the world as a divine afflatus. In the Old Testament, the Spirit of God came upon men to enable them to

---

[34] See Prov. 12: 10, 23: 20, Eph. 5: 18, and Matt. 16: 24, 6: 24.

[35] In *The Task*, Cowper castigates the systems of commerce, empire, luxury, and clerical pomposity (I. 719–24; I. 736–8, II. 37; IV. 580–6; and II. 372–462). His portrait of the 'bloated' monarch, contrasted with his 'penurious' subjects (V. 283, 319), is strikingly like the description of the king in *Queen Mab* (III. 30–122). See *Cowper: Poetical Works*, ed. H. S. Milford, 4th edn., rev. N. Russell (1934; London, 1967).

perform specific tasks, such as prophesying or making war (Judg. 3: 10;
1 Sam. 10: 6). Although the descent of Shelley's evanescent spirit may
suggest a comparable inspiration (ll. 59–60), it is in fact quite different;
for the poet doubts the potential for transmundane revelation—the
'voice from some sublimer world' (l. 25).[36] And the poem's speaker
only superficially resembles the Hebrew *nabi*, the prophet who articu-
lates a revelation; for the accent is on poetic ecstasy itself, rather than on
the content of any particular message. It is worth mentioning that
Shelley wrote the 'Hymn' during the summer of 1816, when he was
reading Rousseau's *Julie, ou la nouvelle Héloïse*. Characteristic of the
effusions of the protagonist Saint-Preux in this novel is recourse to
terms such as *égarement* or *mes transports* to describe his emotional
responses to Julie.[37] The effect of such a state of mind in Shelley is to
shift the focus from the power (and its spirit) to the self. These height-
ened states of awareness effectively supplant biblical revelation.

There are two sets of terms which define the operation of the
shadow of power (the Spirit of Beauty) in the poem. One is that of reli-
gion ('grace', 'mystery', 'consecrate', 'vow', 'worships', etc.); the other
is that of uncertainty ('shadow', 'mist', 'clouds', 'Doubt', 'unknown',
etc.). Seen together, they suggest that Shelley's fundamental scepticism
was imbued with a reverential awe normally reserved for religious
experience.[38] The Psalmist had written that dwelling 'under the shadow
of the Almighty' meant security (Ps. 91: 1). Shelley's similar image
inspires no such feeling. But the poem does not end on a note of
lamentation; for, as Donald H. Reiman has observed, the visitations of
divine power are attended by feelings which link the poet not only ver-
tically (with the power itself) but also horizontally (with humanity and
the natural creation). Reiman sees the 'Hymn' as a statement of faith in
which these fleeting intimations of harmony and love point in an
almost eschatological way to an ameliorated state.[39]

[36] My text for the 'Hymn' is that of the *Examiner* clipping corrected in Shelley's hand
(*PS*, i. 528–31). As in the case of 'Mont Blanc', the Scrope Davies MS version of the
poem (in Mary's hand) may be consulted in the Longman edition (*PS*, i. 525–8, 538–41).

[37] In *Œuvres Complètes de Jean-Jacques Rousseau*, ed. B. Gagnebin and M. Raymond (4
vols.; Paris, 1959–69), vol. 2; I. xiv. 65, I. liv. 147. Documentation is by section, letter
number, and page. Shelley's Assassins are noted for their spiritual states of transport (*PW*,
i. 128–9).

[38] Spencer Hall sees in the poem's myth of Power a fundamental scepticism; see
'Power and the Poet', *K–SJ*, 32 (1983), 124.

[39] *Intervals of Inspiration*, 238–9. Shelley's triad of 'Love, Hope, and Self-esteem' (l. 37)
substitutes for St Paul's virtues of love (charity), hope, and faith (2 Cor. 13: 13). As
Harold Bloom has pointed out in *Shelley's Mythmaking* (1959; Ithaca, NY, 1969), the sub-

In the companion poem to the 'Hymn', Shelley again explores the possibility of union with power, the origin of which is metaphorically the peak of Mont Blanc. But whereas in the earlier poem, power was seen as an influence on the mind, it is now seen as a force affecting the material universe. And it provides Shelley with a way of responding to the religious impulse behind Coleridge's statement concerning Mont Blanc and its environs: 'Who *would* be, who *could* be an Atheist in this valley of wonders!'[40] As in the earlier period of Shelley's radicalism, power in 'Mont Blanc' is an alternative to the God of Christians like Coleridge. In the Bible, mountains are frequently associated with moments of revelation. The mountains of Ararat, Moriah, and Sinai all purport to bring heaven into proximity with earth in some way, and each is caught up in the redemptive typology of the Church. Likewise, Christ's most famous sermon, his transfiguration, and his crucifixion are all associated with mountains. In this light, the 'revelation' communicated to Shelley appears all the more extraordinary.

Shelley begins 'Mont Blanc' in language which brings to mind the God-like necessity of *Queen Mab*. The landscape is one

> Where power in likeness of the Arve comes down
> From the ice gulfs that gird his secret throne,
> Bursting through these dark mountains like the flame
> Of lightning through the tempest . . .
>
> (ll. 16–19)

Similarly, the book of Isaiah represents heaven as the throne of Yahweh's divine power: 'OH that thou wouldest rend the heavens, that thou wouldest come down, that the mountains might flow down at thy presence' (Isa. 64: 1).[41] Shelley thus deals with two worlds, that of the Mont and that of the ravine of the Arve. Living in the world of the ravine, he is himself part of the world of generation, of cycles and successions. In *Queen Mab*, Shelley had spoken of continuing generations as a constant, with reference to Ecclesiastes 1: 4 (v. 1–4). The ravine of the Arve too is a realm where all things participate in the

stitution of self-esteem for faith introduces the idea of a divinity within (pp. 39–40). The alternate reading of 'Demon' for 'God, and ghosts' (l. 27) effects a typical Shelleyan transposition. As self is divinized, orthodox Divinity is demonized. Variants are noted by Judith Chernaik and Timothy Burnett, 'The Byron and Shelley Notebooks in the Scrope Davies Find', *Review of English Studies* NS 29/113 (1978), 45.

[40] In *The Poetical Works of Samuel Taylor Coleridge*, ed. E. H. Coleridge (London, 1912), 377 n.

[41] See also Isa. 66: 1. Rieger suggests that the lines be read with reference to Rev. 22: 1 (*Mutiny Within*, 95); Bloom suggests Job 38: 25, 29 (*Shelley's Mythmaking*, 12).

cycles of birth and death (l. 95), where there is 'ceaseless motion' (l. 32). The state of mind in the poet which corresponds to this tumult is that of the Gadarene demoniac named Legion on account of the spirits which possessed him (Mark 5: 9). By contrast, the mountain is static, and the contemplation of it effectively exorcizes from the poet the 'legion of wild thoughts' (l. 41). The poet's meditation parallels the Psalmist's statement that 'I WILL lift up mine eyes unto the hills, from whence cometh my help' (Ps. 121: 1). But the Psalmist's source of help is the personal God who made the hills; Shelley, by contrast, acknowledges a mysterious impersonal power from which he receives no succour apart from instruction.

In stanzas III and IV the biblical language of the poem expresses a recognition of human inability either to grasp the idea of ultimate power or to transcend the ephemerality of life. The 'unknown omnipotence' of line 53 could well descend from the 'UNKNOWN GOD' of the Athenians that St Paul identified as the Christian God (Acts 17: 23). To illustrate the inadequacy of the mind to comprehend this 'remoter world', Shelley uses the following figure of speech:

> . . . For the very spirit fails,
> Driven like a homeless cloud from steep to steep
> That vanishes among the viewless gales!
>
> (ll. 57–9)

The image of the vanishing or dissipating cloud, a biblical simile for death (Job 7: 9), is mirrored in the assertion that human accomplishments 'Vanish, like smoke' (l. 119).[42] Mont Blanc, on the other hand, is emblematic of that which is 'infinite' and 'eternal' (ll. 60, 75). Curiously, Shelley evokes prophetic images of desolation to describe its summits.[43] Yet, according to him, 'The wilderness has a mysterious tongue' (l. 76):

> Thou hast a voice, great Mountain, to repeal
> Large codes of fraud and woe; not understood
> By all . . .
>
> (ll. 80–2)

This is Shelley's alternative to the voice crying in the wilderness to announce the coming of the Lord (Isa. 40: 3). This revisionist voice teaches a reliance on nature and on the unknown power which is its

---

[42] See also Jas. 4: 14.
[43] Cf. ll. 67–70 with Isa. 13: 21, Zeph. 2: 13–14, and Joel 2: 3.

Providential aspect (l. 79). The credal significance of the lines quoted is suggested in Shelley's use of the word 'doctrine' for 'voice' (l. 80) in the 'Scrope Davies' version of the poem.[44] That doctrine is the scepticism summed up in Shelley's 'secret strength of things' (l. 139)—the recognition of which conduces to the serenity of either doubt or faith (l. 77). Doubt will question the natural religion whereby the contemplation of nature leads to an acknowledgement of the Creator. 'Faith' will reconcile man with nature by allowing the mountain (a synecdoche for nature) to speak, rather than any world-transcending God who is the conclusion of all who demand the certitude of a First Cause. The message of the mountain is therefore one of scepticism.

The imperceptibility of power in the 'Hymn' and in 'Mont Blanc' indicates that the idea had undergone some modification since the period of *Queen Mab*. In the earlier work, Shelley had affirmed its operation (as necessity or the Spirit of Nature) as inherent in the material universe itself. However, in the works written at about the same time as the 'Hymn' and 'Mont Blanc', it is described in terms of idealism. In the preface to *Alastor* (written in December 1815), it is portrayed in language comparable to that of the blinding light of the ultimate reality in Plato's allegory of the cave (*PS*, i. 463). And according to the essay 'On Christianity' (drafted *c.*1817), Power is equivalent to the universal Being which authenticates the lesser beings who acknowledge its perfection (*PW*, i. 251–2). But in the philosophy of Hume, to which Shelley frequently refers during this period, the idea of power (or necessary connection) arises in the mind, for it cannot be observed empirically. According to the *Enquiry concerning Human Understanding*, 'power' is an idea resulting from the determination of the mind to establish 'necessary connexion', to assign the designations of 'cause' and 'effect' to phenomena perceived conjointly. Whether this act of the imagination has anything to do with the material universe is another question. Hume refers to such a correspondence as 'mysterious and unintelligible' (p. 66), 'unknown and inconceivable' (p. 67). Such is the language of the 'Hymn' and 'Mont Blanc'.

Shelley had already dealt with this sceptical notion of 'power' in the

---

[44] This alteration appears in the recently discovered Scrope Davies notebook, which presents Shelley's revised transcription of the original notebook draft (Bodleian MS Shelley adds. e. 16). 'Mont Blanc' was first published by Mary Shelley in *History of a Six Weeks' Tour* (1817), the source of the text quoted here. The Bodleian draft is reproduced by Chernaik in *The Lyrics of Shelley* (Cleveland, 1972), 288–93. For more information on the textual problems of the poem, see Chernaik and Burnett, 'Byron and Shelley Notebooks', and *PS*, i. 532–49.

Refutation of Deism (1814). In the second half of the dialogue, Eusebes refutes the deistic assertion of the God of order and design, concluding his speech by criticizing the connection made between the Creator and power. Echoing Locke's definition of power as the idea we derive from observing in objects the capacity to initiate or undergo change, he says that the 'word power expresses the capability of any thing to be or act' (*PW*, i. 121).[45] But Shelley's note directs us to Sir William Drummond, who in opposition to Locke posits the sceptic's 'occult cause' of power, for the '*vis movendi* is no object either of sense, or of understanding'.[46] Drummond says that 'Power . . . cannot be both the consequence and the origin of existing substance' (p. 5). Likewise, Shelley says that 'power is the attribute, not the origin of Being' (*PW*, i. 122). By divorcing power from Being, he undermines both the hypothesis of a First Cause and the biblical concept of the *malkuth*. In the New Testament, the Kingdom of God is mentioned at several points in connection with divine power.[47] But in examining power in terms of the occult necessity of 'necessary connexion', Shelley dissolves the link between existence and power by which the Kingdom of God subsists.

For the Shelley of 1816, power remains fundamentally unascertainable, as indeed is the enigmatic God of the Bible, who tells his prophet that 'my thoughts *are* not your thoughts, neither *are* your ways my ways' (Isa. 55: 8). What Leslie Brisman says of Shelley's 'Hymn' is equally true of 'Mont Blanc': 'the Power itself could no more be perceived by the natural poet than could the face of God by the traditional Christian or Hebrew. Moses saw not God's face but God's departure, the trail of His glory.'[48] The self-disclosure of God in the Bible is proportioned to man's ability to grasp his nature. But such proportion does not exist in the sceptic's apprehension of necessity, or power. Shelley never tires of repeating the assertion of Hume in the *Enquiry concerning Human Understanding* that all we can know about causality is the '*constant conjunction* of objects' (p. 92). He cites the principle as early as the Notes on *Queen Mab* (*PS*, i. 382) and as late as the *Defence of Poetry* (*SPP*, 489). Yet it is clear that in the poems discussed in this chapter, the idea of power has changed. In spite of the lip service to Hume's idea of necessity in *Queen Mab*, Shelley plainly sees necessity in that

[45] John Locke, *An Essay concerning Human Understanding*, 4th edn. (1700), ed. P. H. Nidditch (1975; Oxford, 1979), II. xxi. 1; p. 233.

[46] *Academical Questions* (London, 1805), 10–11.

[47] See Matt. 6: 13, Mark 9: 1, and 1 Cor. 4: 20.

[48] 'Mysterious Tongue', *Texas Studies in Literature and Language*, 23/3 (1981), 413.

work as inherent in the natural order, as did Godwin and Hartley.[49] For Hume, however, the natural order (that is, 'external objects') cannot be the source of the notion of power, or necessary connection, which is ultimately an 'idea of reflection' arising in the mind (p. 64). Necessity is simply the determination of the mind to infer causal relationships in the natural world based on its customary experience of observed phenomena (p. 82). Since necessity is thus divorced from the universe outside the mind, it is an essential feature of Hume's radical scepticism. Hence the frequent recourse to the language of the enigma, mystery, and uncertainty in the discussion of causes (particularly the First Cause) in the *Enquiry*. There are strong resonances of this view in the companion poems written in the summer of 1816. For Shelley increasingly appropriates the *malkuth* for the self (or mind). As Jesus in patristic theology embodied the *malkuth* in his person, the Kingdom of God is assimilated in the divinized self which is described in the essay on Christianity (*PW*, i. 251, 259).[50] However, it must be emphasized that this is a tendency, a general development in Shelley's philosophy. The idea of a millennial state, which for a time will remain as the spiritual model for his vision of a reformed society, will once again find expression in the revolutionary poem *The Revolt of Islam* (written in 1817). In the preface to this work, Shelley identifies love as the moral law which will reanimate 'the social institutions of mankind' (*SPW*, 37). Not surprisingly, the essay 'On Christianity' also dates from this period.

[49] The point is made and developed by F. B. Evans III, 'Shelley, Godwin, Hume, and the Doctrine of Necessity', *Studies in Philology*, 37 (1940), 639–40.

[50] Origen names Jesus αὐτοβασιλεία ('the Kingdom itself') in his *Commentary on Matthew* (XIV. vii). See Karl Schmidt, 'βασιλεία', in *Theological Dictionary of the New Testament*, ed. G. Kittel and G. Friedrich, trans. G. W. Bromiley (10 vols.; Grand Rapids, Mich., 1964–76), i. 589.

3

The Jacobin Jesus

The nature of the Kingdom of God as an expression of human fraternity is an ancillary theme of Shelley's essay 'On Christianity'. As a visible form of the *malkuth*, the early Church is construed as 'the infant republic of the Christian sect' (*PW*, i. 270), conspicuous by its communal ownership of property (*PW*, i. 269).[1] Thus the earliest Christians are conscripted into Shelley's service as model practitioners of the political philosophy which eradicates the artificial distinctions in society. The chief concern of the essay 'On Christianity', however, is with the proper understanding of Jesus and his message. Pervasive throughout is the insistence that the traditionally Christian view of Jesus is attributable to mere superstition, or as Shelley puts it, 'to the mistaken conceptions of the multitude' (*PW*, i. 251). The familiar dualism of 'the enlightened' and 'the vulgar' thus re-emerges in Shelley's attack on the 'popular' view of Christ, an attack which is more fundamentally a refusal to grant any textual or spiritual integrity to the gospels.

In his zeal to refute the error of orthodoxy (or custom), Shelley occasionally makes mistakes about the content of the scriptural account of Jesus and his teaching, a circumstance that is understandable in an essay that did not reach the form of a final draft. For example, he says that the notion of 'a peculiar Providence' by which men are judged is 'explicitly denied by Jesus Christ' (*PW*, i. 252). The denial, he claims, is expressed in Matthew 5: 44–5, a passage in which Jesus tells his followers to love their enemies because God causes 'the rain to fall on the just and the unjust' (*PW*, i. 253). However, Shelley's interpretation of the passage is at odds with several recorded sayings of Christ.[2] Furthermore, he mistakenly identifies the assertion that in helping one's enemies one 'would heap coals of fire upon his head' (*PW*, i. 260) as a saying of Jesus. Shelley feels that it is 'utterly incredible' that the benign Jesus could have said such a thing, and on this occasion has it his way, for the statement is St Paul's rather than Christ's (Rom. 12: 20). Particularly difficult for Shelley to believe is the teaching of Jesus concerning hell:

---

[1] Acts 2: 44, 4: 32.   [2] See e.g. Matt. 12: 50, 16: 27, 25: 31–46.

'It is not to be believed that Hell or punishment was the conception of this daring mind' (*PW*, i. 256). The gospel record is simply mistaken.[3] Where such 'contradictions' arise, the poet simply denies the record. The written accounts of Jesus are comprised, he says, of 'imperfect and obscure information which his biographers, persons certainly of very undisciplined and undiscriminating minds, have transmitted to posterity' (*PW*, i. 260). That statements about hell could be ascribed to Jesus is therefore due to the superstitiousness of those who wrote the gospels.

The criterion by which to accept or reject the various actions and sayings of Jesus is formulated by Shelley as follows: 'We ought to form a general image of his character and of his doctrines and refer to this whole the distinct portions of action and of speech by which they are diversified' (*PW*. i. 260). This notion of character is related to eighteenth-century speculation on necessity. Hume had referred the judgement of behaviour to its origin in human character, for '[a]ctions are by their very nature temporary and perishing'.[4] It is the 'necessary connexion' of cause and effect (in character and action) which validates the conception of judgement. A person possessing a completely virtuous character and acting only on the purest motives (as Jesus would have done) would utter only virtuous statements and perform only benevolent deeds. As a means of reconstructing a portrait of Jesus, this approach to judgement allows Shelley considerable freedom. He can say that Jesus could not have taught the existence of hell, for example, because the belief in retribution is inconsistent with his teaching on love and forgiveness. Statements about hell in the gospels are therefore to be disregarded.

The Jesus that Shelley reconstructs is to a large extent a projection of his own self-image as an apostle of enlightenment defying inquisitorial college dons, authoritarian judges, and the quislings of the Anglican hierarchy. This updated Christ, like an eighteenth-century philosopher of moral sentiments, has a mild disposition. He is an avatar of 'gentleness and benignity' (*PW*, i. 246). And, like the poet himself, he is something of a Spinozist, for he thinks of God as a 'power . . . mysteriously and illimitably pervading the frame of things' (*PW*, i. 250). Such is the 'general image' that Shelley establishes. He does, however, allow for his own abrogation of character consistency, for he depicts his itinerant rabbi as a proletarian activist who preaches a gospel of social

---

[3] See e.g. Matt. 18: 9, 25: 41, and Mark 9: 43.

[4] *A Treatise of Human Nature*, ed. L. A. Selby-Bigge, 2nd edn., rev. P. H. Nidditch (1978; Oxford, 1981), 411.

revolution. In a sense, then, his Jesus has not dispensed with hell. The fire of eternal judgement has simply been temporalized as incendiary defiance, the nature of which makes for an interesting contrast with the pacific image that Shelley creates. Concerning Christ's abhorrence of Jewish Law as custom, the poet writes:

He descants upon its insufficiency as a code of moral conduct, which it professed to be, and absolutely selects the law of retaliation as an instance of the absurdity and immorality of its institutions . . . . He tramples upon all received opinions, on all the cherished luxuries and superstitions of mankind. He bids them cast aside the chains of custom and blind faith. (*PW*, i. 262–3)

It would be easier to understand this characterization as a description of the poet himself than as any recognizable picture of Jesus. Shelley goes the extra mile by rendering Jesus an enlightened perfectibilist:

Jesus Christ, instructed his disciples to be perfect as their father in Heaven is perfect, declaring at the same time his belief that human perfection required the refraining from revenge or retribution in any of its various shapes. The perfection of the human and the divine character is thus asserted to be the same: man by resembling God fulfills most accurately the tendencies of his nature, and God comprehends within itself all that constitutes human perfection. Thus God is a model thro' which the excellence of man is to be measured. (*PW*, i. 259)

By understanding perfection here in terms of sinless conduct, Shelley interprets the meaning of the passage to which he refers (Matt. 5: 48) in the same way that many Churchmen have read it. However, the aspiration toward wholeness and maturity—the actual meaning of the word for 'perfect' ($\tau\acute{\epsilon}\lambda\epsilon\iota\circ\varsigma$)—is meant to reflect the completeness and perfection of the Father.[5] The poet uses the verse as an occasion to conflate the spheres of the divine and the human. Herein lies the kernel of Shelley's mature theology, of what Timothy Webb has called '[t]he most radical of his re-orderings . . . his re-location of the centre of power in man rather than God, the enthronement of man as his own divinity'.[6] The idea of God becomes for the poet a projection of the loftiest human virtues imaginable, while the God of orthodox Christianity retains 'the character of an evil daemon' (*PW*, i. 259). This confident anthropocentrism thus yields a humanized divinity and a messiah who is in many respects a persona of the poet himself. This acknowledgement, however, does not mean that Shelley's representa-

[5] H. G. Liddell and Robert Scott, *A Greek–English Lexicon*, 9th edn., rev. H. S. Jones (1940; Oxford, 1953), 1769; hereafter cited as Liddell and Scott.

[6] *Shelley* (Manchester, 1977), 171.

tion of Jesus is altogether an inversion of the biblical original. His general emphasis on Christ's teaching of love (*PW*, i. 253, 264–5) and on the need for living as simply as the birds of the air (*PW*, i. 264) have an almost orthodox Christian resonance. But the Jesus who is a proponent of the doctrine of equality and of what we would now recognize as a forerunner of liberation theology is a creation of the poet (*PW*, i. 262–3, 266, 269–71).

One of the Shelley notebooks in the Bodleian Library reveals the extent to which Shelley's recasting of Jesus as a revolutionary was taken. In the notes on the gospel of Luke which it contains, for example, the poet records an interesting response to the following portion of the Magnificat of the Virgin: 'He hath put down the mighty from *their* seats, and exalted them of low degree' (Luke 1: 52). Noting this passage, which anticipates the birth of Jesus, Shelley remarks, 'Jacobinism—the story of the shepherds in Luke alone'.[7] And in commenting on several of the beatitudes further on (Luke 6: 20–6), Shelley again sees a radical message in the scriptural text. That the poor, the hungry, and the reviled are 'blessed' invokes the response: 'Magnificent Jacobinism . . . better than any where else' (fo. 1). As a critic of the life of Christ, then, Shelley has a point to make. His persistent allusion to the Sermon on the Mount as a code of ethics aligns Jesus with the ethical monotheism of the prophets. Further on in the notebook, located between some scribblings for *Adonais* and draft material for his letter to Leigh Hunt concerning *Queen Mab* (22 June 1821), Shelley writes: 'The people which sate in darkness saw great light: to those who sate in the region & shadow of death, light is sprung up.—Blessed are the poor in spirit—the mourners; ye shall be comforted. The meek ye shall inherit the earth' (fo. 210).

This juxtaposition of paraphrased texts from Isaiah (9: 2) and from the Sermon on the Mount in the gospel of Matthew (5: 3–5) suggests that Shelley sees Jesus to be in full accord with the ethical teaching contained in the prophets. And by its panoramic surveying of empires destined to collapse, a mode Shelley employed in *Queen Mab*, that prophetic tradition is 'Jacobinist'. On the next page of the notebook, Shelley comments on the 'burden of Babylon' (Isa. 13: 4): 'The destruction of the old French Tyranny: then the destruction of the spirit of it surviving in Buonaparte—Ferdinand of Spain. The attempt in Italy. The fermentation of Germany. Greece & its liberty. *The Lord* hath broken the staff of the wicked & the sceptres of the rulers'[8] (fo. 211).

---

[7] Bodleian MS Shelley adds. e. 9, fo. 1.   [8] Isa. 14: 5.

While it is true that these notes were made approximately four years after the composition of the essay 'On Christianity', their tone is consistent with that of the essay. Paradoxically, the ethos expressed is both meek and benevolent, while at the same time revolutionary in the sansculottist sense.

The idealized figure of Christ which links Shelley with the Enlightenment survived into the Victorian era. Matthew Arnold asserted in *God and the Bible* (1875) that 'all the reporters of Jesus, understood him but imperfectly', that '[w]here the *logia* are suited to the character of Jesus, they come from Jesus'.[9] Other sayings may be brought into question. None the less, he insisted in *Literature and Dogma* (1873) that the Bible was indispensable, because 'we need the *epieikeia*, the sweet reasonableness, of Jesus' (vi. 405). Such remarks are characteristically Shelleyan, though Arnold's Jesus is certainly purged of the Jacobinist element. In Shelley's fictional Christ-figure of Laon, there is no such compromise. Laon simultaneously embodies the spirit of love and that of overturning tyranny, as does the Christ of Shelley's essay.[10]

The affinity of *The Revolt of Islam* with the essay 'On Christianity' is in part suggested by the circumstance of their composition in approximately the same year, 1817. Beside draft work for 'Ozymandias' (1817) in the Bodleian notebook containing the draft of the essay appears the phrase 'Revolt of Islam' (fo. 85ᵛ), the title by which Shelley's longest poem was to become known. The sonnet about the Egyptian pharaoh may be seen as an abstract of the idealized revolution in the poem about Laon and Cythna, for both works communicate the prophetic insight into the doom of empire.[11]

One link between the essay on Jesus and his teachings and *The Revolt of Islam* is an almost identical conception of the divine Spirit, or power, a conception stemming from the 'Hymn to Intellectual Beauty'. In the essay on Christianity, Shelley writes:

There is a power by which we are surrounded, like the atmosphere in which some motionless lyre is suspended, which visits with its breath our silent chords,

---

[9] *The Complete Prose Works of Matthew Arnold*, ed. R. H. Super (11 vols.; Ann Arbor, Mich., 1960–77), vii. 323, 325.

[10] The idealism of Laon's revolution may be compared to (or contrasted with) that of the Anabaptists who occupied Münster in 1534. These sectarians believed in brotherly love, communal ownership, and of course the overthrow of existing forms of government. See Norman Cohn, *The Pursuit of the Millennium* (1957; London, 1972), 252–80.

[11] See Bodleian MS Shelley e. 4, fo. 85ᵛ (*BSM*, iii. 343). Note the similar fate of the pharaoh and his empire in 'Ozymandias' and in the prophet Ezekiel (chs. 31–2).

at will. Our most imperial and stupendous qualities . . . are the passive slaves of some higher and more omnipresent Power. This Power is God. (*PW*, i. 251–2)

At the outset of the Bodleian notebook draft for *The Revolt of Islam*, Shelley has a stanza beginning with the lines

> There is a Power whose passive instrument
> Our nature is—a Spirit that with motion
> Invisible & swift its breath hath sent
> Amongst us like the wind on the wide Ocean . . .[12]

The lines were not retained, though the thought may have influenced the reference to 'Power of holiest name' in the printed form of the poem (I. xxxii. 5). Opposed to this genuine notion of Power is the 'one Power' that exists as the human conception of God as a tyrant (II. viii. 3). This anthropomorphic God is unveiled in the poem by the Christian priest before the multitude:

> And Heaven above seemed cloven, where, on a throne
> Girt round with storms and shadows, sate alone
> Their King and Judge . . .
>
> (x. xl. 4–6)

This image corresponds with the misconception in the essay on Christianity of God as 'paternal Monarch', the 'King of Heaven' seated on a golden throne (*PW*, i. 250–1). And it appears again in some lines written sideways just prior to the notebook draft of the essay, the lines subsequently titled '*Pater Omnipotens*' (*SPW*, 634):

> Serene in his unconquerable might
> Endured the Almighty King, his steadfast throne
> Encompassed unapproachably with power
> And darkness & deep solitude & awe
> Stood like a black cloud on some aery cliff
> Embosoming its lightning—in his sight
> Unmunbered [*sic*] glorious Spirits trembling stood
> Like slaves before their Lord—prostrate around
> Heavens multitudes hymned everlasting praise.[13]

The scene seems a parody of the vision of the divine throne in the book of Revelation (ch. 4), and it reveals that Shelley's dislike of this particular anthropomorphism had not diminished since the writing of *Queen Mab*.

[12] MS Shelley adds. e. 19, fo. 5.

[13] MS Shelley e. 4, fo. 5ᵛ (*BSM*, iii. 23). These lines are Miltonic in character. Cf. *Paradise Lost*, I. 174–7, 637–9; II. 237–46, 262–70; VI. 671–2; and VII. 254–9.

Another concern shared by the poem and the essay is the ideal of love. There are some seventy-six occurrences of the noun 'love' in *The Revolt of Islam*.[14] But Shelley does not always mean the same thing by it. Both in the essay on Christianity (*PW*, i. 269) and in Cythna's sermon to the mariners (VIII. xxii), love is an effect of some form of knowledge. An alternative view is expressed in the first canto, where love is inspired by the benevolent Spirit (I. xl–xli). In this sense, it becomes a means of reform, rather than a consequence. Thus Shelley's statement in his preface that 'Love is celebrated everywhere as the sole law which should govern the moral world' (*SPW*, 37) contains an element of ambiguity. It may be either cause or effect. Furthermore, it signifies at some points the ideal of brotherly love (e.g. V. xiv. 3–4) and at others the eroticism of Laon's incestuous relationship with Cythna. As John Taylor Coleridge said in his rather grim review of Shelley's poem, 'Love is a wide word with many significations, and we are at a loss as to which of them he would have it now bear.'[15]

The theme of incest is for Shelley a natural expression of his impatience with 'faith' and 'custom'. It was not, however, an unusual subject in his day. John Donovan has recently revealed the extent to which Shelley's contemporaries were concerned with it.[16] What was unusual was the frank sensuality of the description. Shelley clearly has in mind the erotic imagery of the Song of Solomon. In Bodleian MS Shelley adds. e. 14, which contains much draft material for the poem, the inside of the front cover bears the memorandum: 'The aloe and the China Rose | Solomon's Song Cap. 4—v.9 | particularly 4. v. 2 | or Cap. 5. v. 2'.[17] These verses, which feature the endearments 'my sister, my love' and 'my sister, *my* spouse' have a direct bearing on the relationship of Laon with his sister Cythna, as Neville Rogers has noted.[18] The orthodox readings of the male–female relationship in the Song as representing Yahweh and Israel or Christ and the Church, of course, have little to do with an understanding of Shelley's poem. What is important

---

[14] F. S. Ellis, *A Lexical Concordance to the Poetical Works of Percy Bysshe Shelley* (London, 1892), 418–20.

[15] Review of *Laon and Cythna* and *The Revolt of Islam*, by Percy Bysshe Shelley, *Quarterly Review*, 21 (1819), 468. Brian Wilkie suggests that Laon's love for Cythna symbolizes 'the bond of love which should unite all human beings'. See 'Shelley', in *Romantic Poets and Epic Tradition* (Madison and Milwaukee, Wis., 1965), 142.

[16] 'Incest in *Laon and Cythna*', *K–SR*, no. 2 (1987), 49–90.

[17] Quoted by Neville Rogers (ed.), *Complete Poetical Works of Percy Bysshe Shelley* (2 of 4 projected vols.; Oxford, 1972, 1975), ii. 363.

[18] Ibid.

is that the previously forbidden expression of love is celebrated in the very terms of the Bible.[19]

The differing theories of love in the first canto and in the remainder of the poem highlight the fact that the poem is comprised of two distinct structures. Of its framework, Shelley once wrote in a letter to a prospective publisher that 'The whole poem, with the exception of the first canto & part of the last is a mere human story without the smallest intermixture of supernatural interference. The first canto is indeed, in some measure a distinct poem, tho' very necessary to the wholeness of the work.'[20] He admits to having written two poems, a symbolic, metaphysical one and a concrete, narrative one. The precise relation between them is the pressing question. Heinz Brandt complains that in this dichotomy, Shelley separates symbol from event, internal process from external. He feels that the struggle of the eagle and the serpent in Canto I is a representation of the inner struggle trying to externalize itself, a conflict which becomes a figure of speech for the processes of the human heart, processes which are divorced from the narrative action.[21] Carlos Baker likewise sees two separate poems, but thinks that the first is 'meant to heighten and universalize the significance of the struggle' for social and political freedom.[22] Whether the twofoldness is a strength or a weakness is thus open to question. One way of seeing their relation is to view the first canto as an apocalypse which has its basis in a heavenly portent and the narrative as a prophecy of the coming era of justice and peace. As a biblical genre, apocalyptic directs the reader toward the open heaven, while the latter mode of prophecy emphasizes earthly restoration of an Edenic state. Each of these implies the kingship of God over his realm, analogous to which is the sovereign Necessity prophesied by Cythna (IX. xxvii).

In the wake of the French Revolution, on which *The Revolt of Islam* is an idealist's commentary, writers in the Protestant, English-speaking world began linking contemporary events with those prophesied in the book of Revelation. Since Meyer Abrams has already discussed several of these sources, they will not be introduced here.[23] What matters for

[19] The eyes of the beloved are of special interest to the author of the Song, as they are to Shelley (VI. xxiv. 5; IX. xxvi. 4–5).

[20] 13 Oct. 1817, *Letters*, i. 563.

[21] 'Der Protest Shelleys in den Symbolen', in *Das protestierende Element in der Dichtung Shelleys* (Wrocław, 1934), 45, 48.

[22] *Shelley's Major Poetry* (1948; Princeton, NJ, 1973), 64.

[23] 'English Romanticism', in *Romanticism Reconsidered*, ed. N. Frye (New York, 1963), 34–72, *passim*.

the purpose of the present discussion is Shelley's own use of biblical models, chiefly his interpretive treatment of apocalyptic imagery. The inherent apocalypticism of the first canto is at first suggested by a series of cataclysmic events which includes an earthquake (I. i. 8), darkened sun (I. ii. 6), and 'cloven' sky (I. iv. 1–4). All these are included in the upheaval that results from the opening of the sixth seal in the book of Revelation (6: 12, 14). These effects prelude a vision of five angels, one of whom announces the selection of 144,000 Israelite 'servants'. Curiously, the number 1,444,000,000 is written at the beginning of Shelley's draft for this canto.[24]

The governing symbol of the canto, the conflict between the eagle and the serpent, has provoked much speculation. Shelley may have got the image from the Aztec emblem of an eagle wounding a serpent, an emblem adopted by the Mexicans for their national flag shortly after their revolution, which the poet had earlier commemorated in one of the Esdaile poems. There is, however, a close proximity between Shelley's vision of this conflict and the apocalyptic account of the battle between the archangel St Michael (usually depicted with wings) and the dragon ('that old serpent'), or Satan (Rev. 12: 9). It is a battle that Milton had dramatized in *Paradise Lost* (VI. 281–353).

Both biblical and Shelleyan scenarios feature the visionary characters of an eagle, a serpent, and a mysterious woman. The eagle was a standard of the Roman empire, and could have been Shelleyan shorthand for the Napoleonic empire. But the eagle was also identified with St John the Evangelist, traditionally the writer of the biblical book of the Apocalypse. Because of its ability to soar upward until out of sight, yet remain able to gaze directly into the sun, it has been seen to be symbolic of Christ.[25] The biblical associations of the eagle are therefore positive. However, when it was depicted in conflict with the serpent, according to one book of emblems published in the eighteenth century, it was meant to illustrate oppression.[26] Shelley, too, seems to understand the eagle as an oppressive force.

The second symbol, that of the serpent, was one which was closely linked with Shelley, as previously noted. Thus arises a natural antithesis between the poet (nicknamed 'the Snake') and the Christ-symbol of the eagle, an antithesis dating from his early identification with the

[24] MS Shelley adds. e. 19, fo. 4.
[25] George Ferguson, *Signs and Symbols in Christian Art* (1954; Oxford, 1980), 17.
[26] *Choice Emblems, Natural, Historical, Fabulous, Moral, and Divine* (London, 1788), 125.

Antichrist.[27] Kenneth Neill Cameron and Gerald McNiece both observe that Shelley used the serpent as an emblem of revolution.[28] Political revolution was in theory based on seasonal cycles, or 'revolutions'. Drummond's *Oedipus Judaicus* featured an illustration of a serpent swallowing its tail (p. 346) and the explanation that 'the tail of the serpent is placed in his mouth to show, that time is still resolved into time' (p. 356). Volney presented a similar view in *The Ruins* (p. 154). For this reason, it seems that Shelley associates the serpent of the first canto with the revolution, for revolutions occur within time.

The third character portrayed in the canto is the woman sitting by the sea (I. xvi) who becomes the speaker's visionary guide. She is in part derived from Peacock's poetic fragment *Ahrimanes*, in which the central character, standing by the shore, confronts a female genius wearing a crown of twelve stars.[29] From this source Shelley may have borrowed the Zoroastrian dualism of good and evil. But Shelley does not retain the crown of twelve stars. He simply depicts the woman on the shore as clothed in a 'star-bright robe' (I. xviii. 6). Peacock's ultimate source for the crown was most likely the woman of the Apocalypse 'clothed with the sun, and the moon under her feet, and upon her head a crown of twelve stars' (Rev. 12: 1).[30]

The significant details in the narrative that follows are that the serpent, wounded in the struggle, falls into the sea, swims ashore, and is embraced by the woman. The scene of the woman holding the snake contributes to G. Wilson Knight's argument that *The Revolt of Islam* is 'continually approaching a *Kubla Khan* symbolism'.[31] The fact that the term 'Demon Lover' is written above Shelley's working draft of this stanza (I. xxi) supports Knight's assertion.[32] What Shelley accomplishes in the first canto is a subversion of the archetypal conflict in Revelation 12. The celestial woman of St John who is about to give birth in this

[27] Letter to T. J. Hogg, 3 Jan. 1811, *Letters*, i. 35.

[28] See Cameron, 'A Major Source of *The Revolt of Islam*', *PMLA*, 56 (1941), 201, 203–4, and McNiece, *Shelley and the Revolutionary Idea* (Cambridge, Mass., 1969), 196.

[29] *Works of Thomas Love Peacock*, vii. 266–7. In *SHC*, iii. 211–44, Cameron presents a full treatment of the *Ahrimanes* fragments, arguing that their anticlerical and antimonarchist elements reflected the influence of Shelley's *Queen Mab* (p. 236). He goes on to discuss the influence of *Ahrimanes* on *The Revolt of Islam* (pp. 240–4).

[30] Shelley initially featured an additional character in his draft: a boy standing near the woman, 'who, adorning / Her hair with seaweed—sometimes sought his home / In her deep bosom . . .' (MS Shelley adds. e. 19, fo. 25). The child quickly disappears in revision. St John's vision also features a 'man-child' born to the woman (Rev. 12: 5).

[31] 'The Naked Seraph', in *The Starlit Dome* (1941; London, 1959), 189.

[32] MS Shelley adds. e. 19, fo. 31.

spectacle is confronted by a dragon who stands poised to devour her child at birth. The dragon fails, however, and the child is 'caught up unto God' (Rev. 12: 5). In the disjointed verses that follow, St Michael does battle with the dragon/serpent, who is cast out into the earth, where he threatens the woman (Rev. 12: 13). However, the woman is given eagle's wings, by which she escapes (Rev. 12: 14).[33]

That Shelley inverts the biblical source is clear from two significant details. First, the heavenly woman in the Apocalypse who is 'clothed with the sun' and who escapes by her eagle's wings is supplanted by Shelley's earthly woman who dislikes the sun (i. xvii. 3–4). Like the eagle, the sun is another emblem of God as Sky-Father, a negative association for Shelley. Secondly, the woman in Revelation flees from the serpent, whereas the woman in Shelley's poem embraces it. Thus the woman identifies with the chthonic symbol of the snake, rather than with the emblems of the upper world, as opposed to the woman in the Bible. She subverts the pattern of conflict between the woman and the serpent established in the book of Genesis, when God relegated the serpent to the lower world of dust with the following curse: 'And I will put enmity between thee and the woman, and between thy seed and her seed; it shall bruise thy head, and thou shalt bruise his heel' (Gen. 3: 15). The verse is traditionally seen as a prophecy of the Messiah, though its implications extend into the apocalypse, where the serpent is finally expelled for all eternity (Rev. 20: 10). In *The Revolt of Islam* it is the eagle who disappears, while the serpent becomes a medium of continuity.

The most potent inversion of all in the first canto is the characteristically Gnostic demonization of Yahweh as 'the Fiend' and the identification of the morning star with the serpent. The 'Fiend' becomes the lord of the lower world, over which he reigns as the spirit of evil. His ability to 'soar aloft with overshadowing wings' (i. xxviii. 3) reverses the biblical association of this image with security in God. As the eagle broods over her young ones and 'beareth them on her wings' (Deut. 32: 11), so the Lord upholds the people of Israel. Thus Shelley's winged spirit is fundamentally an inversion of the Old Testament God. Like the Satan of the Apocalypse, who 'knoweth that he hath but a short time' (Rev. 12: 12), this Fiend

---

[33] The verse recalls the biblical assurance of God's Providence: 'Ye have seen what I did unto the Egyptians, and *how* I bare you on eagles' wings, and brought you unto myself' (Exod. 19: 4).

Omnipotent of yore, now quails, and fears
His triumph dearly won, which soon will lend
An impulse swift and sure to his approaching end.

(I. xxxiv. 7–9)

Shelley's corruption of Yahweh is thus defined by the biblical models of both God and Satan.

The morning star, on the other hand, is a positive symbol. The mysterious woman tells the narrator that she 'loved; but not a human lover' (I. xl. 7), and proceeds to describe her experience of the morning star (Venus) as it shone through her casement inspiring love:

Even like the dayspring, poured on vapours dank,
The beams of that one Star did shoot and quiver
Through my benighted mind—and were extinguished never.

(I. xli. 7–9)

The love of Venus is like the love of God, which is 'shed abroad in our hearts by the Holy Ghost' (Rom. 5: 5). The 'dayspring' is a suggestive echo of the rising of the day-star in 2 Peter 1: 19. The word for the star here ($\phi\omega\sigma\phi\rho\acute{o}s$) is traditionally identified with Christ, the 'morning star' in Revelation 22: 16. However, here we confront an ambiguity, for 'morning star' also refers to Lucifer; it is identified with the fall of the light-bearing angel in Isaiah 14: 12 ($\dot{\epsilon}\omega\sigma\phi\acute{o}\rho s$ in the Septuagint).[34] In classical literature no distinction was made between $\Phi\omega\sigma\phi\acute{o}\rho s$ and $\dot{}E\omega\sigma\phi\acute{o}\rho s$, both names referring to the planet Venus as the morning star.[35] There has been a tendency in Christendom, however, to link the fall of Lucifer with Christ's statement that 'I beheld Satan as lightning, fall from heaven' (Luke 10: 18), thereby establishing a distinction. More in keeping with the common reference of the Greek names, Shelley conflates the identities of Christ and Lucifer. He has in mind a kind of Blakean cosmic fall from a unity in eternity that existed '[w]hen the morning stars sang together, and all the sons of God shouted for joy' (Job 38: 7). For the 'Twin Genii' manifest in the comet and morning star are 'equal Gods' born from a common womb (I. xxv. 8–9). Shelley combines the positive associations of Jesus as the morning star with the Satanic implications of the Luciferic fall. To this unorthodox alliance he attributes the character of love (I. xli. 4).

Canto I comes to a conclusion in the Temple of the Spirit, which

---

[34] Shelley explicitly rejects the identification of Lucifer as the Devil in 'On the Devil, and Devils' (Jul. vii. 103).

[35] Liddell and Scott, 752, 1968.

Shelley compares to heaven (I. xlix. 4). The use of precious stones—
sapphire, jasper, and amethyst—to describe the temple and its environs
recalls the use of such minerals to adorn the New Jerusalem in the final
two chapters of the biblical Apocalypse. The Temple of the Spirit is
clearly a variation on this idea of the extraterrestrial city.[36] Once inside
it, the serpent of the earlier part of the canto is transformed into a radi-
ant form seated on a 'crystalline throne' (I. lvi. 9). This protean manifes-
tation of Shelley's good Spirit, the morning star, may be derived as
Baker suggests in *Shelley's Major Poetry* (pp. 73–4) from the scene of
Satan's return to Pandemonium in *Paradise Lost* (X. 441–59). But the
scene is also suggestive of the apocalyptic vision of God:

. . . behold, a throne was set in heaven, and *one* sat on the throne. And he that
sat was to look upon like a jasper and a sardine stone: and *there was* a rainbow
round about the throne, in sight like unto an emerald. . . . And before the
throne *there was* a sea of glass like unto crystal. (Rev. 4: 2–3, 6)

Shelley's temple, surrounded by a 'crystal sea' (I. li. 4) and built with
'jasper walls' (I. liii. 5), may be constructed in part from St John's vision
of the throne in heaven. The outstanding difference of course is that
the occupant of Shelley's throne is the Luciferic spirit. The first canto
ends in the spirit of biblical inversion that governs it.

The remainder of *The Revolt of Islam* is an attempt to present in the
form of a temporal struggle the cosmic warfare of mild morning star
with sanguinary comet. But because of Shelley's allegorical intention,
derived partly from his model of Spenser's *Faerie Queene*, his characters
tend to become abstractions. Between its two poles of apocalypse in the
first and final cantos, Shelley's tale continually aspires toward the condi-
tion of the morning star, from which it fell. It incarnates love in its
hero, just as it embodies all moral turpitude in its tyrant. The parallel
between Laon and Christ has not gone unnoticed.[37] However, it is
clear that Shelley's hero descends not from the gospel figure but from
the Christ of the essay on Christianity. Laon is a revolutionary figure in
the mould of Shelley's Galilean, and the chronicle of his movement is
one of a millennium which is short-lived (in Canto V).

Laon begins to fulfil his messianic aspirations when he kills three of
the tyrant's henchmen who have abducted Cythna. His punishment, as

[36] Shelley's debt to Peacock's *Palmyra* in this description is noted by Reiman in
Intervals of Inspiration, 218–19.
[37] See Knight, 'Naked Seraph', 192, and Weaver, *Toward the Understanding of Shelley*,
231.

Knight observes, resembles the crucifixion of Christ (p. 192). Chained at the top of a column, Laon finds psychological release through delirium (III. xv. 4). Like Christ, he endures mockery (III. xxiii. 4–9).[38] And like Christ, he suffers thirst (III. xxi. 2).[39] He is rescued by an elderly hermit who

> . . . did enfold
> His giant arms around me, to uphold
> My wretched frame, my scorchèd limbs he wound
> In linen moist and balmy . . .
>
> (III. xxix. 4–7)

The scene is reminiscent of Christ's burial. In this case, the hermit corresponds to Joseph of Arimathea, who requested of Pilate the privilege of burying Jesus: 'And he bought fine linen, and took him down, and wrapped him in the linen, and laid him in a sepulchre which was hewn out of a rock' (Mark 15: 46). The sepulchre in Shelley's narrative is the 'tower of stone' where Laon is taken to recover his health (IV. i. 2). Here Shelley inverts the Renaissance Christian type of Archimago/Comus by presenting the hermit as a benevolent sorcerer whose attentions induce a 'resurrection' over the course of seven years (IV. xi. 6). This recovery is accompanied by a growing linguistic-propagandistic proficiency learned from the hermit (IV. xii. 5, xvii. 3) along with the ethic of love associated with Shelley's Jesus (IV. xv. 2).

Having completely recovered by the end of Canto V, Laon departs for 'the great City' of Constantinople (V. xxxviii). In Revelation, 'the great city' is Jerusalem, where Jesus was crucified (11: 8). Laon, too, is ultimately executed in the metropolis. On his arrival in the encampment surrounding the city, he joins the revolution in progress. In a skirmish between rebel and imperial forces, he rushes to prevent a confederate from killing one of the tyrant's 'slaves'. Crying 'Forbear, forbear!' (V. viii. 9), Laon intervenes only to be wounded inadvertently by a spear in the arm (V. ix. 1). Thus transfixed, he continues to preach 'the truth of love's benignant laws' (V. ix. 9) and the ameliorative possibilities in forgiving one's enemies (V. xi–xii). This second anticipation of his eventual martyrdom again recalls Christ on the cross, pierced with a spear by one of the soldiers after uttering a prayer asking God's forgiveness of his executioners (Luke 23: 34). Now the unquestioned leader of the antimonarchist forces, Laon makes his triumphal entry into the city:

[38] Matt. 27: 39–43.   [39] John 19: 28.

> Bright pennons on the idle winds were hung;
> As we approached, a shout of joyance sprung
> At once from all the crowd . . .
>
> (v. xv. 4–6)

This vivid evocation of Palm Sunday (Matt. 21: 8–9) is followed by an
incident which clearly corresponds to Christ's experience with the
woman caught in the act of adultery. When the scribes and Pharisees
confronted him with the Mosaic law requiring her death by stoning,
Jesus forgave the woman (John 8: 1–11). In Shelley's narrative, the
emancipated masses surround Othman, the fallen tyrant, with the inten-
tion of executing him. They shout, '. . . He who judged let him be
brought / To judgement! blood for blood cries from the soil' (v. xxxii.
1–2). Their code of justice refers the reader back to the Old Testament.
When God speaks to Cain, he says, 'the voice of thy brother's blood
crieth unto me from the ground' (Gen. 4: 10). He further tells Noah
that whoever sheds human blood must forfeit his own life (Gen. 9: 6).
But, like the Jesus of the essay on Christianity, Laon rejects the law
based on retribution. Exploiting Christ's metaphor of the second birth
in the third chapter of St John's gospel (v. xxxiii. 9), he insists that since
the people have obtained freedom, there is no need for vengeance.
Before the accusers of the adulterous woman, Jesus had said, 'He that is
without sin among you, let him first cast a stone at her' (John 8: 7).
Laon too directs the attention of the group to the inner self and its
motives:

> What call ye *justice*? Is there one who ne'er
>   In secret thought has wished another's ill?—
> Are ye all pure? . . .
>
> (v. xxxiv. 1–3)

Like the accused woman, Othman walks away forgiven and unharmed.
    The precise relationship of Cythna to Laon's messianism is not clear
from the details in the narrative. Her own account of her mysterious
origin suggests a range of theological meanings:

> Some said I was a maniac wild and lost;
>   Some, that I scarce had risen from the grave,
> The Prophet's virgin bride, a heavenly ghost:—
>   Some said, I was a fiend from my weird cave,
>   Who had stolen human shape, and o'er the wave,
> The forest, and the mountain came;—some said
>   I was the child of God, sent down to save

Women from bonds and death, and on my head
The burden of their sins would frightfully be laid.

(IX. viii)

The stanza suggests that Cythna may be, among other things, a messianic figure herself. The book of Isaiah had featured an account of the Suffering Servant on whom God had laid 'the iniquity of us all' (53: 6). And Jesus said that 'the Son of man is come to save that which was lost' (Matt. 18: 11). In the narrative itself, however, Cythna assumes an apostolic-hierophantic function. She seems to embody the more cognitive, cultic features of the ideals proclaimed by her counterpart. Just as Moses had to wear a veil to conceal the divine radiance of his face in the book of Exodus (34: 30–5), so Cythna, seated on an ivory throne as a high priestess, wears a veil to conceal the brightness of her countenance.

In general, Cythna appears to embody the qualities of an apostle, rather than those of Christ. The heart of her teaching is the sermon delivered to the slave-trading mariners who rescue her. Indeed, the circumstance of her maritime adventure has a cast reminiscent of the Pauline missionary voyages in the book of Acts. The message itself makes for a stark contrast with the speech of St Paul to the Athenians (Acts 17: 22–31).[40] Whereas St Paul is a monotheist addressing polytheists, Cythna is an enlightened sceptic addressing monotheists. The apostle would make known the Unknown God (Acts 17: 23). In the spirit of 'Mont Blanc', Cythna insists that God is by definition unknowable:

'What is that Power? ye mock yourselves, and give
   A human heart to what ye cannot know:
As if the cause of life could think and live!
   'Twere as if man's own works should feel, and show
   The hopes, and fears, and thoughts from which they flow,
And he be like to them! . . .'

(VIII. v. 1–6)

St Paul too disparages the anthropomorphic God of human workmanship by saying, 'Forasmuch then as we are the offspring of God, we ought not to think that the Godhead is like unto gold or silver, or stone, graven by art and man's device' (Acts 17: 29). But the difference is obvious. The Christian missionary denounces iconographic representations

---

[40] Shelley's awareness of this speech is revealed in a portion (usually deleted) of the draft for the essay on Christianity, in which a hypothetical speech of Jesus begins with the salutation 'Men of Athens', the opening used by St Paul. See MS Shelley e. 4, fo. 18ʳ (*BSM*, iii. 73).

of God; Cythna's more radical iconoclasm denounces the anthropomor-
phic ascription of any attributes of personality to God. St Paul teaches
that one day God 'will judge the world in righteousness (Acts 17: 31);
Shelley's hierophantess claims that the belief in such a judgement stems
from a tyrannous conception of power, which in the final analysis must
remain unknown (VIII. v–viii). Mere custom maintains that God pun-
ishes wrongdoing (VIII. viii. 1).

Unlike the oration of St Paul, Cythna's message is a political gospel.
If the apostle could be seen as a proponent of equality, it was only in
the sense that all men shared a common origin. The sovereign Lord of
heaven and earth, he tells his listeners at the Areopagus, 'hath made of
one blood all nations of men' (Acts 17: 26). Likewise, Cythna begins by
affirming the common humanity of all men and women (VIII. iii. 6–7).
All bear the same likeness. However, this likeness does not imply that
men and women were made either by God or in the image of God.
Justice for her is not grounded in any transcendent norm. It is governed
by 'human love' (VIII. x. 6), an equalizing force that subverts all hierar-
chies, including domestic ones:

> 'But children near their parents tremble now,
>   Because they must obey—one rules another,
> And as one Power rules both high and low,
>   So man is made the captive of his brother . . .'
>   (VIII. xiii. 1–4)

Thus Shelley undermines the basis for the Pauline instruction that chil-
dren are to obey their parents (Eph. 6: 1) in obedience to the source of
all power, the 'One God and Father of all, who *is* above all' (Eph. 4: 6).
He equally subverts the Pauline teaching that wives should submit
themselves to their husbands (Eph. 5: 22). Cythna refers to the tradi-
tional status of women as one of slavery (VIII. xv), and the essence of her
gospel is a proclamation of freedom and equality (VIII. xvii). The oration
has its desired effect, for the mariners swear to renounce custom. They
free their slaves, who assemble on the ship's deck (VIII. xxviii. 6–8).
Shelley again seems to have in mind the book of Isaiah, which records
that 'the LORD hath anointed me to preach good tidings unto the meek
. . . to proclaim liberty to the captives, and the opening of the prison to
them that are bound' (61: 1). And he quotes Christ's citation of this
passage (Luke 4: 18) in the essay 'On Christianity' (*PW*, i. 263).
Cythna's sermon thus complements the more militant activism of Laon.

In establishing the ethic of loving one's neighbour as oneself (Matt.

19: 19) as universally normative, Shelley differs from his chief mentor. Godwin had written in the *Enquiry concerning Political Justice* that the maxim of Jesus was strictly for the vulgar (i. 126). Some neighbours were obviously more useful to society than others, and were therefore to be preferred. There is no such utilitarian casuistry in Shelley. But the son-in-law of Godwin is no less heterodox in appropriating some of the ideals of Christian love. He is free to abrogate the moral teaching of the biblical Christ when he chooses. As Gerald McNiece has noted, the glowing affirmations of love in *The Revolt of Islam* appear in the context of armed retaliation and bloodshed (p. 201). Correspondingly, the Jesus of the essay 'On Christianity' is at once a benign teacher of love (*PW*, i. 253) and a radical who 'tramples upon all received opinions' (*PW*, i. 263). Shelley says in 'The Moral Teaching of Jesus Christ' that if his admonitions were actually practised, 'no political or religious institution could subsist a moment. Every man would be his own magistrate and priest' (Jul. vi. 255). For this reason, Weaver certainly misses the mark in asserting that the 'briefest survey of the *Essay* reveals a deep kinship with the spirit of the New Testament'.[41] The New Testament is replete with references to hierarchy and submission to authority. In Shelley's longest poem, the judgement of God in the afterlife is exchanged for the earthly judgement of revolution. The Logos of the Apocalypse, with his armies arrayed in white, finds in Shelley's poem a local habitation and a name. And that name is Laon.[42] For the popular hero, the divine right of kingship has given way to the divine right of rebellion as the apocalyptic realm of spiritual freedom is temporalized in the fifth canto as a classless society established by military upheaval.

As an analysis of social corruption, *The Revolt of Islam* stands between Shelley's juvenile poem 'Zeinab and Kathema' and the later antimonarchist fragment of *Charles I*. In *Hellas* (written in 1821), he would return to Constantinople as the golden city, and would sustain by a persistent lyricism the apocalyptic mode which *The Revolt of Islam* resists. Shelley's *beau ideal* of the French Revolution ends by escaping time, but not in the apocalyptic sense. Its heroes simply die. However, McNiece feels that their revolution did not fail, since '[i]t has been achieved in the minds of men' (p. 213). There are indeed prophetic murmurings of change among the masses following the burning of Laon and Cythna at the instigation of a 'Christian Priest' (identified subsequently as an

---

[41] *Toward the Understanding of Shelley*, 104.
[42] *Laon* could be seen as a different case of λαός, 'the people', or 'the men' (soldiers). See Liddell and Scott, 1029.

Iberian) in the final canto. Shelley's heroine had earlier told her brother
to look inward:

> Alas! gaze not on me, but turn thine eyes
>   On thine own heart—it is a paradise
> Which everlasting Spring has made its own . . .
>
>   (IX. xxvi. 4–6)

The myth of the 'paradise within', suggested here by Milton in *Paradise
Lost* (XII. 587), stems ultimately from Christ's statement that 'the king-
dom of God is within you' (Luke 17: 21). As Shelley's secularized ver-
sion of the millennium fails to materialize as a political reality, he is
increasingly impelled to pursue it as an internal quest. Following his
departure from England in 1818, the sphere of change in his poetry
tends to become that inner *malkuth* of the mind, or self.

PART TWO

1818–1820

4

A Protestant Apprehension

Prompted by the needs of escaping creditors, social calumny, and the harsh English climate, Shelley left England in March 1818. He found sanctuary, in every sense of the word, in Italy. Despite the rich cultural opportunities presented by this new life on the Continent, however, there were two features of Italian society about which he as an Englishman had reservations. In the first place, Italy to the English had been for centuries a land of sinister intrigue, Machiavellian duplicity, and political treachery. For Shelley, this image would have been justified by exposure to Sismondi's history of the Italian republics, a single chapter of which provided not only the source for the fragmentary poem 'Marenghi', but also some highly unsavoury instances of betrayal and tyranny in the late Middle Ages. Shelley would have read of the 'épouvantable boucherie' of rival factions of the Cavalcabò clan at a banquet of reconciliation sponsored by their trusted mediator, Gabrino Fondolo, who thereby gained control of Cremona in 1406.[1] He would also have read the account of how the treacherous Boucicault, a 'maréchal de France' who governed Genoa, had his ally Gabriello Maria Visconti of Pisa stripped of power and executed in 1408 (viii. 143). Such vignettes could only reaffirm a stereotype of Italy held by the English since Renaissance times.

Another lamentable characteristic of the Italians, from Shelley's viewpoint, was their religion. Italy was the very nest of the inquisitorial Roman Church that Shelley had depicted in the person of the Iberian priest in *The Revolt of Islam*. Living in this Catholic, 'southern' country heightened his awareness that he was from a Protestant, northern European nation. What Shelley found distressing about this Latin society was its tacit acceptance of behaviour and customs that were either sad or shocking to his English perception. The sight of 300 chained criminals hoeing weeds between stones in the square of St Peter's in Rome became 'the emblem of Italy: moral degradation contrasted with

---

[1] J. C. L. Simonde de Sismondi, 'Conquête de Pise par les Florentins', in *Histoire des républiques italiennes du Moyen Âge* (16 vols.; Paris, 1809–18), viii. 139.

the glory of nature & the arts'.[2] His witnessing the fatal stabbing of a
youth in the streets as he entered Naples was made all the more
appalling by a fellow traveller subsequently making light of the event:
'a Calabrian priest who travelled with me laughed heartily and
attempted to quiz me as what the English call a flat.'[3] It is not difficult
to imagine how the two incidents could have represented for the poet
the indifference of the Catholic Church to human suffering.

Both what the Italians tolerated and what they prohibited tended to
draw out the Puritan in Shelley.[4] Lord Byron's bargaining with
Venetian parents for access to their daughters was for him a 'sickening
vice . . . a melancholy thing'.[5] That such a practice could be accepted
was all the more ironic in the light of what the Catholic society of that
time could not accept: the sacred book of the Protestants. Medwin
records the following anecdote of Shelley's travels in Italy: 'On entering
Rome, the *Doganieri* laid hands on his books, among which was the
very Spinoza, and the Bible. "Which do you suppose", said he, with
one of his peculiar laughs, "they confiscated?—the Bible"!' (p. 350).
This incident could only underscore the fact that the Scriptures were in
Shelley's time a Protestant book. As such, they were connected with his
ideals of morality. In *A Defence of Poetry* he included 'the Hebrew
poetry' (translated into vernacular tongues) in a list of literary works
that he felt to be indispensable to the moral condition of mankind
(*SPP*, 502).

Such an acknowledgement does not mean that Shelley's fundamental
view of the Bible had changed. In Italy he heard of the trial of Richard
Carlile, who, like Eaton before him, had published the blasphemous
Age of Reason. The news prompted him to write a response in the form
of a letter to Leigh Hunt at the *Examiner*. The similarities between this
letter and the earlier *Letter to Lord Ellenborough* are evident. Both the
essay and the letter assert that the members of a jury prejudiced against a
deist are not legitimately peers of the defendant and that the accused is a
man of good character; both relegate the supernatural content of the
gospel record to the credulity of an epoch some eighteen centuries in
the past.[6] In the letter to Hunt, Shelley expressly denies that 'the whole

---

[2] Letter to T. L. Peacock, 6 Apr. 1819, *Letters*, ii. 94.

[3] Letter to T. L. Peacock, 18 Dec. 1818, *Letters*, ii. 60.

[4] The 'Puritan' streak in Shelley is discussed by Richard Holmes in *Shelley* (1974; London, 1976), 203, 248, 264, 297, 448, 515.

[5] Letter to T. L. Peacock, 18 Dec. 1818, *Letters*, ii. 58.

[6] Letter to Leigh Hunt, 3 Nov. 1819, *Letters*, ii. 137, 147, 143. The corresponding passages in the *Letter to Lord Ellenborough* are found in *PW*, i. 64, 71, 67.

mass of antient Hebrew literature is of divine authority' (ii. 137). Yet he once again affirms the ethical teaching of the Bible in his denunciation of those who support the cause of liberty by principles of 'revenge & retribution' (ii. 148). Such was the sort of response condemned in the preface to *The Cenci* (*SPP*, 240), where the poet specifically identifies retaliation and moral indifference as features of Catholic Italian society. Protestant England ought to be different, for, he writes in his letter to Hunt, 'Christianity, or that system which is founded on the maxim of "Do unto others as thou wouldst they should do unto thee" has been declared to be part of the law of the land' (ii. 139). This appeal to a scriptural text is of course no indication of a change of mind on Shelley's part. Near the end of his life, he exclaimed to Hunt in the cathedral at Pisa, 'What a divine religion might be found out, if charity were really made the principle of it, instead of faith!'[7]

As Shelley looked more closely at the Roman Church from within a Catholic culture, he eventually developed a critique that faulted the Catholic faith for its dissociation of religious faith from morality. This stricture had been foreshadowed in *An Address, to the Irish People*, in which he enumerated historical instances of Catholic wrongdoing: the establishment of the Inquisition, the burning of heretics, the Massacre of Saint Bartholomew in 1572, the 'vices of Monks and Nuns in their Convents', and the purchasing of absolution from sin (*PW*, i. 11–12). Naturally, Shelley was presenting himself as an impartial arbiter, insisting that 'I am not a Protestant, nor am I a Catholic' (*PW*, i. 10). Yet, as P. M. S. Dawson has remarked, his caricature of the Roman Church 'seemed to stem from typical Protestant prejudices'.[8] Once in Italy, however, the poet's analysis of Catholicism began to transcend the cataloguing of shortcomings and atrocities. A cursory look at the prose written during his first two years in Italy reveals a deepening scrutiny of the intrinsic difference between the two camps.

In the fragmentary story 'The Coliseum' (written in 1818 or 1819), set in Rome at Easter time, Shelley describes how the adherents of the 'most awful religion of the world . . . had assembled to wonder at and worship the creations of their own power' (Jul. vi. 299). Shelley plainly has in the mind the iconic, material features of the Roman Church. His is the familiar 'Pauline' and Protestant lament over the vanity of men who converted the notion of an eternal God into man-made idols and

[7] Hunt, 'Mr Shelley', i. 297.
[8] *The Unacknowledged Legislator* (Oxford, 1980), 151.

anthropomorphisms (Rom. I: 23).[9] Correspondingly, he writes in *A Philosophical View of Reform* (composed c.1819–20) that the egalitarian 'system preached by that great Reformer' was eventually 'perverted to support oppression' by the Catholic Church (*SHC*, vi. 963). What Shelley had previously attributed to the Christian faith in general, he now attributes to the Roman Church in particular. In the fashion of a Protestant, he further weighs 'intolerant & oppressive hierarchies' against a sincere 'unbiassed' reading of the New Testament, judging that the teachings of his recalcitrant Jesus are inconsistent with the former (*SHC*, vi. 968–9). The want of Scripture thus leads to a want of moral emphasis. In the undated and fragmentary essay 'On the Revival of Literature' written in Italy, Shelley faults in the same breath monastic disputations and the discussions of scholastic philosophers. His charge is that the scholastic wars of words 'had no relation to morality. Morality,—the great means and end of man' (Jul. vi. 214). Finally, the preface to *The Cenci* explores the nature of a particular Catholic society. Where religion touches all the outward aspects of life, it has little to do with morality itself.

To a Protestant apprehension there will appear something unnatural in the earnest and perpetual sentiment of the relations between God and man which pervade the tragedy of the Cenci. . . . Religion coexists, as it were, in the mind of an Italian Catholic with a faith in that of which all men have the most certain knowledge. It is interwoven with the whole fabric of life. It is adoration, faith, submission, penitence, blind admiration; not a rule for moral conduct. (*SPP*, 240–1)[10]

A key term in this indictment is the 'certain knowledge' which Shelley links with convention and with Catholicism in general. In the hymns of 1816, he revealed a fundamental scepticism about the ultimate source of power. The sources for this scepticism were to be found in the philosophy of the eighteenth century. Now, however, he associates the intellectual foundations of doubt with the Protestant Reformation. In the essay *A Philosophical View of Reform*, the poet claims that the Reformation inaugurated a new era which 'was marked by the com-

---

[9] See *The Revolt of Islam*, VIII. vi. 4, and *Queen Mab*, VI. 84–7, 94–107.

[10] In his essay 'Hot and Cold' (*The Plain Speaker*), Hazlitt contrasts the Catholicism of Italy with the Reformed worship of northern Europe, and makes essentially the same point: 'In morals, again, Protestants are more precise than their Catholic brethren. The creed of the latter absolves them of half their duties, of all those that are a clog on their inclinations, atones for all slips, and patches up all deficiencies.' See *The Complete Works of William Hazlitt*, ed. P. P. Howe (21 vols.; London, 1930–4), xii. 178. I am indebted to Roy Park for pointing out to me the affinity between Hazlitt and Shelley on this point.

mencement of deeper enquiries into the forms of human nature, than
are compatible with an unreserved belief in any of those popular mis-
takes . . . with all their superstructure of political & religious tyranny'
(*SHC*, vi. 969–70). It erred in not going far enough, and Shelley's own
secular Protestantism has as a goal the fulfilling of this initial promise. It
may well represent what he calls in the preface to *The Cenci* 'a gloomy
passion for penetrating the impenetrable mysteries of our being, which
terrifies its possessor at the darkness of the abyss' (*SPP*, 240).

The vaguely spatial language of descending into the abyss of the self
brings to mind Keats's comparison of life to a 'Mansion of Many
Apartments'; for the younger poet makes the same correlation between
the act of penetrating the mysteries of the mind and gradual emancipa-
tion from Rome. To illustrate the development of the mental processes
in man, Keats uses the analogy of a 'Chamber of Maiden Thought', the
intoxicating and enjoyable condition of thinking which

becomes gradually darken'd and at the same time on all sides of it many doors
are set open—but all dark—all leading to dark passages—We see not the bal-
lance [*sic*] of good and evil. We are in a Mist—We are now in that state—We
feel the 'burden of the Mystery'.[11]

According to Keats, Wordsworth explored these labyrinthine corridors
of the mind more deeply than did Milton, who lived during a time
when England was only partially emancipated from the parochialism of
the Church. Like Shelley, he recognizes the benefits of the
Reformation; but he also acknowledges that there are 'remaining
Dogmas and superstitions' in Protestant Christianity (i. 282).

For Shelley, the quest to explore this inner self is prerequisite to the
twofold nature of his moral purpose. Primarily, it leads to self-know-
ledge, 'in proportion to the possession of which knowledge, every
human being is wise, just, sincere, tolerant and kind' (*SPP*, 240). The
implicit connection between knowledge and morality is that the under-
standing of the self, as Earl Wasserman observes, is grounded in 'the
true understanding of universal human nature'.[12] The self-respect
inherent in self-knowledge is thus universalized to encompass others.
Secondly, self-knowledge will tend 'to convert' one's injurer 'from his
dark passions by peace and love' (*SPP*, 240). Here then is a conception

[11] Letter to J. H. Reynolds, 3 May 1818, in *The Letters of John Keats*, ed. H. Rollins (2
vols.; Cambridge, Mass., 1958), i. 281. See also the stimulating discussion of this passage
by David Morse in 'From Protestantism to Romanticism', in *Perspectives on Romanticism*
(London, 1981), 156.
[12] *Shelley* (1971; Baltimore, 1977), 111.

of salvation at the individual and social levels. It is true that Shelley still conceives of salvation along the lines of enlightenment and knowledge. But by bringing in the Pauline language of 'justification' and 'redemption' from an attitude of vengeance and 'atonement', he approximates a view of inherent sinfulness (*SPP*, 240, 241). In spite of this apparent recognition of human depravity, belief in original sin is the rationale used by Count Cenci to justify his malevolent behaviour; his sinful nature was inherited from Adam (I. iii. 12). As Wasserman says, the doctrine of original sin precludes hope by positing evil as inherent in the soul (p. 109). Explicitly, Shelley denies it by linking it with Cenci's hubris. Implicitly, the evil contrivances of the play's characters query this denial. Can the determination to commit rape, parricide, and acts of vengeance ultimately spring from a lack of knowledge? Shelley's position, in theory, is to maintain his belief in the moral aptitudes of the dictum 'Know thyself'.

The language of conversion in the preface to *The Cenci* reflects Shelley's belief that the idea of repentance is by its very preoccupation with the spiritual direction of the inner man a Protestant idea.[13] In a comparison of the four gospels (*c.*1819), for which he appropriately drew four columns in one of his notebooks, Shelley makes the observation on the first chapter of St Mark's gospel that 'Repent in Greek is μετανοειν v. 15.'[14] It is a concept which colours both *Prometheus Unbound* and *The Cenci*. As the cosmos in the lyrical drama is redeemed by the willed repentance of Prometheus, it is ultimately reduced to a prison in the Italian tragedy by Beatrice's refusal to renounce her desire for vengeance. Both dramas thus deal with the potential for transformation at the level of the self.

In so far as the theme of *The Cenci* has a biblical source, that source would be the story recorded in 2 Samuel 13 of the rape of Tamar by her half-brother Amnon and the account of Amnon's murder by the order of Tamar's brother Absalom. Just as the sexual sin of David's adultery with Bathsheba led to his arranging the death of her husband (2 Sam. 11), so the sexual sin of his son's incest leads to a murder that breaks apart a family. The same pattern is found in *The Cenci*. Shelley

---

[13] Cf. the following statement by John Mason in his devotional book *Self-Knowledge* (1745; London, 1810), 204: 'A man is what his heart is. The knowledge of himself is the knowledge of his heart, which is intirely an inward thing.'

[14] See *The Mask of Anarchy Draft Notebook*, ed. M. A. Quinn (New York, 1990), *The Manuscripts of the Younger Romantics: Shelley*, gen. ed. D. H. Reiman (5 vols. to date; 1985–91), iv. 352. This notebook also contains draft material for the prefaces to both *Prometheus Unbound* and *The Cenci*.

was reminded of this series of events in the reign of David by his read-
ing of Calderón's *Cabellos de Absalón* in 1819. Writing about it to Maria
Gisborne, he especially notes the scene depicting Amnon with Tamar,
and asserts that incest may involve selfless, giving love, in some cases, or
selfishness and cynicism in others.[15] Ostensibly, *The Revolt of Islam* and
the poem *Rosalind and Helen* dealt with the positive sort, the lust of
Count Cenci and of Calderón's Amnon with the negative.[16]

The pervasive New Testament element in the play is the Christology
that is overtly identified with Beatrice. She is described by Camillo

> As that most perfect image of God's love
> That ever came sorrowing upon the earth.
> She is as pure as speechless infancy!
>
> (v. ii. 67–9)

Incarnate Christ-child or the self-humbling Messiah of St Paul's kenosis
(Phil. 2: 5–8), she is perceived in terms of the human perfection
embodied in Jesus. And she is furthermore described by her mother as a
mediatrix, standing between Cenci's paternal wrath and the other
members of her family (II. i. 46–8), just as Christ stands between God
and man as a mediator (1 Tim. 2: 5). She is the Johannine Logos,
though only initially; for Shelley's play is an inversion of the idea that
'the light shineth in darkness; and the darkness comprehended it not'
(John 1: 5). Beatrice is originally one whose 'bright loveliness / Was
kindled to illumine this dark world' (IV. i. 121–2). She is the 'light of
life' (IV. iii. 42; V. iv. 134)—in a phrase borrowed from John 8: 12—
which shines to illuminate the sombre interiors of her world, that of the
Cenci family, and which is ultimately extinguished by its darkness (II. i.
179–81; IV. iii. 40–2). Unlike her New Testament model, she is, by a
reverse form of conversion, spiritually seduced by the lord of that
world, who in the governing scene of Act I diabolically institutes the
sacrament of death. For Cenci is an inversion of the Christ who,
according to St Paul, was 'appointed' to 'judge the world in righteous-
ness' (Acts 17: 31). He likens himself to 'a fiend appointed to chastise /
The offences of some unremembered world' (IV. i. 161–2).

The Cenci itself can be seen as an inversion of the mass, presided over

---

[15] Letter to Maria Gisborne, 16 Nov. 1819, *Letters*, ii. 154. Cf. the more conventional
horror of incest expressed in the letter to Countess Guiccioli, 9 Aug. 1821, *Letters*, ii. 326.
[16] See *The Revolt of Islam* (VI. xxxvi) and *Rosalind and Helen* (ll. 276–98). Mary notes
that in Rome on 1 Apr. 1819, Shelley was reading Euripides' *Hippolytus*, a work dealing
with the similar situation of a stepmother's illicit desire for her husband's son. See *JMS*, i.
256.

by a priest who is both a spiritual and a physical father. At the banquet in his palace which is attended by an assembly of guests, Cenci performs his priestly office:

> Cenci (*filling a bowl of wine, and lifting it up*).
> Oh, thou bright wine whose purple splendor leaps
> And bubbles gaily in this golden bowl
> Under the lamp light, as my spirits do,
> To hear the death of my accursed sons!
> Could I believe thou wert their mingled blood,
> Then would I taste thee like a sacrament,
> And pledge with thee the mighty Devil in Hell . . .
>   (I. iii. 77–83)

The image of the sacramental cup of death is not an unfamiliar one in Shelley's works of this period. Bennett Weaver has traced it to a conflation of Socrates' cup of hemlock and the visionary cup of death that Jesus prays to have removed in the garden of Gethsemane (Luke 22: 42). It is related to the chalice that yields a life of 'incarnate death' for the Wandering Jew in *Alastor* (ll. 675–81).[17] In 'Marenghi' (ll. 15–22) it commemorates, as it does in *The Cenci*, the pattern of violence that Shelley viewed as characteristically Italian. And in the conversation poems 'Julian and Maddalo' (ll. 435–8) and *Rosalind and Helen* (ll. 1129–30), it is associated with escape from persecution and suffering. The poet Lionel in the latter work dies in a deliciously decadent fashion, attended by Aeolian strains and his devoted lover in an aesthete's temple, where he drinks the cup of the nightingale's song.

The sacrament of violent intention in the Cenci palace portends the two violations of the blood kin relationship that are the play's themes: incest and parricide. They are the same violations of the familial relationship that bring about the tragedy of Oedipus. But Oedipus is the pawn of forces beyond his control, as he simply enacts the decrees of the oracle. In *The Cenci* the deeds are consciously willed, and deviously executed. Cenci's own murder is implicit in his own words, for he sacramentally institutes the pattern of vengeance by which the play operates. Like Jesus, he is to be arrested by religious authorities in the middle of the night. But unlike the acquiescent Galilean, he is a prince of darkness whose malign spirit triumphs over his own death. Betrayed by his own, he fulfils the destiny of his own eucharist. Beatrice, as his disciple, re-enacts with resolve in Act IV the mass she witnessed with horror in Act I.

---

[17] *Toward the Understanding of Shelley*, 214–18.

The induction of Beatrice into this cycle of violence and blood viola-
tion is the business of the third act. Emerging from the momentary hys-
teria that is her only comfort following rape, she laments,

> But now!—O blood, which art my father's blood,
> Circling through these contaminated veins,
> If thou, poured forth on the polluted earth,
> Could wash away the crime, and punishment
> By which I suffer . . . no, that cannot be!
>
> (III. i. 95–9)

The underlying principle here, according to the Mosaic code, is that
'the life of all flesh *is* the blood thereof' (Lev. 17: 14). The strictures
forbidding the consumption of animal blood in the Pentateuch (Lev.
17) quickly develop into prohibitions of incest (Lev. 18). The penalty
for parent–child incest was death for both persons involved (Lev. 20:
11). Cursing a parent, since it was equally subversive of the natural
order, also meant execution (Lev. 20: 9). In violating the blood kin
relationship, by this reckoning, Cenci had corrupted Beatrice's inner
life, her soul. But the Mosaic code was synonymous with tyranny for
Shelley. Cenci merely says that his intent was to 'poison and corrupt
her soul' (IV. i. 44). In the preface, Shelley denies that any person 'can
be truly dishonoured by the act of another' (*SPP*, 240). Since the death
penalty operated on this principle, it formed part of the 'Catholic'
tyranny that Shelley inveighs against in the play. The fact that Beatrice
appeals to the Old Testament penalty for incest implicates her in the
very system she initially loathes. For, by the Mosaic code, she too
incurs the death penalty, both for incest and for reviling her father.

If the blood of Christ washed away men's sins (Rev. 1: 5), Beatrice
momentarily ponders whether her blood might effect the same result
(III. i. 98). Rejecting both this option of suicide (III. i. 99, 132) and the
ethical response of brotherly love associated with the New Testament
(III. i. 387–90), she chooses the Hebraic demand for atonement (III. i.
215). She embraces the biblical principle that 'without shedding of
blood is no remission' (Heb. 9: 22). For Shelley, of course, this choice
constitutes her error. According to the book of Leviticus, the high
priest annually sprinkled the mercy seat of the most holy place in the
temple with blood to atone for the sins of the Israelites (16: 15).
Shelley's own detestation of such an image is reflected in the inverted
world witnessed with horror by the violated Beatrice: 'The beautiful
blue heaven is flecked with blood!' (III. i. 13). Yet, by the end of this

scene, she has opted for this very Levitical scheme. She will see to it that the death penalty for incest is enforced, a determination which ironically means imposing the death penalty on herself.

The death of Beatrice marks the end of the play, which, as a celebration of the eucharist of violence, is also a mass. We do not witness her execution. But in the account of the Cenci family which Shelley read and translated, Beatrice in her final words on the scaffold officiates much like a priest:

'Most beloved Jesus, who, relinquishing thy divinity, becamest a man; and didst through love purge my sinful soul also of its original sin with thy precious blood; deign, I beseech thee, to accept that which I am about to shed at thy most merciful tribunal, as a penalty which may cancel my many crimes, and spare me a part of that punishment justly due to me.' (Jul. ii. 165)

The Beatrice of the play itself, however, does not share the sacerdotal function with her father. She dies much like the Agnus Dei of the Church, but for her own sins, not those of the world. Nevertheless, she tells her brother that she

> Though wrapped in a strange cloud of crime and shame,
> Lived ever holy and unstained. And though
> Ill tongues shall wound me, and our common name
> Be as a mark stamped on thine innocent brow
> For men to point at as they pass, do thou
> Forbear . . .
>
> (v. iv. 148–53)

Christ too lived a holy life, yet was 'numbered with the transgressors', and mocked by those who passed by 'wagging their heads' (Mark 15: 28–9). The mark upon the brow (l. 151) recalls the ironic conflation of the mark of Cain (Gen. 4: 15) with Christ's crown of thorns (Mark 15: 17). It is a fusion that would reappear in *Adonais* (ll. 305–6). Appropriately, Lucretia echoes the words of Christ to the penitent thief on the cross in Luke 23: 43: 'ere night / Think we shall be in Paradise' (v. iv. 76–7).

Following the precedent of the historical Beatrice, who died reciting Psalm 130, *De profundis* (Jul. ii. 165), Shelley's protagonist plays on the significance of the Psalter. Here the poet is again ironic. In the Bible, the Psalmist typically moves from a state of dejection or fear to one of trust and hope in God. Like the Psalmist (Ps. 6: 6), Beatrice spends 'long sleepless nights' in prayer (I. iii. 117–20). But whereas the Psalmist concludes that 'the LORD will receive my prayer' (Ps. 6: 9), she says that her prayers 'were not heard' (I. iii. 119). After her arrest, she is therefore doubtful about following her mother's advice (v. iv. 75) and that of the Psalmist (Ps. 118: 8)—to put her trust in God:

> You do well telling me to trust in God,
> I hope I do trust in him. In whom else
> Can any trust? And yet my heart is cold.
>   (v. iv. 87–9)

What makes trusting God difficult is the spiritual chain of authority linking all the play's father figures—Cenci, the Pope, and God. If one understands the God of the other world by the father in this one, belief could be demanded, but not inspired. In the play, Shelley links father-hood with tyranny (II. ii. 80), papal authority (II. ii. 52–6), and finally with God, the ultimate Father (IV. i. 126). All are characterized by intractability and hardness. Cenci himself claims to feel inhuman (IV. i. 160). Likewise, the Pope is transformed into 'a marble form, / A rite, a law, a custom: not a man' (v. iv. 4–5), whose pastoral cross becomes something akin to the rod of the oppressor in the Old Testament (v. iv. 37; Isa. 9: 4). What creates the play's tragedy, according to Stuart Curran, is Beatrice's very 'Christianity'—that is, her opting to join this hierarchical model of it, by which evil has its sanction, rather than choose the interpretation whereby Christianity becomes a rule for morality.[18]

Nevertheless, the death of Beatrice means that Cenci's spiritual line has come to an end, despite the old man's wish to see his malignity pro-liferate. The biblical mandate to 'Be fruitful, and multiply' (Gen. 1: 28) had become for him a license to propagate offspring through his daugh-ter who would be deviant both in conception and spirit (IV. i. 143–52). Cenci's desire to manufacture such progeny is expressed in terms which distort the Christian idea of spiritual rebirth. He says,

> There shall be lamentation heard in Heaven
> As o'er an angel fallen; and upon Earth
> All good shall droop and sicken, and ill things
> Shall with a spirit of unnatural life
> Stir and be quickened . . . even as I am now.
>   (IV. i. 185–9)[19]

---

[18] See Curran's study *Shelley's Cenci* (Princeton, NJ, 1970), 67–9, 93–6, and *Shelley's Annus Mirabilis*, 135.

[19] The lines are dense with both literary and biblical allusion. Cf. *Macbeth*, III. ii. 52–3 and IV.iii. 22–3, 171–3.

He parodies both the rejoicing in heaven over each repentant sinner (Luke 15: 7) and the angelic gloria at the birth of Jesus: 'on earth peace, good will toward men' (Luke 2: 14). Doubly ironic is the fact that he succeeds—though not in the way he expected—in promoting 'unnatural' spiritual activity in his family.

There is both an inward and an outward significance in the moral teaching of *The Cenci*. By probing the vexed mazes of the inner life, Shelley intends to arrive at self-knowledge, the attainment of which generates the outward-moving impulses of love and benevolence. Yet, if the play teaches anything, it reinforces the biblical assertion that the heart is 'deceitful above all *things*, and desperately wicked: who can know it?' (Jer. 17: 9). Orsino observes in the play that the obsession with analysing the mind, a trait of the Cenci family, has its dangers:

> Such self-anatomy shall teach the will
> Dangerous secrets: for it tempts our powers,
> Knowing what must be thought, and may be done,
> Into the depth of darkest purposes . . .
>
> (II. ii. 110–13)

These fears seem to be justified, for there is a God-like presumption in the soul scrutiny of Beatrice that alarms Orsino. Her looks

> . . . anatomize me nerve by nerve
> And lay me bare, and make me blush to see
> My hidden thoughts . . .
>
> (I. ii. 85–7)

Such analysis is meant to be the province of the all-knowing God, who searches the mind of the Psalmist from 'afar off' (Ps. 139: 2). In *Shelley: A Critical Reading*, Wasserman has perceptively distinguished between this self-anatomy and self-knowledge, positing introspection on the part of the individual, particular person as the basis of the former and the discovery of universal human nature as the essence of the latter (p. 111). The uncovering of the general nature produces the Shelleyan fruit of the spirit: wisdom, justice, tolerance, and kindness. Yet, as Milton Wilson says, Shelley was coming to acknowledge 'the thinness of the line that separates "the dark idolatry of self" from self-knowledge'.[20] The Pauline sinful nature is denied in theory, yet Shelley seems to approximate it in the play itself.

---

[20] *Shelley's Later Poetry* (1957; New York, 1961), 92.

Shelley's concern with morality is now defined at least in part by an awareness of the impact of the Reformation on culture. The poet projects his moral critique back on the England which had been only partly emancipated from inquisitorial Christianity. In his poetry of social commentary written during this period, Shelley reveals a concern with the morality of class distinctions in British society. His response to the 'Peterloo' massacre at Manchester, *The Mask of Anarchy*, is a major expression of this consciousness. It is, of course, ironic that Shelley selects the genre of the mask, for as Stuart Curran observes in *Shelley's Annus Mirabilis*, the mask was an artistic form of entertainment favoured by the rich and the powerful (p. 188).

The first third of Shelley's *Mask* borrows heavily from the book of Revelation. Just as St John was an exile recording his vision on Patmos, Shelley was an expatriate living on the Continent. The opening stanza of the poem thus reveals not only the sense of exile 'in Italy', but also the visionary framework. The four horsemen of the Apocalypse become the personified abstractions of murder, fraud, hypocrisy, and anarchy. In this arrangement, the Bible itself merely serves to veil the corruption of Hypocrisy (l. 22), just as dictatorial tyranny is the mask worn by Anarchy. The portrait of this latter figure mounted on a white horse is drawn paradoxically with reference to the figures of both Death and the Logos of Revelation (chapters 6 and 19).[21] The association of the second advent of Christ with bloodshed is of course not unintentional.

At the heart of the *Mask*, however, lies an ethical concern reminiscent of the gospels and New Testament epistles. The virtues of 'Spirit, Patience, Gentleness' (l. 258) may well been suggested by St Paul's fruit of the Spirit (Gal. 5: 22–3). And the emphasis of Hope on 'deeds, not words' (l. 260) recalls the similar concern of St James with good works. The chief irony of the ethical assertions in the *Mask* springs from the association of Christianity with the affluent, rather than the underprivileged. Both Castlereaugh and 'the rich man in his riot' possess fattened hounds (ll. 6–13, 173). This symbol of affluence is better understood with reference to Shelley's poem 'A Ballad' (or 'Young

---

[21] Noting the presence in the poem of comic rhythms and melodramatic elements, Richard Hendrix raises the question of the appropriateness of Shelley's 'visionary mode', concluding that the apocalyptic format would not have appeared unusual to a popular culture familiar with the Bible and with Bunyan. See 'The Necessity of Response', *K–SJ*, 27 (1978), 53, 66.

Parson Richards'), in which the young cleric feeding his dog is
approached by a starving woman with a child.[22] She asks for food:

> 'Give me bread—my hot bowels gnaw—
>   I'll tear down the garden gate—
> I'll fight with the dog,—I'll tear from his maw
>   The crust which he just has ate—'

> 'Priest, consider that God who created us
>   Meant this for a world of love—
> Remember the story of Lazarus,
>   You preach to the people of—'

(ll. 41–8)

As William McTaggart has pointed out, there are two anecdotes from
the gospels to be kept in mind when looking at this scene (p. 24). The
one that Shelley mentions explicitly is the parable of the rich man and
Lazarus (the beggar in Luke 16: 19–31), separated in the afterlife by the
abyss between heaven and hell. Jesus uses the story to illustrate the
divine irony whereby the élite of this world become the outcasts of
the next. Shelley uses it to illustrate the class distinctions that existed in
the early nineteenth century. The implicit reference to the gospel
involves the Canaanite woman who begged Jesus to exorcize the devil
possessing her daughter (Matt. 15: 21–8). When he initially refused on
the ground that his ministry was to Israel rather than to the 'dogs' of
Gentile nations, she persisted, saying that 'the dogs eat of the crumbs
which fall from their masters' table' (Matt. 15: 27). Hearing this, Jesus
responded by granting the woman's request. The irony is that Parson
Richards does not do likewise. Although the *Mask* is not specifically
directed at the Church, it bears undertones of the same anti-ecclesiasti-
cism that informs the ballad. Society as it exists is in the comatose state
of tolerating social injustices, abuses which the exiled visionary
denounces.

In *The Mask*, Shelley targets the sources of social and political tyranny
which he felt lay behind the massacre at Manchester. In *Peter Bell the
Third*, composed at Florence in the autumn of 1819, the poet lampoons
the allied religious and literary movements which he associated with
tyranny. He presents a satire on the Lake school of poetry, particularly

---

[22] In William McTaggart, *England in 1819* (London, 1970), 9. A facsimile of Shelley's
draft for the poem may be consulted in *The Harvard Shelley Poetic Manuscripts*, ed. D. H.
Reiman (New York, 1991), *The Manuscripts of the Younger Romantics: Shelley*, gen. ed.
D. H. Reiman (5 vols. to date; 1985–91), v. 150–5.

on Wordsworth, who he felt had betrayed the movement which had led to the demonstration at Manchester (l. 644). The occasion for this work was the publication of Wordsworth's *Peter Bell* and of John Hamilton Reynolds's parody of it. Along with Shelley's Peter, a triune 'awful mystery' of three Peter Bells, as Shelley calls it in his dedication (*SPP*, 324), is created.

Shelley's Peter Bell is an overly pious version of Job, an oily-haired evangelical who falls ill (l. 12) and must endure the company of his 'holy friends' (l. 16). In their piety, the friends exacerbate Peter's distress by convincing him that he is 'predestined to damnation' (l. 20). From this point on, Shelley veers from his biblical model. Unlike Job, Peter curses his parents and blasphemes before entering the next world, virtually at the outset of the poem (ll. 40–50). In the Old Testament narrative, Yahweh speaks to Job from a whirlwind (38: 1 ff.). In Shelley's satire, it is the Devil who arrives in a 'black storm' (l. 61) to claim Peter's soul. The poet continues in this spirit of inversion by calling the Devil a 'thief, who cometh in the night' (l. 86) after the fashion of Christ's second coming (1 Thess. 5: 2).

Persuaded to become the Devil's footman, Peter arrives in hell, where, under the influence of a great poet (modelled after Coleridge), he is inspired to write assorted lyrics. This mentor

> . . . spoke of poetry, and how
> 'Divine it was—a light—a love —
> A spirit which like wind doth blow
> As it listeth, to and fro;
> A dew rained down from God above . . .'
>   (ll. 388–92)

The twin biblical images whereby the clouds 'drop down the dew' (Prov. 3: 20) and the wind 'bloweth where it listeth' (John 3: 8) illustrate two attributes of poetry. It is divine in origin, and is associated with renewal. Peter, however, bungles the Coleridgean creative act, for he lacks imagination (ll. 298–9), the chief prerequisite for poetic expression. For Coleridge's analogy of the 'infinite I AM' as the basis for the primary imagination in the *Biographia* (i. 304), Shelley (following Wordsworth) substitutes the more homely one of making pottery. Peter, it must be remembered, was a potter before entering into the Devil's service. And the Old Testament speaks of God's sovereignty over Israel as that by which a potter manipulates his clay (Jer. 18: 6). Likewise, 'language was in Peter's hand / Like clay while he was yet a potter' (ll. 443–4). His work is published, but the Devil bribes his reviewers into maligning it. And Peter's critical foes, likened to Job's adversary (ll. 458–61; Job 31: 35), condemn his work to mediocrity.

Shelley's fascination with the diabolical finds a naturally playful expression in *Peter Bell the Third*. But the implications of this use of orthodox Christian materials are serious. That the Devil is 'what we are' (l. 81), that hell is a state of mind, as it was for Milton's Satan (ll. 244–5, 260), and that damnation is the prerogative of the self rather than of God (ll. 217–41) are all suggested in the poem, and illustrate Shelley's growing tendency to reduce the categories of the transcendent to the province of the mind itself. Wordsworth's *Peter Bell* was essentially a poem about repentance, or change of mind. But while Shelley affirms the need for a transformation of the mind, he continues to reject the Christian bases for that change.

Unlikely as it may seem, Shelley began writing his 'Ode to the West Wind' at approximately the same time that he was composing *Peter Bell the Third*. The former was begun 20–5 October 1819 (*SPP*, 221 n. 1), and the latter was largely written in October and November of that year.[23] Shelley had used the wind as a simile for poetry in *Peter Bell the Third* (l. 390). Now it becomes an essential element in explaining the poetic process.

In the Scriptures, the wind heralds the new epochs of the post-diluvian world (Gen. 8: 1) and of the Church age (Acts 2: 2). Jesus compares the person who has been 'born of the Spirit' with the wind, in that both are enigmatic (John 3: 8). What links these three passages is the idea of renewal.[24] Each could apply to the ode in a particular way. The speaker in the poem is aware of an impending new epoch (l. 70); he emphasizes spiritual rebirth (l. 64); and just as the coming of the Holy Spirit brought with it the gift of prophecy (Acts 2: 18), so the ode is self-conscious of a prophetic role (l. 69). Whether it is seen as structurally akin to a prayer, a psalm, a hymn, or even an exorcism (based on l. 3),[25] it is more fundamentally a prophetic lyric. The prophets were

[23] According to Donald Reiman, Shelley may have begun composition on *Peter Bell the Third* as early as July or Aug. 1819, while at Leghorn. See *BSM*, i. 6–9, vii. 4–5.

[24] See the discussion of the wind and the rebirth archetype in Romantic poetry (with some cautionary comments) in M. H. Abrams's essay 'The Correspondent Breeze', 43–52.

[25] See Coleman Parsons, 'Shelley's Prayer to the West Wind', *K–SJ*, 11 (1962), 32–4; White, *Shelley*, ii. 280; Frederick Pottle, 'Wordsworth in the Present Day', in *Romanticism*, ed. D. Thorburn and G. Hartman (Ithaca, NY, 1973), 122; Timothy Webb (ed.), *Percy Bysshe Shelley* (London, 1977), 202; and H. Bloom, *Shelley's Mythmaking*, 75.

masters at employing a controlling image to illustrate a point. The central picture in Shelley's poem is that of the forest, which is analogous to the poet (l. 58). It recalls the biblical simile in which the man who puts his trust in the Lord is compared to a tree planted by the water, whose leaves do not wither.[26] The Psalmist contrasts this picture of the righteous man with that of the ungodly one, who is 'like the chaff which the wind driveth away' (Ps. 1: 4). Steadfastness is the opposite of being subject to the wind. Shelley, however, seems to combine the symbolism of tree and chaff. He likens himself to the trees, but not in the sense of having stability, for his leaves in fact wither only to be driven before the wind like chaff (ll. 63–4). Prophetically, the wind is an agent of judgement, ferreting out that which is perishable (Isa. 64: 6; Ps. 1: 4, 6). Its counterpart is the verdant image, which connotes stability and prosperity (Ps. 1: 3). In prostrating himself emotionally before the wind, the poet reverses its biblical significance, for his 'chaff' is not transitory, but conducive to rebirth.

It is quite possible that in his opening stanza, Shelley may have had in mind one of the visions of the prophet Zechariah. His 'chaff'—a frenetic mêlée of yellow, black, pale, and red leaves which are survived by the wind-borne charioted seeds (ll. 4–7)—is similar to the four chariots seen by the prophet (6: 1–8). Each of these is seen drawn by a group of horses coloured differently from those with the other chariots. Respectively, they are red, black, white, and bay (mixed with 'grisled'). They are the 'four spirits of the heavens' (Zech. 6: 5) which can be linked with the 'four winds of the heaven' described earlier (2: 6).[27] The white and black horses execute God's judgement on Israel's enemy to the north, apparently Babylon. But for failing to observe the Yahwistic ethical norms, the Israelites themselves incur chastisement; they are 'scattered . . . with a whirlwind' sent by God, leaving a verdant land to become wilderness (Zech. 7: 14). As in the imagery of the Psalmist, wind is a means of castigation; its counterpoise is the verdant landscape. Shelley's petitioning of the wind could therefore be an invocation of judgement, a correcting process that may involve revolution. The leaves of the natural world, then, are presented symbolically— at least in terms of the biblical prophecy—as elements subject to a

[26] See Ps. 1: 3 and Jer. 17: 8. I am developing an association made by Wasserman in *Shelley*, 240 n.

[27] Shelley was aware that the Hebrew word for 'spirit', *ruah*, suggests both *breath* and *wind*, as noted in Spinoza's *Theologico-Political Treatise*, 19–20. In the margin beside this discussion of the wind in his personal copy of Spinoza, Shelley writes, '5 senses of πνευμα' (*SHC*, viii. 732).

sovereign power. In Shelley's own life, the dispersed leaves are the pages of the proselytic literature which he had issued, much like the bottles of knowledge that he had deployed at Lynmouth Beach, Devon, in 1812.[28]

Like *Peter Bell the Third*, the ode is Job-like in some key respects. As in the biblical drama, the operations of nature are adduced as mysteries to differentiate the limitations of finite human comprehension from the unlimited capacities of an imperceptible source of power. Answering Job from the whirlwind, the voice of Yahweh declares: 'Who hath divided a watercourse for the overflowing of waters, or a way for the lightning of thunder; To cause it to rain on the earth . . . and to cause the bud of the tender herb to spring forth?' (Job 38: 25–7). Shelley employs the similar imagery of buds (stanza I), rain and lightning (stanza II), and cloven waters (stanza III). Each of their associated emblems of leaf, cloud, and wave is endowed with motion by the wind (ll. 43–5). But the speaker, bound by his temporality, could only fall to the ground in an attempt to respond as they do (l. 54). He feels all too keenly his human limitations, and might have lamented with Job, 'wilt thou bring me into dust again?' (Job 10: 9), or 'Thou liftest me up to the wind . . . and dissolvest my substance' (Job 30: 22). He compensates for this sense of limitation by imaging himself as the instrument which the wind will play, yielding his power of speech to the prerogative of the 'other'.

By transforming the poem into an incantation (l. 65), the speaker in the ode ritually purifies his lips from the custom of merely uttering a poem, as the unclean lips of Isaiah were purified by a live coal taken from the altar by one of the seraphim (Isa. 6: 6–8). The act of purification was necessary for the prophet to become a bearer of God's message.[29] The incantation effectively transforms the main elements of the poem—forest and leaves—into the new elements of 'unextinguished hearth' and '[a]shes and sparks'. As leaves, the latter are merely 'dead thoughts' (l. 63). As the self-consciously uttered words of a poet, they are both prophetic and regenerative. In the Bible, God had instructed the prophet to 'lift up thy voice like a trumpet, and shew my people their transgression' (Isa. 58: 1). In Shelley's ode, the poet's lips

---

[28] Cf. the 'Esdaile' sonnet 'On launching some bottles filled with *Knowledge* into the Bristol Channel' (*PS*, i. 238–9), which associates westerly breezes with the dispersion of the 'night of ignorance'.

[29] Shelley parodies the 'Lips touched by seraphim' in the poem 'A New National Anthem' (l. 36). See *SPW*, p. 574.

become a conduit for the wind, which becomes the 'trumpet of a prophecy' (l. 69) heralding an era of reform symbolized by the seasonal shift from winter to spring.

That the springtime of political reform succeeds the winter of tyranny as part of a natural process is of course a cardinal doctrine for Shelley. But the inference that this new epoch is different simply politically is not entirely correct. When the Shelley of 1812 contrasts the 'leafless branches' of winter with the 'foliage bursting from the buds' in spring, he says, 'Do we not see that the laws of nature perpetually act by disorganization and reproduction, each alternately becoming cause and effect. The analysis that we can draw from physical to moral topics are of all others the most striking.'[30] Shelley was vitally concerned with the revolution that might take place in the mind of man, the exploration of which he saw as a 'Protestant' venture. Like several other of Shelley's poems written in 1819, the 'Ode to the West Wind' ends on the note of rebirth, of resurrection.[31] But this rebirth is not simply social and economic. A major reason for the failure of the poet in *Peter Bell the Third* is that he is a 'moral eunuch' (l. 314). *The Cenci* reveals the devastating consequences of the refusal to reorient the mind morally in a spirit of love and forgiveness. In *Prometheus Unbound*, begun in 1818, Shelley celebrates this very transformation of the mind that leads to moral rebirth.

---

[30] *Proposals for an Association of Philanthropists* (Jul. v. 266, 267).

[31] See 'A New National Anthem' (ll. 40–1), 'Sonnet: England in 1819' (ll. 12–14), and 'Ode to Heaven' (ll. 48–9).

5

Providence and Prometheus

Francis Bacon observed long before Shelley that the name Prometheus signified Providence.[1] In fact, the word $\pi\rho o\mu\dot{\eta}\theta\iota\alpha$, related to the name of the mythical figure, shares with the Latin *providentia* the meaning of 'foresight'. Thus arises an association between Prometheus and the idea of Providence. Bacon distinguished between human and divine providence (vi. 747). But in the case of the Romantic poet, there is a unique fusion of the two. Fundamentally, his protagonist is an embodiment of human qualities. However, Shelley makes it clear in the preface to his lyrical drama that he is writing it with Milton's epic in mind (*SPP*, 133). And we recall that Milton wrote *Paradise Lost* specifically to assert the operation of the divine Providence that works to 'justify the ways of God to men' (i. 26). Although the seventeenth-century poet was a leading figure in the movement that denounced the Roman Church—which Shelley calls the 'oldest and most oppressive form of the Christian Religion' (*SPP*, 134)—the later poet could hardly have appropriated his idea of Providence. In *The Cenci*, the word essentially signifies the tyrannous sovereignty of the Christian God (iii. i. 181–2). And the God of the Christians was for him a human fabrication. In the preface to 'Julian and Maddalo', Shelley describes his persona (Julian) as a believer in 'those philosophical notions which assert the power of man over his own mind, and the immense improvements of which, by the extinction of certain moral superstitions, human society may be yet susceptible' (*SPP*, 113). What Shelley is describing is his own conception of Providence, a conception which involves both the purposes of the divine mind and the flow of redemptive history.

The Christian idea of biblical history involved a typology whereby the Old Testament type, or *figura*, providentially found its fulfilment in the New Testament. Erich Auerbach has observed that the concept of

---

[1] *Of the Wisdom of the Ancients* (1609), trans. J. Spedding, in *The Works of Francis Bacon*, ed. James Spedding, R. L. Ellis, and D. D. Heath (14 vols.; London, 1857–74), vi. 746. Thomas Blackwell likewise saw Prometheus as Providence in *Letters concerning Mythology*, 98. The equation has been noted by both Harold Bloom in *Shelley's Mythmaking*, 56, and Stuart Curran in *Shelley's Annus Mirabilis*, 214 n. 15.

the *figura*, when applied to the flow of human events, defies a conception of history that operates on consecutive or causal connection alone. For the pattern of early type and later fulfilment cannot be superimposed on the 'horizontal dimension' of the temporal world, but 'can be established only if both occurrences are vertically linked to Divine Providence, which alone is able to devise such a plan of history and supply the key to its understanding'.[2] Providence, then, is the unique contribution of the Judaeo-Christian world to the understanding of history. Although it is nowhere formally defined in the Bible, the idea is expressed at several points. The same God who 'removeth kings, and setteth up kings' (Dan. 2: 21)—a thought that is especially relevant to *Prometheus Unbound*—becomes so involved with individuals that St Paul believed 'all things work together for good to them that love God, to them who are the called according to *his* purpose' (Rom. 8: 28). Providence was seen as an all-embracing reality that left nothing to chance. As the thinkers of the Enlightenment construed this idea, it implied necessity. And as the Yahwistic God evolved into 'the Deity' of the post-Newtonian religionists, there was a corresponding mechanization of necessity whereby its progressive autonomy led to a secularization of the concept, a development especially evident in thinkers such as Holbach and Godwin. It is this more materialistic necessitarianism that is characteristic of the young Shelley. Yet, by the time of *Prometheus Unbound*, Shelley's necessitarianism had changed. And this change is expressed in the character of Demogorgon, often identified with (if not as) necessity, who emerges in the drama as a force that must be seen in a complementary relation to Prometheus.

If Providence 'becomes' necessity in Western thought, one could equally say that in a sense Prometheus 'becomes' Demogorgon in Shelley. Providence is simply the larger context in which the necessitarian's causal rigour operates. In *The Statesman's Manual*, Coleridge describes just such a relationship:

In the Bible every agent appears and acts as a self-subsisting individual: each has a life of its own, and yet all are one life. The elements of necessity and free-will are reconciled in the higher power of an omnipresent Providence, that predestinates the whole in the moral freedom of the integral parts.[3]

Providence, then, is a holistic concept, a point to which particular aspects can be referred. Prometheus also stands for an integral unity.

---

[2] *Mimesis*, trans. W. Trask (1953; Garden City, NY, 1957), 64.

[3] In *Lay Sermons*, ed. R. J. White (Princeton, NJ, and London, 1972), 31.

Shelley's vegetarian preceptor John Frank Newton aligned himself with the widely held view that Prometheus represented the human race.[4] The Scriptures, too, speak in a similar way of Adam, the primal man containing the seed of the human race, the 'one man' by whom all men fell into sin and death (Rom. 5: 12, 1 Cor. 15: 22).[5]

There is, however, an alternative interpretation of Prometheus as an emblem of unity which associates him with another figure in the book of Genesis. If the poem is read in epistemological terms, Prometheus would stand for the mind, the point to which the multiplicity of sensory experience is referred.[6] The syncretist mythographer Francis Wilford had linked Prometheus with the Hindu deity Maha-Deva, 'who is called also PRAMAT' HE' SA or the lord of the five senses or servants; because they are to be kept in due subjection to reason'.[7] But in the *New System*, Jacob Bryant summarized the process by which he believed the legend of Prometheus evolved from the biblical account of Noah (ii. 198–204). Bryant said that the Greek word for 'mind' ($voῦs$) was a corruption of the name 'Noah', and that '*the mind was Prometheia; and Prometheus was said to renew mankind, from new forming their minds; and leading them by cultivation from ignorance to knowledge*' (ii. 200).[8]

Superimposing the account of Prometheus on that of Noah thus yielded not only a fresh speculation on the mind, but an interest in the idea of renewal. The apostle Paul also speaks of being 'transformed by the renewing of your mind' (Rom. 12: 2). But the state of spiritual rebirth in the New Testament points back to the flood story, in which safe passage through the waters of death was guaranteed by the hand of God. In the New Testament, the ark's survival of the great flood is a picture of baptism, of rising from the waters of death—symbolic of the death of the old sinful nature—into the new life made possible through the resurrection of Christ (1 Pet. 3: 18–21). Bryant's comparison of Noah to Prometheus is of particular interest in this connection, especially as it illustrates the nature of Providence. According to him, the ancient emblem depicting a serpent surrounding an egg (a cognate of

---

[4] *The Return to Nature* (London, 1811), 8.

[5] See also the discussion of the primal man by Jonas, *Gnostic Religion*, 128–9, 147, 176, 216–33.

[6] Bacon had anticipated this view by identifying Promethean providence as a capacity of the human intellect, or mind (*Wisdom of the Ancients*, vi. 747).

[7] 'On Mount Caucasus', *Asiatick Researches*, Calcutta edn., 6 (1799), 506.

[8] Cf. the statement of Hermes Trismegistus in the *Divine Pymander*. 'As many therefore as understood the Proclamation [of God], and were baptized or dowsed into the Minde, these were made pertakers [*sic*] of Knowledge, and became perfect men, receiving the Minde' (185–6).

the ark) signified for some in the ancient world the providential hand that protected those in the ark during the cataclysm (ii. 359). The experience of the flood is tantamount to a new genesis, for 'Ark' becomes Αρχα [sic], or 'the beginning' (ii. 382). Bryant is here ingenious enough to twist the word 'Ark' into the name of Prometheus. From 'Arca' he derives Aracca, or Erech (mentioned in Gen. 10: 10). He writes: 'The Deity of Erech was undoubtedly the original Erectheus. The Chaldeans expressed it Erech-Thoth, analogous to Pirom-Thoth, or Prometheus; and by it they denoted the Arkite God' (ii. 518). The connection is enhanced by the fact that *Theba* (Hebrew for 'ark') was said to be a daughter of Prometheus (ii. 220, 220 n. 63). Allegorically, enclosure in the ark represented a state of darkness and death, from which one emerged in a second birth or new life (ii. 209, 359). In the Egyptian version of the deluge legend, confinement in the ark—that is, in its cognate form of the coffin of Osiris—symbolized the season of winter (ii. 386), the prelude to the season of rebirth. This movement from winter to spring, which Shelley naturally associates with the idea of resurrection, is one of the thematic undercurrents of *Prometheus Unbound*.

It is ironic that Shelley's only mention of the great flood in his lyrical drama is negative; it is presented as an act of total destruction (IV. 314–16). Yet, typologically, it illustrates the archetype of rebirth, and this regeneration is effected through μετάνοια, the change of mind. In the New Testament, this transformation is the work of the Holy Spirit. But in Shelley the sources of this dramatic reversal do not lie outside the self, for the Promethean mind subsumes in itself the functions of divine Providence. In the Shelleyan fragment 'To the Mind of Man' (written in 1820), the mind is addressed as though it were a divine force. Timothy Webb has observed that the manuscript notebook containing this fragment also contains an apostrophe to the mind as 'Great Spirit'.[9] As the mind therefore exercises its providence over the reality that it perceives, Prometheus deals with the perceptive capacity and with that which can be known. Demogorgon, on the other hand, is emblematic of that which cannot be known. He is 'darkness visible', as Milton Wilson has noted in *Shelley's Later Poetry* (p. 135), the veiled causal force that cannot be perceived. Beyond the depths of his cave lies the abysm of secrets (II. iv. 114–15). Wilson has discussed him with

---

[9] '"Avalanche of Ages"', 8–9. Webb further says that '[t]his concern with the power of mind is closely connected with Shelley's investigations into the existence of God' (p. 9).

reference to Hume's principle of constant conjunction, the basis for the inference of causality (p. 138). But constant conjunction is observable; and Demogorgon is not. It may prove more constructive to consider him along with Hume's principle of necessary connection, the unascertainable mysterious link between the events that are arbitrarily called cause and effect.[10] As mind, Prometheus could be associated with constant conjunction, for this falls within the realm of empirical experience. As that which lies beyond apprehension, however, Demogorgon must be seen in a different light, in this case that of the principle of necessary connection, which does not answer to any impression made upon the mind. It was on this basis that Hume in his *Enquiry* undermined the deistic method of arrival, by pursuing the chain of causes, at the First Cause, the Supreme Being (pp. 72, 137–8). Herein lies the basis of Shelley's own scepticism, a scepticism for which the mystery of Demogorgon is symbolic.

The mystery of causality was not, however, solely the prerogative of the sceptics. It is an essential component of Calvinism. According to John Calvin, the doctrine of Providence is twofold. On the one hand, it is 'lodged in the act'.[11] The action of the wind in creating waves on the sea, for example, testifies to its presence as a cosmological reality (I. xvi. 7; i. 206). And the provision of a ram for Abraham to sacrifice in place of his son (Gen. 22: 8–13) illustrates the divine hand at work in human affairs (I. xvi. 4; i. 202). On the other hand, the ultimate cause of these acts lies in the eternal decree of God, and therefore cannot be known. Calvin says that 'the order, reason, end, and necessity of those things which happen for the most part lie hidden in God's purpose' (I. xvi. 9; i. 208). This distinction has a parallel in Calvin's discussion of the divine will, which he equates with necessity (III. xxiii. 8; ii. 956). The reformer says that God has a revealed will which is disclosed in the Scriptures. And he has 'another hidden will which may be compared to a deep abyss; concerning which Paul also says: "O depth of the riches and wisdom and knowledge of God! How unsearchable are his judgments, and how inscrutable his ways!"' (I. xvii. 2; i. 212–13). The necessity of God's providential acts is therefore shrouded in the diction of mystery and incomprehensibility. God's secret determinations cannot

---

[10] *Enquiry concerning Human Understanding*, 75.

[11] *Institutes of the Christian Religion*, trans. F. L. Battles, ed. J. T. McNeill (2 vols.; Philadelphia, 1960), I. xvi. 4; i. 202. Referencing is by book, chapter, and section of the original, then volume and page number of the modern edition.

be known by man. Like the 'abysm' of Demogorgon's cave, his will is an abyss whose deep truth cannot be imaged.

The typical response to such notions in the Enlightenment was to retain belief in necessitarian dogma without retaining the idea of an actively intervening Providence. Initially this meant the substitution of the First Cause for the Yahwistic God of the Jews. Eventually, even the deist's Supreme Being became unnecessary as atheistic thinkers empha- sized laws of nature. In the *Système de la nature*, Holbach decried Providence as an unjustifiable theory and predestination as fatalistic (ii. 68–9; i. 217 n. 61), retaining a belief in a universally operative necessity based on constant laws (i. 54). He quotes from Thomas Blackwell, who had written that Pan, or universal nature, was without father or mother; he had 'sprung of DEMOGORGON at the same instant with the fatal Sisters the *Parcae*: A beautiful Way of saying, that the Universe sprung from an unknown Power (to them) and was formed according to the unalter- able Relations and eternal Aptitudes of Things; the Daughters of *Necessity*' (p. 55).[12] And in a passage quoted by Shelley in the Notes on *Queen Mab* (*PS*, i. 386), Holbach ridicules the idea of pursuing the chain of causes back to the First Cause. His God is simply a metaphor for ignorance, and exists in the 'abîme ténébreux' of limited human comprehension (ii. 16). Thus Calvin's image of the abyss of God's hid- den will is turned against the Christian view of Providence altogether.

Prometheus and Demogorgon thus stand in their relationship to each other as complementary manifestations of the biblical Logos. The former represents the voluntaristic possibilities of choice (repentance, forgiveness, and love); the latter stands for the unascertainable causal certitudes that govern the world. Prometheus is that aspect of the divine which reveals itself, Demogorgon that aspect which remains hid- den. The pattern of the former is that of the kenosis passage of the New Testament: Christ subsisting in the form of God appeared after the fash- ion of men (Phil. 2: 6–8). The humbling culminates in death on the cross. The tendency of the latter, however, is to remain perpetually undisclosed; as St Paul writes elsewhere of 'the mystery, which from the beginning of the world hath been hid in God, who created all things by Jesus Christ' (Eph. 3: 9). We could say with Wasserman that Prometheus's realm is one of being (p. 319), whereas Demogorgon, according to Wilson, 'exists at the point where nothing becomes some- thing' (p. 135), in the realm of becoming. Both are aspects of the

---

[12] See Holbach's *Système* (ii. 35), where the passage is cited in French.

Logos, of the capacity of the divine to erupt from eternity into time. Demogorgon stands for the idea of incarnation (III. i. 46), but only as a process of incarnating. Prometheus, on the other hand, is the Word made flesh which 'dwelt among us', whose glory was beheld of men (John 1: 14). Appropriately, the two never meet, as Wasserman has observed (p. 318), though each of course has a relationship to Asia.

It is generally agreed that Asia represents love in Shelley's poem. Her union with Prometheus is a foreshadowing of the spirit of unity which will characterize the Promethean new age. This parallel between sexual love and the new spiritual epoch brings into close proximity two conceptions of love which, like Prometheus and Demogorgon, must be seen in complementary terms—Eros and Agape. In pre-biblical Greek, as theologian Ethelbert Stauffer notes, the first of these (expressed in the form ἐρᾶν) denotes 'passionate love which desires the other for itself'.[13] The second (ἀγαπᾶν) indicates a love that 'makes distinctions, choosing and keeping to its object. . . . it is a giving, active love on the other's behalf' (i. 37). It is this latter form of love that prevails in the New Testament. The sacrificial love of God for the world (John 3: 16), the command to love one's enemies (Matt. 5: 44), and the great Pauline virtue of charity (1 Cor. 13: 13) are all expressed by forms of this word.

The basic difference between Eros and Agape led theologian Anders Nygren to see the two concepts as antagonistic. According to Nygren, Eros is acquisitive, of human origin, and is motivated by its response to the intrinsic worth or beauty of its object. Agape, on the other hand, is sacrificial, divine in origin, and inclined to invest its chosen object with value. Eros ascends toward its object while Agape descends.[14] Responding to this view, James Allsup, in a study of Shelley's view of love, asserts that the functions of Agape and Eros are both necessary for metaphysical wholeness:

Human *agape* is divine *Agape* in human reflection and translation—divine love incarnate. Divine *Agape* descends, in ancient metaphor, to inspire our *eros* to ascend to it, to the One. . . . Severely to split *agape* from *eros* and baldly to praise the first at the expense of the second (as Anders Nygren does in *Agape and Eros*) is to be unjust to both. These two are different forms or shapes of the same longing. Love is perhaps best comprehended, then, under the image of a circle commenced by *Agape*, continued by *agape*, and completed by *eros*—a magic circle, as it were, traced by both God and man.[15]

[13] See 'ἀγαπάω', in *Theological Dictionary of the New Testament*, i. 35.
[14] *Agape and Eros*, trans. P. S. Watson (1932, 1939; London, 1982), 210.
[15] *The Magic Circle* (Port Washington, NY, 1976), 5.

Allsup goes on to distinguish images of Agape (those involving descent, such as celestial fire, light, rain, and wind) from those of Eros (images of ascent, such as earthly fire, reflected light, wings, and boats), asserting that the 'creative tension of contraries' informs much of his discussion (pp. 10–11). He explores a number of these images in his analysis of *Prometheus Unbound* (pp. 87–102).

Because of his orientation in Greek literature, Shelley found Eros to be an appealing concept; and Nygren's analysis reveals that it had its loftier goals. Shelley would have realized this from his reading of Plato's *Symposium*, which he had finished translating six or seven weeks before beginning *Prometheus Unbound* in September 1818. Here Pausanias divides Eros into Pandemian (vulgar) love and Uranian (heavenly) love.[16] The former is physical and somewhat immature, whereas the latter is both spiritual and mature. Uranian love is naturally the noblest, for, as Shelley translates the speech of Pausanias, '. . . not all love, nor every mode of love is beautiful, or worthy of commendation, but that alone which excites us to love worthily' (*Plat.* 422). Such a recognition of intrinsic worth or beauty is, as Nygren observed, a feature of Eros. Shelley reflects this view in the Notes on *Queen Mab* by saying that 'Love is inevitably consequent upon the perception of loveliness' (*PS*, i. 368). And in his brief essay on love, probably written shortly after he translated the *Symposium*, Shelley says that love 'is that powerful attraction towards all that we conceive or fear or hope beyond ourselves' which 'connects not only man with man, but with every thing which exists' (*SPP*, 473).[17]

The Scriptures have a unique way of linking the ideals of Eros and Agape. In the Old Testament, God is spoken of as the eternal bridegroom whose love for his bride Israel is everlasting. One of the outstanding examples of this analogy is found in the second chapter of Hosea. In the New Testament, the image comes to represent the ultimate union of Christ and the Church, presented as the Lamb and his Bride, the new Jerusalem (Rev. 21: 9–10). This symbolism has

[16] *Plat.* 422. According to Mary Shelley's note, the poet had originally entitled his poem 'Prince Athanase' *Pandemos and Urania* (*SPW*, 158 n.).

[17] Shelley is here dealing with the classical φιλία (friendship, sentimental love), a notion subsumed in Agape in the New Testament. Neville Rogers explains this aspect of Shelleyan Love by arguing that a humanitarian Agape develops out of Eros in *Prometheus Unbound*. See *Shelley at Work*, 2nd edn. (Oxford, 1967), 144. Donald Reiman dates 'On Love' 20–5 July 1818 in *SHC*, vi. 633, 639. He goes on to explain that Shelley's concept of love changed after the writing of *The Revolt of Islam* and that Shelley's brief essay is a critique of Plato's *Symposium* (vi. 642).

prompted G. Wilson Knight to attribute to the New Testament an underlying pattern of Eros.[18] But such a view superimposes an alien way of thinking on the Scriptures, for, as Northrop Frye points out, the word Eros does not occur in the New Testament.[19] Sexuality is taken up in Agape. Even in his admonitions on love between husbands and wives, the apostle Paul uses the language of Agape (e.g. Eph. 5: 24–5). For, Stauffer notes, it is the selfless form of love that has a teleological orientation: 'Faith and hope bear the marks of this defective aeon. . . . With love the power of the future age already breaks into the present form of the world. As for Jesus, so for Paul $\dot{\alpha}\gamma\dot{\alpha}\pi\eta$ is the only vital force which has a future in this aeon of death' (i. 51). This form of love broadens our understanding of the plainly erotic relationship of Asia to Prometheus, for it is a future-oriented love. But it is not so in exactly the same way as in the biblical Apocalypse. In the first place, there is no theology of Agape (apart from Eros) in Shelley's poem. Furthermore, there is a mingling of apocalyptic and millennial elements.[20] An apocalyptic conclusion in the biblical sense would mean the end of the earth. At this stage of his career, however, Shelley is more interested in redeeming than transcending the world.

Although *Prometheus Unbound* is based on the drama of Aeschylus, several biblical and Miltonic sources have a bearing on the opening act. In different ways, Shelley's protagonist resembles the biblical Job, Milton's Samson, and the Christ of *Paradise Regained*. But the comparison Shelley makes is with Milton's Satan, an overreacher having an affinity with the Lucifer of the Old Testament (like Prometheus a 'light-bearer'), who said 'I will ascend into heaven, I will exalt my throne above the stars of God . . . I will be like the most High' (Isa. 14: 13, 14).[21] The subsequent fall of Lucifer, if it is to be identified with the fall of Satan, suggests the biblical version of the Titan myth, in which 'the angels which kept not their first estate' are 'reserved in everlasting chains under darkness unto the judgment of the great day' (Jude 6). In the drama, Jupiter refers to the 'deep Titanian prisons' where he would

---

[18] *The Christian Renaissance*, rev. edn. (London, 1962), 214–18, 241.

[19] *The Great Code* (1981; London, 1982), 141.

[20] The contrast between prophecy, with its goal of millennial restoration, and apocalyptic is drawn by Paul Hanson, 'The Phenomenon of Apocalyptic in Israel', *The Dawn of Apocalyptic* (1975; Philadelphia, 1979), 4–12. Milton Wilson discusses the difference between apocalypse and millennium as these terms apply to *Prometheus Unbound* in *Shelley's Later Poetry*, 206–11.

[21] R. J. Z. Werblowski has asserted that the appealing features of Milton's Satan have been derived from the Prometheus myth. See *Lucifer and Prometheus*, p. xvii.

like to consign Demogorgon (III. i. 62). St John likewise says in his vision that Satan will be shut up in the bottomless pit during the millennium 'and after that he must be loosed a little season' (Rev. 20: 3). Shelley, on the other hand, plainly identifies the millennium as a period of titanic freedom in speaking of

> . . . the chained Titan's woful doom
> And how he shall be loosed, and make the Earth
> One brotherhood . . .
>
> (II. ii. 93–5)

That Prometheus should be a Titan to whom Shelley ascribes both Christ-like and diabolical characteristics naturally brings to mind the Gnostic hermeneutics attacked by the Church Fathers. According to Irenaeus's treatise against the heresies, one of the possible names of the Antichrist is 'Teitan' [Titan], the six letters answering to the number associated with the Antichrist, 666. He would take the name Teitan because it is associated with the sun, and because he 'pretends that he vindicates the oppressed' (V. xxx. 3; i. 559). Both of these are elements that could be taken to apply to Shelley's Prometheus.

The pivotal points of this first act are the penitent benediction of Prometheus (I. 303–5) and his expression of pity for those who are incapable of suffering the absence of sympathetic love that he feels (I. 633). The first of these follows from an act of memory:

> It doth repent me: words are quick and vain;
> Grief for awhile is blind, and so was mine.
> I wish no living thing to suffer pain.
>
> (I. 303–5)

In the New Testament, repentance indicates a 'turning about', and characterizes the response of the new Christian to the dead works of the old life (Heb. 6: 1). Clearly, this notion informs Prometheus's self-induced 'conversion', which had been foreshadowed as early as line 57. The second of these moments is, like the first, an expression of sympathy which grows out of experience. Prometheus tells his tormenting Fury: 'Thy words are like a cloud of winged snakes / And yet, I pity those they torture not' (i. 632–3). To lack the capacity for suffering is not to be fully human; to express pity for hypothetical beings is.[22]

---

[22] Similar to this is Hazlitt's view of the sympathetic imagination in *An Essay on the Principles of Human Action* (1805): 'The imagination, by means of which alone I can anticipate future objects, or be interested in them, must carry me out of myself into the feelings of others by one and the same process by which I am thrown forward as it were into my

It is an unregenerated Titan, however, that is presented at the begin-
ning. The opening speech of Prometheus is one of Satanic defiance.
Like Milton's truant angels, for whom heaven had been an eternity of
required chapel and 'Forced hallelujahs',[23] Prometheus refuses his heav-
enly Monarch 'knee-worship, prayer and praise' (I. 6). By the fact that
he suffers for his own sin and retains his defiance, he is characteristically
unlike the crucified Jesus. Ironically, the imagery Shelley uses is that of
Christ's crucifixion. He begins his story very near where the gospel
story ends. Prior to his crucifixion, Jesus had prayed in the garden of
Gethsemane: '. . . O my Father, if it be possible, let this cup pass from
me . . .' (Matt. 26: 39). The symbol of the cup, borrowed from the
Passover rite he had just commemorated, suggests an awareness of his
impending death. And in Shelley's drama, the Titan defiantly tells the
Furies to 'Pour forth the cup of pain' (I. 474). Unlike Cenci, who insti-
tutes a sacramental cup to symbolize violence to others, Prometheus
takes the cup for himself.

As many critics have observed, the imagery of Christ's death on the
cross frequently appears in Act I. The chief details are as follow:

crown of thorns	Matt. 27: 29	I. 290, 563–5, 598–9
robe of mockery	Matt. 27: 28, 31	I. 289
nails of crucifixion	John 20: 25	I. 20
piercing spear	John 19: 34	I. 31–2
succession of mockers	Matt. 27: 39–44	I. 36–8

Both Shelley and the gospel-writer portray a contrast between the
mother, who is present, and a sense of cosmic abandonment. For Christ
on the cross, this means being forsaken by his heavenly Father (Matt.
27: 46). Looking down, he says to the earthly mother witnessing his
death, 'Woman, behold thy son!' (John 19: 26). Prometheus, defying
the idea of a heavenly Father, feels abandoned instead by the elements
of earth, sea, and sky (I. 24–30). When his mother, Earth, finally speaks,
he addresses her as Jesus did his mother: 'Know ye not me, / The Titan
. . .?' (I. 117–18). The Earth, as a source of beginnings, embodies the
faculty of memory and the attempt to bring time back to the Fall. But
she is also the fallen world itself, the cosmos which must be redeemed.

As part of the cosmic sympathy with this Fall, a series of plagues rem-
iniscent of those which afflicted the Egyptians in the book of Exodus

future being, and interested in it. I could not love myself, if I were not capable of loving
others' (*Works*, i. 1–2).

[23] *Paradise Lost*, II. 243.

occurs on the earth—a similarity noted by Wasserman.[24] The comparison seems even more biblical when the similarity between Israel and
Prometheus is taken into account. Israel, both a man and a race of men,
is in bondage in Egypt. The plagues take place to manipulate the tyrannous will of the pharaoh, who finally allows the Israelites to go free.[25]
Likewise, the enchainment of Prometheus (man, and the race of men)
creates a universal upheaval, just as there is cosmic rejoicing following
his liberation. Similar events take place at the death of Christ. Because
he is the Logos, the principle of order underlying nature, the one of
whom St Paul writes, '. . . by him all things consist' (Col. 1: 17), nature
responds by lapsing into chaos at his death. However, there is an event
in the record of the crucifixion that outweighs the significance of the
earthquake and darkness: the rending of the veil in the temple (Matt.
27: 51), an event which finds a parallel in the assault on Prometheus by
the Furies, one of whom shouts 'Tear the veil!' (I. 539).

As in the case of *Queen Mab*, Shelley here apparently employs the
image of the veil to represent time, for just as the quest to recall the
curse was an act of memory, so the temptation of the Furies is a history
lesson. The aim is to show respectively how the teachings of the meek
reformer Jesus were garbled by the inquisitorial Christian Church and
how the egalitarian goals of the French Revolution were twisted into a
new despotism during the Napoleonic era. The rending of the veil thus
points backward in time, and can teach only despair. By contrast, the
rending of the veil in the gospel account points forward in time, and
imports hope. And just as the writer of the book of Hebrews speaks of
'a new and living way' of access to God by Christ 'through the veil,
that is to say, his flesh' (Heb. 10: 20), so Prometheus's flesh is rent as
though it were a veil (I. 478). But the Furies use this history lesson to
inspire hopelessness, to drive home their point that the lessons of the
past promise no redemptive good out of evil experience:

> Past ages crowd on thee, but each one remembers,
> And the future is dark, and the present is spread
> Like a pillow of thorns for thy slumberless head.
>
> (I. 561–3)

The overtones of Gethsemane and Golgotha in the imagery of the
thorns and the 'Drops of bloody agony' flowing from the brow (I.

---

[24] *Shelley*, 291. Cf. I. 78–9, 102, and 170–9 with Exod. chs. 7–12.

[25] The editors of the Norton edition note that the pharaoh of the Exodus was Ramses
II, or Ozymandias (*SPP*, 103 n. 5).

564–5) are reinforced by a vivid reminder of Christ's death.[26] To exac-
erbate the idea of futile suffering, the Fury who is last to leave displays a
crucifix (I. 585). And to reinforce the lesson from the past, that evil
develops out of good, the Fury says that even philanthropists are pre-
vented from acts of kindness by becoming inured to social ills: 'they
know not what they do' (I. 631).[27]

In the final third of Act I, Shelley leaves behind the preoccupation
with the past and with memory. Prometheus indicates that his sufferings
have already become sacramental in the context of love:

>   . . . I feel
> Most vain all hope but love, and thou art far,
> Asia! who when my being overflowed
> Wert like a golden chalice to bright wine
> Which else had sunk into the thirsty dust.
>
>   .   .   .   .   .   .
>
>   . . . I would fain
> Be what it is my destiny to be,
> The saviour and the strength of suffering man,
> Or sink into the original gulph of things . . .
>   (I. 807–11, 815–18)

Unless he assumes a messianic identity like that of the new Adam, or
Christ (1 Cor. 15: 45–7), Prometheus will sink like Jupiter into the
abyss with Demogorgon. And unless knowledge, the content of mind
(Prometheus) leads to the wisdom of love embodied in Asia—its natural
'chalice'—this overflow of Prometheus's 'being' is wasted. It is spilt on
the ground like the seed of Onan (Gen. 38: 9).[28] The descent of Asia to
the 'original gulph' in Act II is therefore the natural complement and
development of suffering in Act I.

The crucifixion of Christ in the New Testament is followed by his
descent into hell, where he preaches to the spirits of the antediluvian
dead (1 Pet. 3: 19). The second act of Shelley's drama, in which Asia is
the central figure, presents a similar descent following the Golgotha of

---

[26] See Luke 22: 44 and Matt. 27: 29.

[27] These words of Christ in Luke 23: 34 have contributed to the argument of Claude
Jones that this Fury is probably Jesus ('Christ a Fury?', *Modern Language Notes*, 50 [1935],
41). It is true that Prometheus is addressing Christ in I. 603–4, but he is speaking to the
corpus of the crucifix, rather than to the Fury who displays it, as Baker suggests in
Shelley's Major Poetry, 100 n. 28.

[28] The image of the overflowing chalice (I. 809–10) is used by Plato in the *Symposium*
to describe the overflow of wisdom from one man to another. See Shelley's translation
(*Plat.* 417).

Prometheus. Continuing this archetypal pattern, Asia journeys into the underworld, not to impart knowledge, but to find it.[29] In *Shelley's Major Poetry*, Baker says that her querying of Demogorgon takes the form of a catechism (p. 105). However, the questions deal not with religious beliefs but with cosmic origins. Just as the first act dealt with the themes of history and memory, before presenting a new orientation toward the future, so the descent into the underworld represents initially a movement backwards in time. For Asia wishes to arrive at an understanding of the First Cause. However, as we have seen, Demogorgon stands for the principle of necessary connection, the unascertainable causal link. And just as Hume had invalidated the attainment of certain knowledge regarding the First Cause by annulling the causal theory that lay beneath the cosmological argument, so Asia fails to find specific answers to her questions about the beginning of the world. Again Shelley uses the image of the parted veil to introduce this movement into the past (II. iv. 1–2). However, Asia and her sister see that they cannot see; obscurity is the governing metaphor for the entire scene. It is true that Demogorgon's answers seem orthodox—initially three repetitions of 'God'. But when pressed further, he says that the name is simply an anthropomorphic or linguistic convention (II. iv. 112–13). It is used by men to unite all unknown causes in one abstract conception, as Holbach had argued in a passage from the *Système* (ii. 16) quoted by Shelley in the Notes on *Queen Mab* (*PS*, i. 386). To insist upon a God who is the ultimate Cause in the Judaeo-Christian sense would be, as Hume had observed in the *Enquiry*, to posit a God who is the source of evil (p. 103).

Following Hume's tack, Asia thus shifts the question from world origins to the source of evil, only to receive the evasive answer 'He reigns' (again three times). When Asia asks, 'Whom calledst thou God?' (II. iv. 112), Demogorgon responds by saying, 'I spoke but as ye speak . . . .' There is a mirror-like quality to Demogorgon, from whom, it is evident, Asia learns nothing. What she discovers is that she has become her own oracle (II. iv. 121–3). She answers her own questions, and ends by presenting a replete account of cosmic and human beginnings (II. iv. 32–109). Her quest for knowledge thus becomes self-referential. If the beginning of wisdom is the fear of the Lord in Scripture (Ps. 111: 10), the beginning of wisdom in Demogorgon's cave is agnosticism, a state

[29] On the archetypal patterns of ascent and descent, which are reflected in the New Testament account of Christ, see Mircea Eliade, *Images and Symbols*, trans. P. Mairet (London, 1961), 47–51, 164–9, and Northrop Frye, *Great Code*, 129, 175–6.

of mind for which the mystery of the abyss is emblematic.[30]
Demogorgon says,

> —If the Abysm
> Could vomit forth its secrets:—but a voice
> Is wanting, the deep truth is imageless . . .
>   (II. iv. 114–16)

The scene of Asia's transformation which follows the realization of
the self as oracle in Demogorgon's cave involves the archetypal pattern
of ascent. St Paul wrote of Christ: 'Now that he ascended, what is it but
that he also descended first into the lower parts of the earth?' (Eph. 4:
9). The transfiguration of Jesus in Matthew 17, like his subsequent
ascension in Matthew 28, takes place on a mountain, as does Asia's.[31] It
is recorded that on the mount 'his face did shine as the sun, and his rai-
ment was white as the light' (Matt. 17: 2). The scene brings to mind his
self-revelation as the 'light of the world' who makes possible the attain-
ment of 'the light of life' (John 8: 12). This language of proclamation
colours the description of the radiant Asia as 'Life of Life' and 'Child of
Light' (II. v. 48, 54). The passage in question reintroduces the image of
the veil:

> Child of Light! thy limbs are burning
>   Through the vest which seems to hide them
> As the radiant lines of morning
>   Through the clouds ere they divide them . . .
>   (II. v. 54–7)

Only a few lines earlier, Panthea had told Asia of the radiance of her
'unveiled' presence (II. v. 20). Moses too, descending from Mount
Sinai, bore a countenance too radiant to look at. The glory of the
divine presence required that he wear a veil when addressing his people
(Exod. 34: 33). However, it becomes evident in Asia's case that the
radiance is not reflected, but intrinsic. The biblical analogue is not
Moses, but Christ, whose light was 'the glory as of the only begotten of
the Father' (John 1: 14).

---

[30] The descent of Asia has a general parallel in the venture of Sophia in the Valentinian
myth to comprehend the ultimate ground of her being. She attempts in vain to discover
the nature of the first aeon, Abyss. See *Irenaeus against Heresies*, I. ii. 1–2; i. 317 and Jonas,
Gnostic Religion, 180–6. The fallen daughter Sophia which separates from her creates the
Demiurge (I. v. 1; p. 322). In *Mutiny Within*, Rieger argues against equating Asia with the
fallen Sophia (140).

[31] On the archetypal significance of the mountain, see Mircea Eliade, *The Myth of the
Eternal Return* (1949), trans. W. R. Trask (1954; Princeton, NJ, 1974), 12–17.

The overtones of the Johannine Logos in Asia's transfiguration suggest that her identity cannot be divorced from that of her masculine counterpart, the central Christ-figure of the poem. As the 'Lamp of Earth' (II. v. 66), she much resembles Prometheus, whose emblem was the lamp (III. iii. 170) and who will arise as 'the Sun of this rejoicing world' (II. iv. 127). One thinks of the sun which appears as an image of the reintegrated whole following Albion's waking in the final book of Blake's *The Four Zoas* (IX. 825, 832, 846). Like Albion, Prometheus is archetypal man who must reverse the Fall and to whom all deity is ascribed. And the sun, which is a circle and therefore eternal, stands for his reintegration.[32]

At the beginning of Act III, Shelley presents the unreal throne world which is opposed to the Promethean enthronement of the self. Jupiter, who boasts an omnipotence that is mere hubris (III. i. 3), and Thetis, 'bright Image of Eternity' (III. i. 36), plainly counterfeit the prospective union of Prometheus and Asia. Jupiter is to Shelley what Lucifer is to Isaiah. Correspondingly, Bloom in *Shelley's Mythmaking* identifies him as 'the Accuser, or contrary, the Self-within' masquerading as a false thesis in a dialectic manipulated by Demogorgon (p. 100). Bloom's idea of the illusory thesis is an attractive one, for Shelley seems to be saying that Jupiter only appears to be God. Since penetrating the veil separating 'things which seem and are' is one of the concerns of *Prometheus Unbound* (II. iii. 60), Jupiter merely seems; Prometheus *is*. As William H. Hildebrand has noted, the world of the former 'has no ontological tone or texture or weight'.[33] The latter, on the other hand, could be compared with the God of the Old Testament, who revealed himself to Moses as pure Being: 'I AM THAT I AM' (Exod. 3: 14).[34] Yahweh is that which is; and the error of Lucifer is to assert that which is not: that he is like the most high. The fact that Jupiter is a non-entity means that he cannot endure experience, as Prometheus does. In the drama, he actually appears in only one scene, and the moment of his assertion 'I am omnipotent' (III. i. 3) is simultaneously the moment in which he is cast out with 'Eternity' into the 'bottomless void' (III. i. 76), as Satan was

---

[32] Thomas Blackwell claimed that later Platonists related the idea of the sun's power to that of mind and eternal Providence (405).

[33] 'Naming-Day in Asia's Vale', *K–SJ*, 32 (1983), 192.

[34] In *Observations upon the Plagues Inflicted upon the Egyptians* (London, 1794), Jacob Bryant links the sun with 'the *Living God, the self-existing Being*' (p. 216). The Egyptian word for the sun ('On' or $\tau\grave{o}\,{}^{\prime\prime}O\nu$) becomes $\mathring{o}\nu\tau\alpha$ (p. 217), the Greek word which denotes that which actually exists. Bryant relates this idea of pure Being to the self-disclosure of Yahweh to Moses in Exodus 3: 14 (p. 219).

cast into a bottomless pit for the duration of the millennium (Rev. 20: 3).[35] The false assertion of Jupiter stands eternally refuted by the corrections of Being, for 'to be' without experience is as much as having no existence, a condition symbolized by the void.

Equally as unreal as Jupiter is the 'fatal Child' he claims to have engendered (III. i. 19). In *Shelley's Mythmaking*, Bloom contrasts its non-existence with the reality of the frosty 'winged Infant' and the Spirit of the Earth in the final act (p. 132). In his view, the two cherubic infants evince the final paradisiacal state of man (p. 142). Ione's description of the 'winged' child is saturated with biblical imagery:

> Its countenance, like the whiteness of bright snow,
> Its plumes are as feathers of sunny frost,
> Its limbs gleam white, through the wind-flowing folds
> Of its white robe, woof of aetherial pearl.
> Its hair is white,—the brightness of white light
> Scattered in strings, yet its two eyes are Heavens
> Of liquid darkness, which the Deity
> Within, seems pouring, as a storm is poured
> From jagged clouds, out of their arrowy lashes,
> Tempering the cold and radiant air around
> With fire that is not brightness . . .
>
>   (IV. 220–30)

The whiteness of countenance and the infant's arrival in a chariot with wheels of clouds (IV. 214) bring to mind the appearance of the enthroned Ancient of days in the book of Daniel (7: 9). More precisely, the whiteness of hair and the flaming eyes suggest the Christophany of St John (Rev. 1: 13–14). If the 'winged Infant' is described in terms of apocalyptic, the Spirit of the Earth is associated with the idea of the millennium; for as a little child leads the subdued animal kingdom in Isaiah's picture of the millennial state (11: 6), the Spirit of the Earth leads Prometheus and Asia to their bower-cave, the locus of Edenic restoration.

The biblical Apocalypse, which provides some of Shelley's imagery in the final act, transcends the world and its ills by dissolving time in eternity. The seventh angel of St John's vision announces that 'there should be time no longer' (Rev. 10: 6). And Shelley seems to imply the same by having his frenetic pallbearers, the past hours, sing 'We bear Time to his tomb in eternity' (IV. 14). As Wasserman says in

[35] Satan is later cast into the lake of fire for eternity. Shelley's verbal echo of Rev. 20: 3 (rather than 20: 10) supports the view that Jupiter may return.

his critical reading of Shelley's poetry, the illusion of time has indeed disappeared in so far as the prototypical Promethean Mind is concerned (p. 362). Act IV of Shelley's drama, however, deals with the cosmos itself. It is clear that Shelley does not intend to say that human time will end, but rather that it will assume a different character: 'Let the Hours, and the Spirits of might and pleasure / Like the clouds and sunbeams unite' (IV. 79–80).[36] The world is to be redeemed, not abandoned; consequently, Shelley's vision is more millennial than apocalyptic.

The redemptive ideal is present in each of the three announcements of the millennium, which are presented by the Spirit of the Earth (III. iv. 33–85), the Spirit of the Hour (III. iv. 98–204), and Panthea (IV. 236–318).[37] Each of these suggests temporal transformation, as opposed to transcendence. When the Spirit of the Earth reports that 'All things had put their evil nature off' (III. iv. 77), he is describing a divestment of sinful nature reminiscent of the resurrection life described by St Paul. In order for the new man to emerge, according to the apostle, the nature of the old man, which is 'corrupt according to the deceitful lusts' must first be 'put off' (Eph. 4: 22). The Spirit of the Hour goes a step further in speaking of a world transformed by a 'sense of love' (III. iv. 100–3). Finally, the beams emanating from the Spirit of the Earth seen by Panthea are emblematic of 'Heaven and Earth united now' (IV. 273). Like the kingdom of heaven proclaimed by Christ, the new spiritual age simultaneously exists within or among individuals (Luke 17: 21), yet is 'not of this world' (John 18: 36). This paradox is reflected in the rhapsodies of the Earth (now masculine) and Moon, which celebrate the merits of both Eros and Agape.

It is evident that Shelley intends the antiphonal duet of the Earth and Moon to be the cosmic counterpart of the love of Prometheus and Asia, who have recovered the Edenic bower in a cave. Both are sexual relationships representing society's new character of charity: men now are 'a chain of linked thought, / Of love and might to be divided not' (IV. 394–5). In the apocalyptic marriage that concludes the New Testament, Agape and Eros are fused in the image of the self-sacrificing Lamb and his Bride, the new Jerusalem (Rev. 21). The image is naturally reminiscent of the Canticle of Canticles. Like the Song of Solomon, *Prometheus Unbound* is a paean to spring, the time of love.

---

[36] Cf. *Queen Mab*, VIII. 202–11. See also Wasserman's excellent discussion of the idea of time in his critical reading of Shelley (*Shelley*, 366–8).

[37] These passages are discussed in more detail by V. A. de Luca in 'The Style of Millennial Announcement in *Prometheus Unbound*', *K–SJ*, 28 (1979), 78–101.

The departure of the Urizenic 'Sceptred Curse' (IV. 338) prepares the
way. The Moon says: 'The snow upon my lifeless mountains / Is loos-
ened into living fountains' (IV. 356–7). 'Living fountains' are of course a
provision of the Lamb's eternal paradise (Rev. 7: 17). But the image of
the seasonal thaw recalls the season of the Song of Songs: 'For, lo, the
winter is past . . . . The flowers appear on the earth . . . . Arise, my
love, my fair one, and come away' (S. of S. 2: 11–13).

There had initially been a suggestion of the Old Testament Canticle
in the vigil of Ione and Panthea over Prometheus:

> O thou of many wounds!
> Near whom for our sweet sister's sake
> Ever thus we watch and wake.
>
> (I. 228–30)

The young woman of the Song of Solomon says, 'I charge you, O ye
daughters of Jerusalem . . . that ye stir not up, nor awake *my* love, till
he please' (S. of S. 2: 7). The sisters of Asia here assume the role of the
attendant daughters of Jerusalem until the wintry season of
Prometheus's glacial enchainment is over. When finally released by
Hercules, Prometheus addresses Asia in language which at points recalls
the Song of Songs, referring to the 'low voice of love' and to 'dove-
eyed pity's murmured pain and music' (III. iii. 45–6). And just as the
beloved and her lover speak antiphonally in the biblical love-song,
Moon and Earth alternate in the final act of Shelley's lyrical drama. The
imagery used by Moon to describe Earth especially brings to mind the
biblical love-poem. The simile of the eclipse as a form of kiss (IV. 451)
in which Earth's shadow falls on the beloved (IV. 453) and Moon's
referring to her lover as a brother whom she desires to pursue (iv.
476–7) strongly suggest the Old Testament Canticle.[38] Shelley uses the
language of Eros to characterize even the astronomical aspects of the
redeemed cosmos.

Prometheus Unbound began with the defiance of Prometheus; it con-
cludes with a speech by the drama's order figure, Demogorgon. Just as
the Titan discovered in his opening speech that his 'words had power'
(I. 69), so Demogorgon's words will 'never pass away' (IV. 553)—like
those of Christ (Matt. 24: 35). As Wasserman has indicated (*Shelley*,
373), the final passage seems to mock the binding of Satan in the book
of Revelation (20: 1–3), for it celebrates the end of 'Heaven's
Despotism' (IV. 555). If the Psalmist could say that God has 'led captiv-

[38] See S. of S. 1: 2, 2: 3, and 8: 1.

ity captive' (Ps. 68: 18), Shelley uses the same language (IV. 556) for quite the opposite thought. What keeps captivity captive for Shelley are the New Testament virtues of 'Gentleness, Virtue, Wisdom and Endurance' (IV. 562).[39] Yet even this recitation of moral qualities is not orthodox in so far as it constitutes an act of perpetual conjuration to ward off evil (IV. 568). The ethos of the New Testament again emerges in the final stanza:

> To suffer woes which Hope thinks infinite;
> To forgive wrongs darker than Death or Night;
>   To defy Power which seems Omnipotent;
> To love, and bear; to hope, till Hope creates
> From its own wreck the thing it contemplates;
>   Neither to change nor falter nor repent:
> This, like thy glory, Titan! is to be
> Good, great and joyous, beautiful and free;
> This is alone Life, Joy, Empire and Victory.
>
> (IV. 570–8)

According to St Paul, 'tribulation worketh patience; And patience, experience; and experience, hope: And hope maketh not ashamed; because the love of God is shed abroad in our hearts by the Holy Ghost' (Rom. 5: 3–5). In the final stanza, Shelley too emphasizes, as he did in *The Mask of Anarchy*, the emergence of hope out of adversity. Shelley's advocating a refusal to repent in line 575 does not abrogate the repentance of Prometheus in Act I, for the word does not always have the same meaning. In the final passage of the poem, Shelley speaks of the general posture of defiance towards evil. The act of repentance in the first act involves removing the mental blockage that inhibits the natural inclination toward goodness. The Psalmist says, 'If I regard iniquity in my heart, the Lord will not hear *me*' (66: 18). Repenting of iniquity is essential for communion with God. Repentance, or the removal of iniquity, is for Shelley a concept that is inseparable from the idea that the mind comes to resemble the object of its contemplation.[40] St Paul advises Christians to 'think on' things that are honest, pure, lovely, and of good report (Phil. 4: 8). Shelley would agree; but he would base his understanding of the thought on Eros, on the perception of the beautiful. Prometheus must renounce the iniquity of his curse (i. 303–5), but

---

[39] Cf. the Pauline fruit of the Spirit (Gal. 5: 22–3). Timothy Webb further links the qualities listed by Shelley with those of the Sermon on the Mount and the book of James (*Shelley*, 172).

[40] See *Prometheus Unbound*, IV. 483–4, 574, and 'An Exhortation' (*SPW*, 579).

he must also reorient himself toward the lovely and the beautiful that exist in Asia (I. 809–11). Biblical repentance is also twofold, for it involves turning from the dead works of the old life toward the life of the Spirit, out of which proceed good works. The chief difference between the Shelleyan and Pauline notions lies, of course, in the two conceptions of love that are involved.

In his conclusion to the poem, Demogorgon inaugurates the new age of love, which 'folds over the world its healing wings' (IV. 561). He echoes the prophet Malachi, who had spoken of the era in which the messianic Sun of righteousness will arise 'with healing in his wings' (Mal. 4: 2). The Sun of righteousness, who is now Prometheus (II. iv. 127), is the mind that is fully integrated as a knowing self. It knows and is known, but does not encompass the causal power of necessity. The materialistic necessity of Hartley and Godwin in Shelley's early days gives way to an idealistic necessitarianism grounded in Hume. It is a shift which creates Demogorgon, who has been identified in this discussion with Hume's sceptical principle of necessary connection as well as with the abyss of God's hidden purpose. The abyss of mystery, which Calvin had located in the transmundane mind of God, was drawn down from the heavens by Hume and Holbach, who relocated it in the mind of man. In her own descent, Asia (an extension of Prometheus) attempts unsuccessfully to determine the source of causes in the universe outside the one Mind. Prometheus, on the other hand, represents the revealed purpose of a providence that is divine in its anthropocentrism.

In her note on *Prometheus Unbound*, Mary Shelley says that her husband had considered writing a lyrical drama on the book of Job, but that no manuscript material for it had survived (*SPW*, 271). Yet the character of Job survives in Prometheus, who like the Old Testament protagonist, longs for the peace of the grave (I. 638–40).[41] The Pauline perspective is that 'the sufferings of this present time *are* not worthy *to be compared* with the glory which shall be revealed in us' (Rom. 8: 18). In quarrying such biblical models of suffering, redemption, and new birth, Shelley internalizes providential history. Correspondingly, the poet in him is increasingly redefined in accordance with the self-awareness arising from this inclination to remove the sphere of change from society to the self.

[41] See Job 14: 13.

PART THREE

1820–1822

6

The Theology of *A Defence of Poetry*

It is one of the commonplaces of modern criticism that Shelley is a 'prophetic' poet. The Victorian Gilfillan said in his *Gallery of Literary Portraits* that his 'burdened soul' recalled the conscience of the Israelite prophets (p. 73). Bennett Weaver standardized this view of Shelley as one who prophetically addressed the social evils of his time.[1] Yet what is meant by the term 'prophetic' in relation to a post-Christian writer like Shelley is not always clear. Gilfillan reflected an orthodox understanding of the word in saying that Shelley became 'the mere organ of the message he bore' (p. 73). Certainly there is some justification for such a view of the poet. In the 'Ode to Naples' (written in 1820), for example, Shelley speaks as the 'organ' of a higher power. Like the prophet Jeremiah, who cannot contain the word of God which burns within him (20: 9), he cannot refrain from expressing the message of freedom and justice:

> Louder and louder, gathering round, there wandered
> Over the oracular woods and divine sea
> Prophesyings which grew articulate—
> They seize me—I must speak them!—be they fate!
>
> (ll. 48–51)

It is clear, however, that Shelley's conception of prophecy is not that of the biblical writers. In the first place, the prophets of the Old Testament were mouthpieces for the word of God. In the 'Ode to Naples', the poet is not a conduit for a message from the world-transcendent God, but rather a discerner of the world-immanent social and political developments from which 'fate' may be ascertained. These serve as omens of a coming era of love, hope, truth, and justice symbolized by the volcanic rumblings of Mount Vesuvius. This idea of the poet as prophet is clarified in the *Defence of Poetry*, which Shelley drafted in 1821. As a prophet, the poet 'not only beholds intensely the present as it is . . . but he beholds the future in the present' (*SPP*, 482–3). In

---

[1] *Toward the Understanding of Shelley*, 4–5, 59–123.

effect, he comments on the society of which he is a part, addressing its moral ills while at the same time seeing the direction in which it is headed.

In the second place, Shelley believes that the 'prophetic' poet does not actually predict coming events. He denies that poets are 'prophets in the gross sense of the word, or that they can foretell the form as surely as they foreknow the spirit of events: such is the pretence of superstition . . .' (SPP, 483). Like Blake in the annotations of Richard Watson's apologetics, he scorns the view of prophets as dictators of destiny. Blake had written that a prophet 'utters his opinion both of private & public matters. Thus: If you go on So, the result is So.'[2] Like Shelley, he sees the future in terms of the present.

The fundamental anti-supernaturalism in Shelley's view of the prophet is deeply rooted. In the Notes on Queen Mab, he had suggested that successful prophecies were most likely written after their alleged fulfilment (PS, i. 402), and that general prognostications could be made by virtually any informed person. Such was Lord Chesterfield's prediction of a sanguinary revolution in France (PS, i. 402–3). This post-Enlightenment notion of prophecy is reformulated in Shelley's undated fragmentary prose piece dealing with the subject of Zionism, which surfaced this century in Japan. Here the poet presents a Jewish leader who is addressing other Jews on the subject of re-establishing the Jewish nation:

Whether we regard the antient prophecies and prophetic traditions which promise a Redeemer and a Saviour to the people of Israel; or consider the almost miraculous preservation of our institutions, during our past and present captivity and dispersion; this event will appear no less manifestly designed by the will of God, than consistent with and consequent upon the natural and inevitable order of things.[3]

The voice here seems to be that of the Shelley who has been immersed in the theology of Spinoza, who had even gone so far as to undertake the project of translating the Jewish philosopher's treatise on religion and politics. On the basis of his presupposition that God and Nature are inseparable, Spinoza says that 'by the decrees and volitions, and conse-

---

[2] Complete Writings, 392.

[3] In The Shelley Memorial Volume, ed. the English Club at the Imperial University of Tokyo (Tokyo, 1922), 188. Although the fragment could be a translation from an unknown source, its affinity with the philosophy of Spinoza suggests that it may have been inspired by the Jewish philosopher and written by Shelley. Some of its political content is reflected in A Philosophical View of Reform and in the preface to Hellas.

quently the providence of God, Scripture . . . means nothing but nature's order following necessarily from her eternal laws' (p. 82). This is essentially a more dogmatic version of the opinion presented by Shelley's speaker. In both cases there is a tendency to make the divine imperative into an operation of nature. The possibility of prophecy is thus explored with reference to the prophet. Although Spinoza defines prophecy as revelation from God to man (p. 13), it must be remembered that in his philosophy the human mind partakes of the divine nature (p. 14). The fact that a prophet speaks when moved by the Spirit of God is not remarkable; for, as Spinoza says, 'the "Spirit of the Lord" is used as equivalent to the mind of man' (p. 22). Since the prophet's perceptions typically result from his emotional and imaginative states, Spinoza is led to some very unorthodox conclusions. He asserts that the gift of prophecy requires a powerful imagination (p. 19).[4] And he insists that it is the nature of the imagination to be unconcerned with certainty regarding truth (p. 28). The principle of uncertainty, which the author of *The Cenci* had referred to both Protestant and sceptical impulses, is in Spinoza localized in the prophetic imagination.

It is not difficult to see how Shelley might adapt the view of the prophet to his own conception of the poet. Writers as different as Sir Philip Sidney and Thomas Paine had linked poets with prophets, chiefly by referring to the metrical and musical facility of prophetic writers.[5] And by the time of his writing the 'Speculations on Morals', Shelley is prepared to assimilate the idea of prophecy in his poetics. Here the imagination is prophetic in its 'imaging forth' of objects in relation to the moral life (Jul. vii. 75).[6] This thought forms one of the core concepts in the expanded discussion of the imagination in the *Defence of Poetry*. But apart from the metaphysics involved in Shelley's ruminations on the subject of the imagination, there is a theological dimension to his more mature theory. In the preface to *The Cenci*, he writes: 'Imagination is as the immortal God which should assume flesh for the redemption of mortal passion' (*SPP*, 241). The roots of a secular trinitarianism are evident in this passage written two years before the writing of the *Defence*. In this latter work, Shelley amplifies the three

---

[4] Shelley's translation of the passage: 'the qualification to prophecy is rather a more vivid imagination than a profounder understanding than other men' (Jul. vii. 274).

[5] *A Defence of Poetry*, in *Miscellaneous Prose of Sir Philip Sidney*, ed. K. Duncan-Jones and J. van Dorsten (Oxford, 1973), 76–7; Paine, *The Age of Reason, Complete Writings*, i. 475 n. 4, 475–6, 561.

[6] The relevant portion is dated by Dawson in spring 1817, *Unacknowledged Legislator*, 282.

interrelated ideas of imagination, poetry, and love. The first of these, functioning as the 'creative imagination', may be seen as that which constitutes reality for the poet. It is the first person, the 'immortal God' of Shelley's trinity. The second is poetry, or '"the expression of the Imagination"' (*SPP*, 480), which serves as the Logos of Shelley's universe. Finally, there is the Shelleyan holy spirit of Eros, the 'going out of our own nature, and an identification of ourselves with the beautiful which exists in thought, action, or person, not our own' (*SPP*, 487). Presented as 'love' in the essay, it reflects the same paradoxical fusion with Agape that Shelley featured in *Prometheus Unbound*.

That the imagination is somehow a god-like faculty is an essential part of Shelley's mature aesthetic theory. In the *Defence*, it is 'that imperial faculty, whose throne is curtained within the invisible nature of man' (*SPP*, 483). Shelley regards it as a creative capacity (*SPP*, 494, 507). In his biography of the poet, Thomas Medwin recorded that his cousin once gave the following description of poetic creation:

'The poet is a different being from the rest of the world. Imagination steals over him—he knows not whence. Images float before him—he knows not their home. Struggling and contending powers are engendered within him, which no outward impulse, no inward passion awakened. He utters sentiments he never meditated. He creates persons whose original he had never seen; but he cannot command the power that called them out of nothing. He must wait till the God or daemon genius breathes it into him. He has higher powers than the generality of men, and the most distinguished abilities; but he is possessed by a still higher power. He prescribes laws, he overturns customs and opinions, he begins and ends an epoch, like a God; but he is a blind, obedient, officiating priest in the temple of God.' (*Life*, 329–30)

The description brings to mind both the language used by Shelley to characterize the 'possession' of a poet in his translation of Plato's *Ion* (*Plat.* 472) and the ideal of prophetic inspiration which informs such poems as the 'Hymn to Intellectual Beauty' and the 'Ode to Naples'. However, it adds to the conception of the poet as prophet the metaphors of hierophant, legislator, and creator. In the *Defence*, Shelley presents all four analogues as valid representations of the poet (*SPP*, 482, 497, 508). But it is the latter which is of most relevance to the discussion of the imagination as a divine power.

Shelley begins the *Defence* with a contrast between reason and imagination. The former is thought of as analytic in nature, the latter as synthetic. By the faculty of reason (τὸ λογίζειν), we perceive according to particularity, difference, and quality. Using the imagination (τὸ ποιεῖν), on the other hand, we are able to grasp wholeness, similarity, and value. The latter differs from the former by 'acting upon those thoughts so as to colour them with its own light' (*SPP*, 480). In other words, it imparts to the mind's perceptions something of itself. With the phrase 'its own', Shelley veers from the associationist tradition of Hume, who in the *Treatise* denied the existence of the constant 'I' that might unify the mind's perceptions (pp. 252–3). Although Shelley generally takes the empirical associationist tradition for granted in his essay, there are occasional suggestions of such an 'I' in the theory of the mind that he presents.[7] And these have a bearing on the idea of divine creativity in the expressions of the imagination.

In the *Defence*, the biblical idea of God as Creator becomes the supreme metaphor of poetic creation. In that the poet creates fresh associations from the chaos of stale language (*SPP*, 482), he is like the God of Genesis 1: 2. And in that he can create the universe anew at the level of perception (*SPP*, 505–6), he resembles the God of Revelation 21: 1–5.[8] In both cases, he is dealing in poetic recreation from a universe already existing, but in disarray, requiring only to be reordered by Shelley's equivalent of the Coleridgean secondary imagination. In *Shelley: A Critical Reading*, Wasserman asserts that Shelley cannot possibly mean by the poet's role as 'creator' that he is like the God of creation *ex nihilo* in the first verse of Genesis (p. 205 n. 2). His reasoning seems to be that since Shelley's God is implicitly demiurgic rather than Yahwistic, the poet—by way of analogy—assembles his work from materials already at hand. Wasserman is right of course to point out that the poet does not create from nothing, at least in empirical terms. However, there remains a more figurative sense in which the notion of the Creator of the universe is appropriate to Shelley's theory of a creative imagination. In that he is the creator of the eternal city, God in the Greek New Testament (Heb. 11: 10) is a demiurge ($\delta\eta\mu\iota\upsilon\rho\gamma\acute{o}\varsigma$). But in the original creation, he is a poet. The Septuagint version of the Old Testament says that God created ($\acute{\epsilon}\pi o\acute{\iota}\eta\sigma\epsilon\nu$) the heavens and the earth (Gen. 1: 1). Creation from nothing is seen to be poetic. Thus Diotima says in Plato's *Symposium* (Shelley's translation) that poetry is '"a general name signifying every cause whereby anything proceeds

---

[7] For further discussion of Shelley's departure from the associationist tradition and the Coleridgean elements in the *Defence of Poetry*, see Bryan Shelley, 'The Synthetic Imagination', *Wordsworth Circle*, 14/1 (1983), 68–73, and 'The Interpreting Angel' (Oxford Univ. D. Phil. thesis, 1986), 207–43.

[8] This observation is made by John Clubbe and Ernest Lovell, Jun., 'Shelley', in *English Romanticism* (London, 1983), 130.

from that which is not, into that which is"' (*Plat.* 444). The context here is the inventive capacity of all artists, including poets, who, figuratively speaking, bring their works into existence from nothing. The accent is on one's *being* as a creator. Analogous to this is the innate capacity of the imagination not only to interpret its experience, but in a sense to create it. The Shelleyan emphases on synthesis, unity, and the prismatic quality of the imagination to refract or 'colour' the objects of its thought (*SPP*, 480) all suggest the intrusion of a philosophy which is foreign to the empirical basis of the essay. And the immediate source for Shelley's knowledge of this philosophy was Coleridge.

Like Shelley, Coleridge was grounded in the theory of the association of ideas, the view that the mind's construction of reality is based on the linking of simple elements *a posteriori* according to certain principles, such as resemblance, contiguity, and causality. His mature rejection of this explanation of mental operations arose largely from his exposure to the philosophy of German idealism. In the *Biographia Literaria*, Coleridge maintains an earlier distinction between fancy and imagination, presenting it as an opposition between the 'aggregative and associative' faculty and the 'shaping and modifying power' (i. 293). Ideally, the poet 'diffuses a tone, and spirit of unity, that blends, and (as it were) *fuses*, each into each, by that synthetic and magical power, to which we have exclusively appropriated the name of imagination' (ii. 16). The power is revealed in a 'balance or reconciliation of opposite or discordant qualities' (ii. 16). The synthesis now described occurs in the coalescing unitive moment of self-consciousness (i. 272–3), in which the antithesis of subject and object is resolved in a willed moment of truth (i. 270–306). The ultimate source for this reflexive synthesis is the a priori transcendental unity of apperception described by Kant.[9] This self-awareness both precedes and makes possible all experience. And for Kant it constitutes a unity of consciousness (p. 136), something that the materialist Hartley had specifically excluded from the epistemology of the *Observations on Man* (i. 512). According to Kant, the fact that this unity is unchangeable (p. 136) introduces the 'I' whose existence Hume had denied in the *Treatise* (pp. 252–3). In Coleridge's adaptation of the transcendental synthesis in the *Biographia*, the imagination in perception is a diminution of the great 'I AM' of the Bible (i. 304).

The characteristically Coleridgean emphases on unity are evident in

---

[9] *Immanuel Kant's Critique of Pure Reason*, trans. N. K. Smith (1929; London, 1982), 135–7, 152–5.

the *Defence*. Shelley ultimately says that poetry as the expression of the imagination

subdues to union under its light yoke all irreconcilable things. It transmutes all that it touches, and every form moving within the radiance of its presence is changed by wondrous sympathy to an incarnation of the spirit which it breathes; its secret alchemy turns to potable gold the poisonous waters which flow from death through life; it strips the veil of familiarity from the world . . . (*SPP*, 505)

Such phrases as 'subdues to union . . . all irreconcilable things', 'veil of familiarity', and 'secret alchemy' have a Coleridgean resonance.[10] But these verbal echoes do not mean that Shelley had undergone some form of conversion to the aesthetic doctrines of Coleridge.[11] Shelley's mature philosophy of poetry cannot be interpreted as a derivation from any one thinker. Nevertheless, the younger poet would have recognized in his reading of the *Biographia* in 1817 a substantive basis for identifying the poet as a creator. Throughout Shelley's essay, the original distinction between reason and imagination recurs as a contrast between the 'calculating principle' and the 'creative faculty'. Precisely what Shelley means by the word 'creative' here is the vital question. Following the empirical understanding of the term 'creative', Wasserman says that the imagination is 'entirely an organizing force and nothing else' (p. 208). For example, Shelley says that the poet's task is 'to create afresh the associations which have been thus disorganized' (*SPP*, 482). In quoting from a biography of Tasso, however, Shelley says, '*Non merita nome di creatore, se non Iddio ed il Poeta*' (*SPP*, 506). It is difficult to imagine that in making such a claim he means that 'None deserves the name of Organizer except God and the Poet'. More likely, the old empirical notion of 'creation' here gives way, in Shelley's theory of the imagination to the biblical model of Coleridge, who in the *Biographia* considered the primary imagination to be 'a repetition in the finite mind of the eternal act of creation in the infinite I AM' (i. 304).[12]

It is this transcendental self-consciousness, the locus of Coleridge's

[10] See the *Biographia Literaria*, ii. 16, 7, and the *Statesman's Manual* (in *Lay Sermons*), where Coleridge refers to 'a spiritual alchemy which can transmute poisons into a panacaea' (p. 35).

[11] On the vital issue of the role of volition in poetic creation, e.g., Shelley differs from Coleridge, who in the *Biographia* identified the will with the secondary imagination (i. 304). Shelley says that poetry cannot be willed (*SPP*, 503, 506).

[12] It is true that Coleridge uses the 'I AM' to refer to the agency of perception and that Shelley uses it to refer to poetic creation. But Coleridge none the less extends the Yahwistic analogy to the secondary imagination.

synthesis, which lies at the opposite pole from Hume's view of the mind—expressed in the *Treatise*—as 'successive perceptions only' (p. 253) in the spectrum of philosophies that emerge in the *Defence*. In so far as Coleridge is a tutelary spirit here, the poet's imagination cannot be considered as merely demiurgic, dealing with materials already at hand, as Wasserman feels. For the imagination assists in establishing those materials by its activity in perception, an activity suggested by Shelley's reference to 'the principle within' which distinguishes man from the Aeolian harp: 'It is as if the lyre could accommodate its chords to the motions of that which strikes them' (*SPP*, 480). The poet, then, is like the Creator in three ways. Primarily, he resembles the God of the Old Testament in his creation of order from disorder, as does Yahweh in the Genesis creation. Secondly, he is like God in the apocalyptic creation of a new universe (Rev. 21: 1–5). Finally, he may be compared to the Creator in his identity or *being* as a maker, analogous to which is Coleridge's theory of the primary imagination. In dealing with materials *a posteriori*, as he does in the first two instances, he follows the demiurgic model of poetic creation. But in the sense that the imagination is active in perception itself, poetic creation may be seen to be Yahwistic, as the Creator exists before his creation.

The second element in Shelley's trinity, Poetry, is suggested in the initial contrast between the 'making' and the 'reasoning' faculties. Related to the latter of course is the biblical conception of the Logos, the second person of the Christian trinity. The word $\lambda \acute{o} \gamma o \varsigma$ can suggest a variety of meanings (e.g. account, rule, principle, reason, thesis, speech, divine utterance).[13] However, Shelley employs the form $\tau \grave{o}$ $\lambda o \gamma \acute{\iota} \zeta \epsilon \iota \nu$ in a restricted sense. By making the human reason into an analytical and arithmetical faculty, Shelley establishes its inadequacy as a creative principle. He associates it with mere calculation (*SPP*, 480) in order to promote the $\tau \grave{o} \ \pi o \iota \epsilon \iota \nu$ as the chief imaginative principle and as his substitute Word.

Shelley may well have got the idea of using the Greek form from Sidney, his distant relation by marriage, who employed it in his own *Defence of Poetry* to denote the poet's function as a maker (p. 77).[14] The biblical scholar Herbert Braun has pointed out some additional meanings for Shelley's $\tau \grave{o} \ \pi o \iota \epsilon \hat{\iota} \nu$ (in its various forms) as it occurs in the

---

[13] Liddell and Scott, 1057–9.

[14] The principle of making was affirmed in the Hermetic *Divine Pymander*, where the procreative process in the world of generation falls short of the 'Good' in that the passions are involved (p. 86), but is rectified 'in the part of making or doing ($\pi o \iota \epsilon \hat{\iota} \nu$)' (p. 87).

Bible. First, it suggests God's sovereignty in dealing with his people, as reflected in the analogy of the potter's power over his clay (Isa. 29: 16, 45: 9, Jer. 18: 4).[15] Shelley had of course already used the analogy of the poet and the potter in *Peter Bell the Third*. Second, Braun also observes that the verb form denotes the bringing forth of fruits by the earth (vi. 471). It is used in the Apocalypse to describe the tree of life, 'which bare twelve *manner of* fruits' (Rev. 22: 2). According to Shelley, the 'scions of the tree of life' are nourished by poetry, which constitutes 'the root and blossom of all other systems of thought' (*SPP*, 503). The frequent allusion to organic images in Shelley's essay recalls equally the *Biographia* and the Bible. When Coleridge refers to ποίησις here, he adds that 'the *rules* of the IMAGINATION are themselves the very powers of growth and production' (ii. 84). Third, Braun observes that believers themselves, in the life of the resurrection, are examples of God's 'work-manship' (Eph. 2: 10), as seen in the word ποίημα (vi. 464). Christ's followers in effect become the poems God writes. Shelley would substi-tute 'poet' for the individual Christian here, for in his preface to *Adonais*, he refers to Keats as 'one of the noblest specimens of the workmanship of God' (*SPP*, 391).

These biblical associations cast a new light on our understanding of Shelley's idea of poetry. As the substitute for the biblical Logos of John 8: 12, it is 'the light of life' (*SPP*, 493). Shelley calls it 'a sword of light-ning, ever unsheathed, which consumes the scabbard that would con-tain it' (*SPP*, 491). As a 'sword of lightning', poetry becomes the 'word of God' in Shelley's religion, the word that is 'quick, and powerful, and sharper than any twoedged sword, piercing even to the dividing asun-der of soul and spirit' (Heb. 4: 12). Poetry, then, is a kind of revealed scripture—Shelley's equivalent of the Logos. Correspondingly, there is a messianic dimension to the way that it affects self and society. The language associated with its operations is the New Testament language of incarnation, resurrection, and redemption (*SPP*, 495, 505). And its presence in society becomes the means whereby the Edenic paradise is recreated (*SPP*, 497). On the other hand, the absence of poetry, the 'creative faculty', is associated with fallenness (that of mechanistic indus-trial society) and the curse of labour imposed on Adam in the third chapter of Genesis (*SPP*, 503).

As the *Defence* presents the expression of the imagination as both written word and redeeming force, it sometimes echoes the teachings

---

[15] 'ποιέω', in *Theological Dictionary of the New Testament*, vi. 467.

of Christ. Poetry 'subdues to union under its light yoke all irreconcil-
able things' (*SPP*, 505), just as Jesus said 'my yoke *is* easy, and my bur-
den is light' (Matt. 11: 30). In referring to contemporary vilification of
poets (and poetry), Shelley says, 'judge not, lest ye be judged' (*SPP*,
506). He employs the same saying of Jesus that he used to defend his
moral conduct when impugned by Southey (Matt. 7: 1).[16] The most
significant of Shelley's allusions to the teachings of Jesus in the *Defence*,
however, is contained in the statement that 'Poetry, and the principle of
Self, of which money is the visible incarnation, are the God and
Mammon of the world' (*SPP*, 503). This passage may well represent the
theological core of Shelley's essay. When Jesus tells his followers that
they cannot simultaneously serve God and Mammon, he is essentially
subordinating material, temporal concerns to eternal ones (Matt. 6: 24).
Likewise, Shelley is using the term 'Mammon' in a sense that is integral
to his entire world-view. The 'principle of Self', which he opposed to
self-knowledge, descends from the early preoccupation with selfishness
which is reflected in *Queen Mab*. Here it is the 'custom' of failing to
differentiate between the personal self and the higher, universal self
(common to all men) which corresponds to the divine One and longs
to unite with it.[17] And the personified abstraction that Shelley uses to
express this failure is that of Mammon.[18] The term had only recently
been brought to the attention of Shelley, in association with the idea of
selfishness, by Keats, though of course in a very different context.[19]
Shelley may have been drawing from *Paradise Lost*, where the fallen
spirit Mammon proposes that

> This desert soil
> Wants not her hidden lustre, gems and gold;
> Nor want we skill or art, from whence to raise
> Magnificence; and what can heaven show more?
>
>   (II. 270–3)

[16] Letter to Robert Southey, 17 Aug. 1820, *Letters*, ii. 230. In this letter, Shelley con-
tinually promotes the meekness which he felt characterized Jesus.

[17] I here follow the Arnold-like distinction between the two selves made by Barnard
(*Shelley's Religion*, 265). According to Wasserman, Shelley means by 'the One' the tran-
scendent Absolute, of which the poet's spirit is a portion (*Shelley*, 205). It is intuited
through the medium of poetry by the poet (p. 210), who thus, in Shelley's words, 'partic-
ipates in the eternal, the infinite, and the one' (*SPP*, 483).

[18] In his *Address, to the Irish People*, Shelley refers to 'the Mammon of unrighteousness'
(*PW*, i. 36). Cf. the contrast between God and Mammon in Hartley's *Observations on
Man*, ii. 344, 406.

[19] Letter to Percy Bysshe Shelley, 16 Aug. 1820, in *Letters of John Keats*, ii. 322–3.

The attitude is not simply one of materialism, but of rivalry and retaliation, motives condemned by Shelley in *The Cenci*. The high seriousness of Milton's Mammon has its complement in the comic portrait of Mammon in *Oedipus Tyrannus*. As the archpriest of Famine (with whom he rhymes), Mammon in Shelley's satire believes that divine oracles and drunkenness are attributable to the same power (I. i. 120–5). On the one hand, he travesties the pretensions of organized religion. On the other, he slanders the entire enterprise of vatic, poetic activity promoted by Shelley in the *Defence*. Consequently, the principle of Mammon stands diametrically opposed to poetry, the Shelleyan Logos. It is an opposition that has its roots in the young Shelley. Writing to Peacock in 1816, Shelley identifies Mammon and Jehovah as deities whose altars are 'stained with blood or polluted with gold'.[20] In *Queen Mab*, he associates both these desecrations with the principle of selfishness (IV. 195; V. 53–68, 166–76).

The references to Jesus and his teachings are not theological intrusions in the *Defence*. For Shelley, Jesus was a poet, and he is willing to go so far as to say that Christianity was an ameliorating force in Western society in so far as it retained the poetic principle (*SPP*, 495–6). As in the essay on Christianity, Jesus is seen as an avatar of the imagination, a student of the poetry within the Jewish Scriptures (*PW*, i. 249–50; *SPP*, 495). He is part of a particular cultural matrix. This concept of literary tradition is an essential feature of the *Defence*, and is illustrated by the role of Dante, who served as 'the Lucifer of that starry flock which in the thirteenth century shone forth from republican Italy, as from a heaven, into the darkness of the benighted world' (*SPP*, 499–500).[21] Correspondingly, the English literary tradition has in Shelley's time experienced a 'new birth' (*SPP*, 508). Apart from such national traditions, the poets of all ages and nations comprise a succession of prophetic figures who have spiritually enriched the human race. Echoing St Paul, Shelley says that they become 'the words which express what they understand not; the trumpets which sing to battle, and feel not what they inspire' (*SPP*, 508).[22] The poet, then, is not distinguishable from the prophetic Logos. The language, institution, and form of society are both produced and sustained respectively by the

---

[20] Letter to T. L. Peacock, 17 July 1816, *Letters*, i. 490.

[21] Shelley's language here is borrowed from *Paradise Lost* (V. 708–10). For the biblical fall of Lucifer, see Isa. 14: 12. Shelley whimsically refers to himself as the 'Lucifer who has seduced the third part of the starry flock' in a letter to Leigh Hunt, 6 Oct. 1821, *Letters*, ii. 356.

[22] 1 Cor. 14: 8–9.

divine creation and the providence of poets (*SPP*, 492), just as the
Logos-Christ is 'before all things, and by him all things consist' (Col. 1:
17). Thus poetry is the second element in Shelley's trinity.

The idea of love in the *Defence* is sometimes regarded as synonymous
with 'the sympathetic imagination', a conception by no means unique
to Shelley.[23] However, it must be noted that the word 'poetry' has a
moral implication. Herbert Braun has pointed out that ποιέω in the
New Testament is sometimes used in an ethical sense to suggest doing
good (or harm) to one's neighbour.[24] An example in the Greek New
Testament would be Jesus's healing of a man with a withered hand on
the Sabbath (Mark 3: 4). Regardless of whether Shelley was aware of
this ethical dimension of the word, he incorporates it into the *Defence*
under the rubrics of love and sympathy, the outworking of the imagi-
nation (*SPP*, 488–9, 490). Godwin had written that 'imagination . . . it
cannot be too often repeated, is the great engine of morality'.[25] Shelley
amplifies this thought by insisting not only that the imagination is a fac-
ulty that produces moral good, but that poetry enlarges the imagination
by 'replenishing it with thoughts of ever new delight' (*SPP*, 488). As
Ellsworth Barnard has noted in *Shelley's Religion* (pp. 266–7), he once
again approximates the exhortation of St Paul to think on things that
are true, honest, just, pure, and lovely (Phil. 4: 8). Shelley's persistent
concern for the beautiful and the true as objects of contemplation (*SPP*,
482, 486, 488, 493, 494, 497) thus transcends the question of simple
aesthetic response. For Shelley, the 'great secret of morals is Love;
or a going out of our own nature, and an identification of ourselves
with the beautiful' (*SPP*, 487). Thus he does not here abandon the con-
cept of Eros celebrated in *Prometheus Unbound*, for Eros recognizes qual-
ity in the object; it does not, like Agape, create that quality in the
object.

Love, however, is not mere eroticism in the *Defence*. In 'A Discourse
on the Manners of the Antient Greeks', Shelley referred to love as the
'universal thirst for a communion not merely of the senses, but of our
whole nature' (*Plat.* 408). And in the *Defence*, he states that only in so
far as erotic writers were not poets could they be considered corrupt

---

[23] See James Engell, *The Creative Imagination* (Cambridge, Mass., 1981), 257–60. Engell
identifies sympathy as 'that special power of the imagination which permits the self to
escape its own confines, to identify with other people, to perceive things in a new way,
and to develop an aesthetic appreciation of the world that coalesces both the subjective
self and the objective other' (pp. 143–4).

[24] *Theological Dictionary of the New Testament*, vi. 477.

[25] *The Pantheon* (London, 1806), p. x.

influences on society (*SPP*, 492–3). True poetry, which, like love, is the outworking of the imagination, is 'the invisible effluence . . . sent forth, which at once connects, animates and sustains the life of all' (*SPP*, 493), like the pervasive Deity of St Paul's sermon at Mars' hill (Acts 17: 28). And it becomes the basis for 'social renovation' (*SPP*, 493). Shelley thus says that the gallery of artists he has assembled from Dante to Milton was as essential to the moral state of the world as 'the Hebrew poetry' (*SPP*, 502).

For Coleridge in *The Statesman's Manual* (in *Lay Sermons*), love is like wisdom the immanence of the will, which, if allowed to become abstract, develops into 'satanic pride and rebellious self-idolatry' (p. 65). And the comments that he makes in this context on Milton's Satan, comparable to those made by Shelley in the preface to *Prometheus Unbound*, are consistent with the younger poet's denunciation of the 'Pride, that ruined Satan'.[26] By placing his remarks on Satanic pride next to a mention of Plato's ideal state, Coleridge postulates love as an operative force in society (p. 65). As the holy spirit in Shelley's trinity, love is the manifestation of the comprehensive imagination by which one can 'put himself in the place of another and of many others' (*SPP*, 488). Barnard describes it as the 'impelling force' in the struggle to real-ize the thing contemplated (p. 273). It breaks down the barriers of sepa-rateness, allowing the selves of others to fall within the compass of the One Self (p. 220). Since self-knowledge is a realization of this '"self" that is common to all men', as Barnard calls it (p. 265), it must be related to the ideal of love. Sidney had stated in his *Defence* that self-knowledge entailed the 'end of well-doing' (p. 83). And two centuries later, Erasmus Darwin explicitly linked self-knowledge with the moral-ity of the Sermon on the Mount. The Socratic dictum 'Know thyself' is selfish, he said, unless one incorporates with it the notion that one ought also to know others. The maxims 'Do as you would be done by' and 'Love your neighbour as yourself', if followed, would greatly improve the human condition.[27] Shelley provides an impetus for just such an ethic in his doctrine of love that emanates from the oneness achieved in the knowledge of the self. Just as the mystical body of Christ was bound together by the Holy Spirit (1 Cor. 12: 13), so Shelleyan love in this mature formulation becomes the binding force of society.

Foreshadowings of the *Defence* can be detected in the essay

---

[26] Letter to Charles Ollier, 25 Sept. 1821, *Letters*, ii. 354.

[27] *The Temple of Nature* (London, 1803), 124 n. See Luke 6: 31 and Matt. 22: 39.

on Christianity, where Jesus is presented as a poet, with a poet's imagination, and as an iconoclast, whose teaching on love contradicts the anthropomorphic picture of God as a judge who condemns men to hell (*PW*, i. 249–53). These ideals of Imagination, Poetry, and Love are developed in the *Defence of Poetry*. Shelley does not explicitly conceive this triad in terms of a trinity or Coleridgean tri-unity.[28] Neither does the New Testament explicitly present a Trinity. But the *Defence of Poetry* clearly establishes a theologically oriented poetics. Thus it brings to mind the tradition of *theologia poetica* and the defences of poetry so controversial in medieval Italy. The tradition is derived from the writings of Albertino Mussato (1261–1329), a chief influence on the Tuscan triad of Dante, Boccaccio, and Petrarch, who are named together twice in Shelley's apology (*SPP*, 500, 502). Mussato theorized that poetry was both a prophetic and a theological endeavour:

> *Quidni? Divini per saecula prisca poetae*
> *Esse pium caelis edocuere deum . . .*
> *Hique alio dici coeperunt nomine vates.*
> *Quisquis erat vates, vas erat ille dei.*
> *Illa igitur nobis stat contemplanda Poesis,*
> *Altera quae quondam Theologia fuit.*[29]

Petrarch echoed this view in saying: 'One may almost say that theology actually is poetry, poetry concerning God.'[30] He went on to mention the literary features of the Bible, citing as especially poetic the writings associated with Moses, Job, David, Solomon, and Jeremiah (pp. 263–4). It is this affirmation of the Old Testament writers as poets that Shelley continues in the nineteenth century (*SPP*, 495). However, in his humanization of the self and his ascription of divinity to it, he removes the tradition from the Christian milieu of medieval Italy to the more

---

[28] In the essay, Shelley dismisses the Christian Trinity as a garbling of Plato's three faculties of the mind (*SPP*, 495). Holbach had likewise traced the Christian Trinity to Plato in *Christianisme dévoilé*, 89 n.

[29] Quoted in E. R. Curtius, 'Poetry and Theology', in *European Literature and the Latin Middle Ages*, trans. W. Trask (1953; New York, 1963), 216. For translation assistance, I am indebted to Denis Lambert, Chris Pelling, Joyce Hren, and Kathryn McKinley:

> What is it? The divine poets in olden times
>   taught that a gracious God dwelt in the heavens . . .
> Hence they came to be called by another name, 'prophet'.
> He who was a prophet was the receptacle of God.
> Thus Poetry, which was once another sort of theology,
> Remains worthy of our contemplation.

[30] Francesco Petrarca, to his brother Gherardo, 2 Dec. 1348, in *Petrarch*, trans. and ed. J. H. Robinson and H. W. Rolfe (New York, 1898), 261. See *Epistolae familiares*, x. iv.

secular one of the post-Enlightenment era. Shelley has now moved far beyond his early dismissal of the prophetic idea by incarnating the triadic operation of Imagination, Poetry, and Love in the prophet-poet himself.

7

The Myths of Eden

In *Queen Mab*, Shelley had expressed the political hope that 'A garden shall arise, in loveliness / Surpassing fabled Eden' (IV. 88–9). This utopian state was to be brought about by material progress. But when Shelley writes in the *Defence* that in the love lyrics of the Middle Ages 'a paradise was created as out of the wrecks of Eden' (*SPP,* 497), he does not mean that poets create the millennium envisioned in *Queen Mab*. His context is the subject of love, which, like poetry, becomes an imaginative means of apprehending the eternal. It is the imagination that discerns the real Eden which is not subject to time and change. Correspondingly, the idea of an earthly paradise in Shelley's poetry written in 1820–2 gives way to a new understanding in which Eden is relocated in realms not accessible in this life. Shelley intuitively realized that Eden could not exist without Eve, that failure in obtaining the latter precludes realization of the former. Like Eden, Eve comes to be transported to an ideal realm apprehended only by the imagination. In their own unique ways, 'The Sensitive Plant', *The Witch of Atlas*, *Epipsychidion*, and 'The Serpent Is Shut Out from Paradise' all reflect this tendency. That Shelley does not allow these poems to exult in the image of an embowered Eve or a paradisiacal state prepares the way for his growing inclination toward apotheosis and idealization, the natural model for which is the biblical genre of apocalyptic.

The scriptural basis for the image of Eve in her paradise is twofold. When the overtones are maternal, one thinks of Eve, the mother of all living. When they are erotic, the closer parallel is the bride in the Canticle of Canticles. In the Song of Solomon, the woman is metaphorized as a garden replete with a fountain, streams, and trees, which is freely entered by her lover (S. of S. 4: 12–5: 1). And she is frequently described in terms of animal metaphor and simile. As Francis Landy notes, 'the Song is a reflection on the story of the garden of Eden, using the same images of garden and tree, substituting for the traumatic dissociation of man and animals their metaphoric

integration.'[1] The woman and her garden thus come to be closely asso-
ciated.

The great Romantic prototype of Eve was established in Rousseau's
Julie, that embodiment of feminine ideals with whom the protagonist
Saint-Preux becomes obsessed in *Julie, ou la nouvelle Héloïse*. Forbidden
by her father to marry Saint-Preux because of class distinction, Julie is
married to a nobleman, while her lover is left to nurse the infatuation
for his unattainable love. It is not difficult to see how Shelley would
have been drawn toward the story. He had earlier used the analogue of
Abelard and Eloisa to describe the similar situation in which his cousin
Harriet Grove was forbidden to marry him.[2] He would later refer to
Rousseau's novel to clarify his marital relationship for Hogg.[3]

The apotheosis of Julie as the patron saint of a sentimental religion is
the ultimate consequence of Saint-Preux's' unhappy ruminations. As a
prototypical woman, she is identified with the fundamental purity of
instinct and of the passions. Thus she may be linked with the Romantic
criterion of feeling.[4] But she is also associated with her garden paradise
of Elisée at Clarens. Jacques Voisine has noted that the pilgrimage of
Byron and Shelley to Clarens in 1816 was made to pay homage not to
Rousseau so much as to Julie.[5] And in turning to Shelley's Eden poems,
the reader will notice a similar inclination to ascribe a superior reality to
the abstraction of woman than to the flesh and blood models from
which it is derived. Shelley had, of course, dealt with this theme in
Alastor. In that poem he had linked the quest for his ideal feminine pro-
totype with the motif of the primal garden in which the young poet in
the poem first beholds her (ll. 140–91). In these later poems, the failure
of the mundane world to yield an incarnation of this ideal leads to the
Shelleyan 'fall', and consequently the demise of the myth of the woman
in the garden.

Eden in 'The Sensitive Plant', the 'undefiled Paradise' (I. 58) of the
first two parts of the poem, is in the conclusion ascribed the status of
reality, the temporal world the status of shadowy seeming (ll. 9–12). In

---

[1] 'The Song of Songs', in *The Literary Guide to the Bible*, ed. R. Alter and F. Kermode
(Cambridge, Mass., 1987), 318.
[2] Letters to T. J. Hogg, 26 Apr. and 9 May 1811, *Letters*, i. 70, 81.
[3] Letter to T. J. Hogg, *c*.16 Nov. 1811, *Letters*, i. 184.
[4] See Walter Jackson Bate, *From Classic to Romantic: Premises of Taste in Eighteenth-
Century England* (1946; New York, 1961), 53–4.
[5] 'Childe Harold et autres pèlerins', in *J.-J. Rousseau en Angleterre à l'époque romantique*
(Paris, 1956), 268.

the first two parts of the poem, however, the 'Eve in this Eden' (II. 2) obtains glimpses of the extra-temporal paradise in her dreams (as does the sensitive plant). These dreams are the means of imaginatively apprehending the eternal, and consequently become the link between the two Edens.[6] The nameless woman's paradisiacal setting is conceived as the 'sublunar Heaven' (II. 10) over which she has dominion, 'as God is to the starry scheme' (II. 4). In the Psalms, God 'telleth the number of the stars; he calleth them all by *their* names' (Ps. 147: 4). With similar attention to detail, the lady cares for each of the diminutive stars, or flowers, in her sublunar heaven. Like Rousseau's heroine, the *surintendante* of her own arborial paradise,[7] she is the presiding spiritual presence of the garden (II. 31–2), analogous to Shelley's idea of God as the Spirit coexisting with the universe. And just as the Bible speaks of God's sending forth angels as 'ministering spirits' in the book of Hebrews (I: 14), so harmless insects act as the lady's 'attendant angels' (II. 52). The perennial flowers that are her subjects are described as infants (I. 59). Shelley says that 'each one was interpenetrated / With the light and the odour its neighbour shed' (I. 66–7). They are known to each other as individual ones through whom may be discerned the more universal One symbolized by the woman.

The most outstanding of the lady's charges is the sensitive plant, a mimosa. According to Wasserman's allegorical view in *Shelley: A Critical Reading*, the sensitive plant represents man, while the garden stands for the world of animate nature. It is like man in that it 'is a native of the world-garden and yet is alien to it' (p. 157). But in the poem itself, it resembles the lady, in that it is both companionless (I. 12, II. 13) and attended by 'ministering angels' (I. 94, II. 52). These are the sensory impressions which the plant experiences (I. 90–4). Thus they constitute the diurnal empirical perception of the garden-world, a way of knowing which is transient and limited. Their natural complement is the more replete nocturnal world of the dream, which links the plant imaginatively with the ideal and eternal garden and its attendant lady. The aspiration toward union with this transcendent ideal reflects something of the Shelleyan doctrine of love expressed in the *Defence*. The poet writes,

---

[6] I base this analysis in general on Wasserman's definitive reading of the poem in *Shelley*, 154–79. Baker has explored the Miltonic aspects of the Eve figure in *Shelley's Major Poetry*, 197–9.

[7] *Julie, ou la nouvelle Héloïse*, IV. xi. 472.

> But none ever trembled and panted with bliss
> In the garden, the field or the wilderness,
> Like a doe in the noontide with love's sweet want
> As the companionless Sensitive-plant.　　(I. 9–12)

The Psalmist writes, 'As the hart panteth after the water brooks, so pan-
teth my soul after thee, O God' (Ps. 42: 1). In a similar way the sensi-
tive plant aspires toward the beautiful (I. 76–7) which it might discover
in the garden-world. But in that it stands for sensory perception, it is
therefore subject to the limitations of empirical knowledge. And in the
conclusion, beauty is placed in the transcendent realm which '[e]xceeds
our organs' (l. 23).

The death of the lady in late summer means the death of the garden.
The world of part III thus commences with death, the death of both
the potential Eve figure and her Eden, which, in the conclusion,
Shelley concedes are dreams that cannot be sustained by empirical per-
ception. The mutable world of epistemological process is inadequate as
an ontological gauge. By spring, the sensitive plant is 'a leafless wreck'
(III. 115). Its incompatibility with the other plants in the garden—and its
ruined state—are both reminiscent of the account of the Suffering
Servant in Isaiah 53. This enigmatic figure, subsequently identified by
the Church as the Messiah, is described as a 'tender plant' who 'hath no
form nor comeliness' (53: 2), just as the sensitive plant features no
bright flower or lovely smell (I. 74–5). He too would ultimately be
'stricken' and 'bruised' (Isa. 53: 4, 5). And yet, for the Church the
suffering servant Christ would come to represent perfected humanity,
mortal flesh taken up into the Godhead.

According to the eighteenth-century collection *Choice Emblems*, the
sensitive plant in that time stood for purity. The emblem itself depicts a
man touching a sensitive plant, which spontaneously shrinks from his
touch (p. 13). The moral is clear: 'IN this Vegetable we may see the
symbol of a truly virtuous person, who shuns even the shadow of evil,
and starts at the thoughts of vice' (p. 15). Likewise, James Hervey saw
in the sensitive plant a model for the Christian, who 'like a coy virgin
. . . recedes from all unbecoming familiarities'.[8] It therefore becomes a
type of moral purity, which is 'prophetically' fulfilled in the antitype of
the sanctified Christian.[9] For Shelley, such a moralistic correspondence

---

[8] 'Reflections on a Flower Garden', in *Meditations and Contemplations* (1748; Edinburgh,
1802), 179.

[9] See the discussion of 18th cent. typology of the *Imitatio Christi* tradition in Paul J.
Korshin, *Typologies in England, 1650–1820* (Princeton, NJ, 1982), 191–202.

would have been oppressive. But the prefigurative quality of the plant would not. As the type extends towards its antitype, Shelley's mimosa extends in love towards the transcendent realm of purity and beauty, the eternal paradise which is glimpsed in the mutable world only as dream through the imagination. Shelley says in his conclusion that the lady and her garden are more 'real' than the changeable world of the sensitive plant. They are immortal, paradoxically because they have never lived.

The theme of the woman in the garden recurs in Shelley's *The Witch of Atlas* in such a way as to evoke comparisons with many literary and mythic forebears. Shelley's witch has been compared to several of Spenser's heroines, Milton's Eve, Blake's Thel, and Keats's Lamia. Discussions of Byron's *Don Juan*, Wordsworth's *Peter Bell*, and Shelley's own translation of the Homeric *Hymn to Mercury* frequently enter into the discussions of several critics. But the analogy of Eden in the poem (l. 170) suggests that the witch is comparable to Eve, at least initially. Like the woman of 'The Sensitive Plant', she exists on an eternal plane coexisting with the mundane reality. Her realm is that of an arborial, Edenic cave and a river which conveys her *through* the world of men (which she 'providentially' influences), though not *to* it.

The birth of the witch brings to mind the nativity of Christ, for it attracts an array of visitors. But the fact that these visitors are to a large extent animals more strongly suggests the biblical Eden, where God brings all members of the animal creation before Adam to be named (Gen. 2: 19–20). The presence of 'the sly serpent' among the witch's guests further intimates the association with Genesis. But in Shelley's version, of course, there is no Fall in the biblical sense, for the witch's activities do not require her entering the world of mutability. Furthermore, the witch usurps the prerogative of the Genesis Creator in fabricating a hermaphrodite. With her hands, she forms it as a 'living Image' (l. 326), in much the same way that Adam is created 'a living soul' fashioned 'in the image of God'.[10] That Shelley does not permit his Eden to become a world of generation is reflected in this hermaphrodite, which may be thought of as prototypical 'man'. In the Hermetic creation myth of the *Divine Pymander*, the primal man standing in subjection to cosmic Fate is hermaphroditic (p. 25). When the two sexes are finally 'loosed & untied' (p. 27), generation ensues, as it does in Genesis 1: 28: 'And straitwayes God said to the Holy Word, **Encrease**

[10] Gen. 2: 7, 1: 27. The hermaphrodite's beauty and perfection resemble that of Milton's Adam and Eve in *Paradise Lost*, IV. 288–311.

in encreasing, and multiply in multitude all you my Creatures
& Workmanships' (p. 28). Prior to his descent into the world of
matter, then, the primal man of Hermetic myth is a bisexual archetype
of an ideal humanity. And Shelley's hermaphrodite reflects a similar
perfection.[11]

In her arborial world of 'ever blooming Eden-trees' (l. 170), the
witch is a female Comus, related to the hermit of *The Revolt of Islam*,
whose cave is a library of occult lore pertaining to such subjects as love
(ll. 198–9). Her collection includes the scrolls of 'some Saturnian
Archimage' (l. 186) who reveals how the golden age might be
reclaimed. As the editors of the Norton edition have indicated, Shelley
does not here mean to suggest the books of evil charms consulted by
the villainous sorcerer Archimago in *The Faerie Queene* (*SPP*, 354 n.). It
is evident that these writings have the status of scriptures. Since Shelley
had spoken of himself as 'some weird Archimage' in the 'Letter to
Maria Gisborne' (l. 106), these scrolls could be interpreted as represent-
ing a fictitious 'prophetic' tradition with which Shelley himself
identified. He too believed that the golden age might be reclaimed, but
only to the extent that the ordinary world was transformed by the
imagination.

The notion of the imagination is close to the heart of *The Witch of
Atlas*. Despite some caveats about reducing the poem to allegorical cer-
tainties in the recent readings of the poem by Richard Cronin and
Michael O'Neill, both critics see the witch as fulfilling in her playful
manner the imaginative function.[12] Imagination is a faculty of mind,
which is illustrated by the 'deep recesses' of the witch's cave (l. 153).
And it is manifest in various acts of making, such as her embroidering
of 'pictured poesy' (l. 252). But since the imagination for Shelley is an
outward moving capacity which seeks to realize its ideals in the external
world, the witch proceeds from her Thel-like realm of the cave towards
the world of actual men and women, where her pranks inspire a lam-
pooning of Church, monarchy, and military—a comic expression of
what occurs in the millennial vision of *Prometheus Unbound*.

---

[11] Erasmus Darwin updated the myth of hermaphroditic origins by reporting the opin-
ion that the Edenic account of Genesis was 'a sacred allegory' designed by the Egyptian
magi (who presumably educated Moses) to teach obedience to God. See the 'Additional
Notes' to *The Temple of Nature* (p. 42). That Eve was created from the rib of Adam
became for the magi 'an hieroglyphic design . . . showing their opinion that Mankind was
originally of both sexes united' (p. 42).

[12] See Cronin's *Shelley's Poetic Thoughts*, 64, 65, 73, and Michael O'Neill, 'Fictions,
Visionary Rhyme and Human Interest', *K–SR*, no. 2 (1987), 118.

Shelley clearly indicates that his witch is associated with the effort to bring about a millennium in the form of a golden age (l. 188). There are several echoes in the poem of the prophet Isaiah's millennial vision. The pacification of carnivorous animals presented in Isaiah 11: 6–8 recurs in the witch's ability to tame 'sanguine beasts' (l. 93). And in a trance-like state brought about by the witch, soldiers '[beat] their swords to ploughshares' (l. 645), as in Isaiah 2: 4. Furthermore, those imprisoned are set free (ll. 645–8), as are the captives in Isaiah 61: 1. There is also an apocalyptic resonance in her power to overrule death. Those whom she has chosen and who have drunk the panacea from her 'chrystal bowl' attain a form of immortality, as those who partake symbolically of Christ's sufferings in the eucharistic rite ultimately triumph over death. The image of her discarding the coffin into a ditch (ll. 605–8) is at least a crude parallel to the apocalyptic casting of death into the lake of fire (Rev. 20: 14). Shelley refers to such deeds as 'pranks' (l. 665). But in a serious sense they link the witch with an imaginative means of penetrating customary experience to discern the eternity of Eden in the parallel universe. The bower-paradise of *The Witch of Atlas*, then, is 'not of this world'; for the Edenic millennium can be seen only in the momentary insights that imaginative vision (represented by the dream-like somnambulistic state of l. 642) will allow.

The metaphysical landscape of *Epipsychidion* is that of 'a garden ravaged' (l. 187) and subsequently tilled by sages of hope such as Shelley who aspire to generate a new Elysium (l. 189).[13] But the poem's chief concern is the idealized portrait of woman in Emilia, the Italian girl known to the Shelleys as Teresa Viviani. By his own admission, Shelley presents in this poem an 'idealized' autobiography.[14] And since he is dealing with an ideal form of femininity, he ultimately ascribes loftier qualities to Emilia than the more mundane Teresa Viviani can justify. In doing so, he defies the limitations of language in a unique way. By heaping up images and metaphors, he attempts to approximate the repleteness of his idealized object in creating the illusion of infinitude. As Jerome McGann has said, the imagination lying behind *Epipsychidion* 'is an image-making faculty, and its vitality is to be measured in terms of the diversity of its realizations'.[15] Because no one image can be

[13] See the similar portrait in the book of Isaiah, where the Lord 'shall comfort Zion . . . he will make her wilderness like Eden' (51: 3).

[14] Letter to John Gisborne, 18 June 1822, *Letters*, ii. 434.

[15] 'Shelley's Veils', in *Romantic and Victorian*, ed. W. P. Elledge and R. L. Hoffman (Cranbury, NJ, 1971), 210.

allowed to have definitive status, an 'image anthology' thus arises (p. 214). The metaphysical poets attempted to surmount the limitations of metaphorical language simply by exhausting the potential of a given image. The approach here is quite different, for it strives to mimic the fullness of its glorified object with a plethora of images. It is a pattern for which there is a biblical precedent. When the Psalmist considers the eternal God, he likewise resorts to an assemblage of images. In crying out to God, he says, 'lead me to the rock *that* is higher than I. For thou hast been a shelter for me, *and* a strong tower from the enemy . . . . I will trust in the covert of thy wings' (Ps. 61: 2–4). The plurality of metaphors—rock, shelter, tower, and covert—is an attempt to convey from different angles the idea of security in God. In the opening seventy-one lines of *Epipsychidion*, Shelley uses a great many metaphors for Emilia. But they succeed only in increasing the distance between the ideal and its realization, for this opening section concludes with the poet's coming full circle back to the discovery of the self and its 'infirmity' (l. 71).

Recent editions of selected Shelley poems have indicated the affinity of *Epipsychidion* with the Song of Solomon.[16] However, there is a darker side to the sister spirit of the poet's imagination, a side which reflects the Wisdom literature of the Old Testament. In fact, Shelley begins his account with some overtones of the book of Proverbs in describing his encounter with the vision of eternal feminine loveliness:

> She met me, Stranger, upon life's rough way,
> And lured me towards sweet Death; as Night by Day,
>
> .   .   .   .   .   .
>
> And from her lips, as from a hyacinth full
> Of honey-dew, a liquid murmur drops,
> Killing the sense with passion . . .
>
> (ll. 72–3, 83–5)

The Keatsian nuance of this final line represents the culmination of knowledge gained through bitter experience. And this is the perspective of the admonitions on sexual conduct in the book of Proverbs. Here 'the lips of a strange woman drop *as* an honeycomb, and her mouth *is* smoother than oil: But her end is bitter as wormwood . . . . Her feet go down to death' (5: 3–5). The portrait of the seductress is amplified further on:

---

[16] See *SPP*, 372, and Timothy Webb (ed.), *Shelley: Selected Poems*, 217.

For at the window of my house I looked through my casement, And beheld among the simple ones, I discerned among the youths, a young man void of understanding, Passing through the street near her corner; and he went the way to her house, In the twilight, in the evening, in the black and dark night: And, behold, there met him a woman *with* the attire of an harlot, and subtil of heart. . . . So she caught him, and kissed him. . . . He goeth after her straightway, as an ox goeth to the slaughter. . . . Her house *is* the way to hell, going down to the chambers of death. (Prov. 7: 6–10, 13, 22, 27)

The preferable course is to heed the voice of that other feminine guide, Wisdom, whose ways are public, not clandestine (Prov. 8: 1). In the poem, Emilia is the embodiment of wisdom, but it is (not surprisingly) not the wisdom of the Hebrew ethos. Apostrophizing her, Shelley writes: 'Thy wisdom speaks in me, and bids me dare / Beacon the rocks on which high hearts are wreckt' (ll. 147–8). Shelley would warn others, as does the writer in Proverbs. However, the remainder of the stanza asserts that this wisdom concludes monogamy to be unsatisfactory. When he says that the slaves of matrimony 'travel to their home among the dead' (l. 156), he seems to echo the even more despondent wisdom of Ecclesiastes: 'desire shall fail: because man goeth to his long home, and the mourners go about the streets' (12: 5). And in some rejected lines, Shelley writes,

> Perhaps we should be dull were we not chidden,
> Paradise fruits are sweetest when forbidden.
> Folly can season Wisdom, Hatred love.
>   (Fragments, ll. 115–17; SPW, 428)

The prohibited fruit of Eden is here acclaimed necessary to the poet's spiritual existence as he redefines the meaning of wisdom. Shelley seems to endorse the suggestion of the 'foolish woman' who says that 'Stolen waters are sweet, and bread *eaten* in secret is pleasant' (Prov. 9: 17). His criticism of monogamy in the mundane world is not based on libertinism, as one might surmise from lines 149–59, but rather on a 'monogamous' fidelity to the ideal portrait he has created. This allegiance naturally recalls the experience of the young poet in *Alastor*. But it also suggests the lack of fulfilment in Shelley's marriage. His wife remains the 'cold chaste Moon' to Emilia's sun (ll. 281, 335).[17] Yet prior to his relationship with Mary, the poet's quest for love was chaotic:

---

[17] See the discussions of White, *Shelley*, ii. 261–5, and K. N. Cameron, 'The Planet-Tempest Passage in *Epipsychidion*', PMLA 63 (1948), 950–72; repr. *SPP*, 637–58.

> In many mortal forms I rashly sought
> The shadow of that idol of my thought.
> And some were fair—but beauty dies away:
> Others were wise—but honeyed words betray . . .
>
> (ll. 267–70)

Shelley again echoes Proverbs, where feminine beauty is said to be vain (31: 30) and pleasing words are compared to a honeycomb (16: 24). The poet's vision of Emilia, and the attempt to locate her in the ordinary world, thus yield the acknowledgement that the vision itself is like the seductive harlot of Proverbs. He can only ascend into the realm of the ideal and sigh, '. . . how / Shall I descend, and perish not?' (ll. 124–5).[18]

The dilemma of being drawn irresistibly toward that which causes one's destruction is reflected in Shelley's image of the moth which burns its wings in the flame towards which it is attracted (ll. 53, 220). Like the image of the sensitive plant, it appears in *Choice Emblems* (p. 53). And it illustrates the consequences of indiscretion. The moral is clear:

> Avoid the glitt'ring evil, shun the snare,
> Which Sin and Guile for artless youth prepare;
> Lest with the Moth one common fate you prove,
> And perish by th' excesses which you love.

To avoid this destiny, one 'must be careful to take Wisdom for his companion' (p. 55). Certainly both the imagery and its lesson here have relevance to at least one aspect of *Epipsychidion*. But this didactic message is not precisely Shelley's, for in his case the 'glitt'ring' attraction is not only the earthly flame, but the star-like transcendent ideal which, like the Wisdom of Proverbs, condescends to a form of revelation in the ordinary world.

The disparaging account of the vision of Emilia as temptress is countered in three redemptive portraits: first, that of the eschatological bride depicted in prophetic and apocalyptic literature; second, that of the sister-lover, a picture derived from the Song of Solomon; and third, that of the Haidée-like new Eve whose Eden is located unattainably on a remote isle. They are all, however, interrelated.

Prior to these portraits, the poet's visionary encounters with his *anima* are cast in messianic terms: 'She met me, robed in such exceeding

---

[18] Cf. 1 Sam. 26: 10.

glory, / That I beheld her not' (ll. 199–200).[19] She is not beheld because, like the transfigured Asia, she is too bright to be seen. Her prospective union with the poet reveals her in a different role: 'Even as a bride, delighting and delighted. / The hour is come:—the destined Star has risen' (ll. 393–4).[20] The Christological element here can be linked with the marital analogy of Yahweh's union with his bride Israel (Isa. 62: 5).

As in *Prometheus Unbound*, the eschatological union of bride and bridegroom in *Epipsychidion* is closely involved with the more amorous imagery of the Canticle of Canticles. The poet apostrophizes his feminine ideal: 'Spouse! Sister! Angel! Pilot of the Fate / Whose course has been so starless!' (ll. 130–1). The spouse–sister association appears in the Song of Solomon as an expression of intimacy and endearment (4: 9, 10, 12, and 5: 1). And it reminds us that in the primitive Hebrew culture, a man might marry one as close as his half-sister.[21] Shelley's preoccupation here with the overtones of incest, of course, has little to do with primitive Semitic marriage customs, but rather is connected with the nature of his quest. The perpetual pursuit of an ideal 'one' has clearly proved to be fruitless. Each metaphor in the succession of images slips into oblivion as it fails to embody the ideal. Given such a failure, Bloom observes, the natural inclination is to abandon the idea of becoming one with another, in order to discover the relationship to the other with whom the poet is already one.[22] Shelley exclaims, 'Would we two had been twins of the same mother!' (l. 45), again echoing the biblical love-poem (S. of S. 8: 1). The sister motif is related to the idea of self-knowledge, and the temporary glimpses of Shelley's spiritual *Doppelgängerin* as sister constitute a mid-point between the quest to find an ideal consort outside the self and what is ultimately the self-referential nature of this search (l. 71). The epithalamium of the Canticle is thus undermined in Shelley's poem. In the biblical love poem, the man says to his beloved, 'Set me as a seal upon thine heart . . . for love *is* strong as death' (8: 6). Shelley writes:

> . . . I love thee; yes, I feel
> That on the fountain of my heart a seal
> Is set . . .
>
> (ll. 138–40)

He too compares love with death (ll. 401–4), asserting in very Christian language the greater strength of the former to overrule the latter. But

---

[19] See 2 Cor. 4: 17 and John 1: 14.
[20] Cf. John 12: 23 and 2 Pet. 1: 19.
[21] See Gen. 20: 12 and 2 Sam. 13: 13.
[22] *Shelley's Mythmaking*, 211.

the only real triumph of love in the poem is its phoenix-like capacity to resurrect itself from the dead metaphors it abandons and to continue the celebration of the sexual union that is perpetually held in eschatological tension without being realized.

Just as the hermaphrodite was the witch's creature, Emilia is the poet's. And in the final section of the poem (ll. 408–604), Shelley suggests a voyage to a hypothetical far-away Eden, similar to the journey of the witch with her hermaphrodite. In fact, Shelley refers in a rejected line to Emilia as a hermaphrodite (Fragments, l. 57; *SPW*, 427). But she is so only in the sense that she combines an aspect of himself with that of the 'other', and in that she is the poet's creation. The poem does not depart from the spouse-sister conception of the Old Testament love-poem.[23] Rather, it refers this conception of the *anima* back to the *locus* of a hypothetical Eden (ll. 387, 417, 423, 427, 459, 539). As Knight has observed, such an Elysium cannot arise again in terms of Christian theology, given the nature of sin.[24] And although Shelley avoids the question of sin in *Epipsychidion*, his Eden remains in the realm of the unrealized ideal. Just as the witch travelled through the mundane world without actually entering it, he can only venture toward his ethereal Eden without ever arriving, for it is as far removed from the ordinary world as is Emilia. In this light, Hazlitt's complaint that Shelley fabricated his poetic world out of non-existent materials 'disdaining the bars and ties of mortal mould' is understandable.[25] Ultimately, the reward of love is 'in the world divine' (l. 597), not in the world of the ravaged garden.

Shelley's poem 'The Serpent is Shut Out from Paradise' (enclosed in a note to Edward Williams) reveals that the quest for an Eve figure was grounded in an unfulfilled domestic relationship with Mary.[26] As the poet found some consolation in the company of Jane Williams, the common-law wife of another English expatriate, the attention formerly devoted to 'Emilia' was redirected toward her. Shelley's consequent affection for Jane, like that for Teresa Viviani, found primarily a literary rather than a literal expression. In 'To Jane. The Recollection', Shelley writes, '. . . thou art ever fair and kind' (l. 85), paraphrasing an endearment found in the Song of Solomon (1: 15, 16). And as the maiden of the Canticle is wooed with the line 'Arise, my love, my fair one, and come away' (2: 13), Shelley addresses Jane in 'To Jane. The Invitation': 'Radiant Sister of the day, / Awake, arise and come away . . .' (ll. 47–8).

---

[23] See *Epipsychidion*, ll. 491–2.   [24] 'The Naked Seraph', 240.
[25] *Works*, xvi. 265.   [26] The point has been discussed by White, *Shelley*, ii. 346–7.

The spirit is that of Marlowe's 'The Passionate Shepherd to his Love'. For understandable reasons, Mary Shelley objected to this rather intimate relationship between the Williamses and her husband. Hence the opening lines of the poem Shelley sent to Edward Williams:

> The serpent is shut out from Paradise—
> The wounded deer must seek the herb no more
> In which its heart's cure lies . . .
>
> (ll. 1–3)

The serpent here is Shelley himself; paradise is the presence of the Williamses. In the book of Genesis, the serpent is the agent lying behind the fallen spiritual and domestic state of man (Gen. 3: 14–16). The metaphor shifts, however, and Shelley becomes a deer wounded by an arrow which has penetrated so deeply that he 'Should quickly perish if it were withdrawn' (l. 24). Since this image unites both domestic and spiritual concerns, it calls for some analysis.

The image of the deer in pursuit occurs in the Old Testament for instructive purposes. The man of understanding is told to deliver himself 'as a roe from the hand *of the hunter*'—that is, from the pitfalls created by personal improvidence (Prov. 6: 5). Jeremiah measures the spiritual decline of the Hebrews by the image of her rulers running before their enemies like harts (Lam. 1: 6). More vividly, the earth in divine chastisement will be 'as the chased roe' before God's anger (Isa. 13: 14). This image of the pursued or stricken deer (hind, fawn, doe, etc.) recurs throughout Shelley's poetic career. His early 'Esdaile' poem 'Dares the llama' deals with the predicament of his flight from the Judaeo-Christian God:

> When the tiger awakes, can the fast-fleeting hind
> Repose trust in his footsteps of air?
>
> .   .   .   .   .
>
> For in vain from the grasp of Religion I flee;
> The most tenderly loved of my soul
> Are slaves to its chilling control . . .
> It pursues me, it blasts me. Oh! where shall I fly . . .
>
> (ll. 3–4, 32–5)[27]

Although the issue at hand is a religious matter, these lines probably stem from the broken courtship with Harriet Grove, as Kenneth Neill Cameron has noted.[28] For Shelley, the spiritual and the sexual were

---

[27] See *PS*, i. 161–2.
[28] Kenneth N. Cameron (ed.), *The Esdaile Notebook* (London, 1964), 248.

inextricable. The spiritual-erotic conflict in *The Cenci*, for example, is likewise focused through the depiction of the deer in the words of Orsino to Beatrice:

> Because I am a Priest do you believe
> Your image, as the hunter some struck deer,
> Follows me not whether I wake or sleep?
>
> (I. ii. 11–13)

The image thus reflects the power of Eros.[29] In the emblem tradition of the Renaissance, however, the image of the wounded deer was spiritualized. J. H. Owen has pointed out that it could symbolize sinful man pricked by conscience or the Christian wounded by the arrows of the world, the flesh, and the devil.[30] Owen points out the affinity between this tradition and the iconographic use of the hunted deer in Cowper's *The Task* (p. 67). What is curious is that Cowper's description of himself as a wounded deer occurs in the context of a discussion of sexual matters in the third book of this work, significantly entitled 'The Garden'. The earlier Romantic poet writes: 'Domestic happiness, thou only bliss / Of Paradise that has surviv'd the fall!' (III. 41–2). Indirectly, he says that unless there is Eve, there can be no Eden. And his own experience of disappointment in life is reflected in the imagery of the hunt:

> I was a stricken deer, that left the herd
> Long since; with many an arrow deep infixt
> My panting side was charg'd, when I withdrew
> To seek a tranquil death in distant shades.
> There was I found by one who had himself
> Been hurt by th' archers. In His side he bore,
> And in his hands and feet, the cruel scars.
> With gentle force soliciting the darts,
> He drew them forth, and heal'd, and bade me live.
>
> (III. 108–16)

Whereas Cowper, at the time of his writing *The Task*, found consolation in Christ, the young Shelley found in him only the cause of his

---

[29] For other references to the wounded or pursued deer, see *Queen Mab*, III. 109–12; *The Revolt of Islam*, x. iv. 3–4; *Prometheus Unbound*, I. 454–7, 603–9, II. iii. 63–7, IV. 7, 73–6; *Peter Bell the Third*, ll. 604–8; 'Letter to Maria Gisborne', ll. 187–92; *The Cenci*, I. ii. 89–91; 'Orpheus', ll. 45–53; *Epipsychidion*, ll. 272–4; *Adonais*, ll. 243–4, 296–306; *Hellas*, ll. 536–40; and 'The Triumph of Life', ll. 405–10.

[30] 'The Stricken Deer and the Emblem Tradition', *Bulletin of the New York Public Library*, 75 (1971), 71–2.

wounds, for it was the Galilean who had personally deprived him of Harriet Grove.[31] Unlike the evangelical Romantic, the mature Shelley of 'The Serpent is Shut Out from Paradise' has no Christ to extricate the arrows. He can only look around himself in vain for such consolation, acknowledging to Edward Williams that 'I sought / Peace thus, and but in you I found it not' (ll. 31–2). Without this companionship, he is like those who, according to the Old Testament, 'shall seek peace, and *there shall be* none' (Ezek. 7: 25). The friendship that was the consolation for the reality of an increasingly cool marriage had become forbidden medicine. Shelley finally likens himself to a bird without a nest (l. 42), an image Jesus used in reference to himself (Matt. 8: 20). Neither marriage to the woman at hand (Mary) nor locating his idealization of femininity in Jane Williams succeeded in embodying the image of Eve.

In each of these portraits of Eve in the garden, Shelley celebrates the beauty of the Eden that lies beyond the veil of time. His epithalamia are of the infinite, not of this world. Nevertheless, the mundane world has its window on to this deeper reality through poetry. 'Emilia' exists in the same sense as the woman of 'The Sensitive Plant', the witch, and the Jane of the poems that bear her name. But these idealizations have only an incidental connection with the women Shelley knew. Eden, too, is presented only as an island retreat from the world-weariness of marriage; it becomes a place where the fantasy of the woman and the garden can assume its own life in the realm of the imagination. The dream of a return to a temporal Eden through either political reform, vegetarian diet, or the discovery of Eve has finally exhausted itself, and made way for the greater vision, that of eternity.

[31] Letter to T. J. Hogg, 26 Apr. 1811, *Letters*, i. 70.

8

Apocalyptic Vision and the Angelic Guide

Shelley's gradual loss of faith in the attempt to bring about a new Eden or an ideal society in the temporal world has an interesting parallel in the development of Hebrew prophetic literature. The decline and cessation of prophecy in the canonical Old Testament is accompanied by the emergence of the new biblical genre of apocalyptic. This newer conception of things to come cannot be separated from the political realities of the Jewish nation during the intertestamental period. Prophets such as Isaiah and Jeremiah had pronounced judgement on the enemies of the chosen people, and had projected a vision of God's restoring Israel to a position of eminence among the nations. The opening chapters of the book of Isaiah, for example, present Zion as the spiritual centre of world civilization. The unpleasant reality of the Seleucid dynasty (312–64 BC), however, was that Jewish identity itself was threatened by the newly disseminated Hellenistic culture. The chosen nation had become an occupied territory.

Apocalyptic developed in a milieu in which Judaism had come into contact with other religious systems, the most influential of these being Persian dualism. It arose chiefly as a response to the frustrated hopes of a Jewish nation governed by outsiders; and it may be seen either as an alternative to prophecy or as a refinement of it. Nevertheless, there are some key distinctions to bear in mind. The prophets saw future developments from a fixed point in their own historical situation; the apocalyptists in general spoke from an ambiguous point in time. The concerns of this world in the prophetic writings were countered by an other-worldliness in the apocalypses. Whereas prophetic eschatology dealt with historic events which, although supernaturally ordained, did not violate the natural order, apocalyptic eschatology involved a shattering of the cosmos. There are strange portents in the heavens while whole empires collapse on earth. The poetic, providential way of seeing God in relation to history in prophecy gave way to determinism, plain fortune-telling, and the interpretation of dreams in many of the apocalypses. The prophets emphasized restoration of the kingdom; the apocalyptists stressed transcendence. The authority of a sovereign God in prophecy came to be overshadowed by a concern with the intermediary functions of angels in apocalyptic.[1]

An essential prerequisite for apocalyptic vision is disillusionment with the political prospects offered by history. And the Shelley of 1821–2 shared this general dismay to a considerable extent. In *Epipsychidion*, the ideal of Eden remains unrealized, just as Hellas in the poem of that name is a timeless ideal not to be confused with the local state. The local state was all too likely to be inhabited by vulgar moderns, like the Greek sailors whom Trelawny and Shelley observed, and of whom the latter complained, 'I had rather not have any more of my hopes and illusions mocked by sad realities.'[2] In 1822, Shelley wrote to John Gisborne, criticizing as 'demoniacal' Wordsworth's sentiment that this world '. . . is the world of all of us, & where / *We find our happiness or not at all*'.[3]

The point of these observations is not that Shelley suddenly 'discovered' the apocalyptic books of the Bible, but that his inclination toward the apocalyptic sensibility was inseparable from his experience of disappointment in life. *Queen Mab*, Canto I of *The Revolt of Islam*, and *The Mask of Anarchy* had all used revelatory techniques which resembled those of the book of Revelation. But in each case the apocalyptic element was subordinated to some other concern. In *Queen Mab*, that concern was the millennium which was to arise as the result of intramundane perfectibilist forces. In *The Revolt of Islam*, the apocalyptic section was simply divorced from the heart of the poem. And in *The Mask of Anarchy*, the elements drawn from the book of Revelation functioned allegorically, not anagogically. Since the concerns were primarily moral, there was no 'αναγωγή, or 'leading upward'. In *Hellas*, *Adonais*, and 'The Triumph of Life', however, there is an other-worldly bent that can more conveniently be identified with the vision of the open heaven which is the essence of apocalyptic spiritual experience.

[1] This contrast is drawn with particular reference to C. H. Dodd, *The Authority of the Bible* (1929; Glasgow, 1978), 80, 180–1, 206; Gerhard von Rad, *The Message of the Prophets*, trans. D. M. G. Stalker (1968; London, 1982), 272–3; R. E. Clements, *Prophecy and Tradition* (1975; Oxford, 1978), 84; and J. J. Collins, 'Apocalyptic Eschatology as the Transcendence of Death', *Catholic Biblical Quarterly*, 36 (1974), 21–43; in *Visionaries and Their Apocalypses*, ed. P. D. Hanson (London, 1983), 66–70.

[2] Quoted in Trelawny's *Recollections*, ii. 201.

[3] Letter to John Gisborne, 10 Apr. 1822, *Letters*, ii. 406. The lines, misquoted from a passage that eventually formed part of *The Prelude* (XI. 142–4), had appeared in *The Friend* for 26 Oct. 1809.

One indication of the shift toward an apocalyptic form of expression is Shelley's increasing interest in Wisdom literature.[4] Some recent scholars argue that apocalyptic either stems from the Wisdom tradition (rather than from prophecy) or is integrally related to it. Each reveals an underlying pessimism regarding the temporal order of things, a prerequisite for the 'unveiling' (the etymological meaning of the word 'apocalyptic') of the true order. In the Old Testament, the worldly-wise ethos of Proverbs gives way to the scepticism of Ecclesiastes—a development akin to the apocalyptists' disillusionment with prophecy—for the voice of Wisdom is seldom heeded on earth. Furthermore, the authors of both Wisdom and apocalyptic literature were interested in the idea of an élite group of learned men. According to Jonathan Z. Smith, they 'hypostatized the scribe and scribal activities in the figure of Divine Wisdom'.[5] In the last two years of Shelley's life, Wisdom literature assumes a more prominent role in his writings than it previously had. As we have seen, the book of Proverbs and the Song of Songs colour much of *Epipsychidion*; the framework device of the heavenly court in Job helps to structure the abandoned prologue to *Hellas*; and the theme of the community of scribes (poets) who are wise men is an important feature of *Adonais*. Finally, Shelley transcribes (occasionally paraphrasing) several passages from the apocryphal Wisdom books of Ecclesiasticus and the Wisdom of Solomon in one of the Bodleian notebooks amid draft material for *Epipsychidion*. Much of this material praises the personification of wisdom.[6]

In the Scriptures, Wisdom serves as a link between the temporal and eternal realms, thus mediating the increasingly evident dualism in Hebrew thought between divine and human spheres. She descends from the heavens, and her voice is heard among men. But there remains the tantalizing alternative to her message of folly, and in the apocryphal book of Enoch, first published in a complete English version in 1821, she returns to her heavenly dwelling among the angels.[7]

---

[4] In the broadest sense, canonical Wisdom literature includes Proverbs, Ecclesiastes, the Song of Songs, Job, and some of the Psalms. See James Williams, 'Proverbs and Ecclesiastes', in *Literary Guide to the Bible*, 263.

[5] 'Wisdom and Apocalyptic', in *Religious Syncretism in Antiquity*, ed. B. A. Pearson (Missoula, Mont., 1975), 131–56; repr. in *Visionaries and their Apocalypses*, 103.

[6] Bodleian MS Shelley adds. e. 8, fos. 166–158, 156. The passages cited are Wisd. 2: 19–21, 5: 7–15, 20–1, 6: 13, 15, 16–18, 7: 1–5, 17–30, 8: 16, 19–20, 12: 10, and Ecclus. 37: 11–14. In *A Lay Sermon*, Coleridge suggests that these two apocryphal books ought to have been included in the canon (*Lay Sermons*, 128 n.–129 n.).

[7] 1 Enoch 42: 1–2, trans. E. Isaac in *Old Testament Pseudepigrapha*, ed. J. H. Charlesworth (2 vols., Garden City, NY, 1983), i. 33. See also Prov. 1: 20–30, 9: 1–4, and Wisd. 9: 10.

Since Wisdom obviously represents a source of order in society, her departure reveals the apocalyptic need for reordering the nature of things. In the *Vita Nuova*, a major influence on Shelley's *Epipsychidion*, Dante has a vision in which he hears that Beatrice—who embodies wisdom, among other things—has died (ch. xxiii). Like Wisdom, she returns to heaven, but the thought of her departure from earth (a fore-shadowing of his own) instils in the poet the feeling that the entire cosmic order is dissolving. The sun and stars are altered, birds fall from the air, the earth quakes, and the poet sees angels ascending heavenward.[8] In the Scriptures, such phenomena are characteristic of apocalyptic passages.[9] And they help establish the 'apocalyptic' dualism between an older corrupted order and newer perfected one.

Joseph Barrell noted long ago in *Shelley and the Thought of his Time* (pp. 173–4) that the general adulation of the One in *Adonais* is inconsistent with the dualism inherent in such a phrase as 'th' unwilling dross' (l. 384). The phrase is not uncharacteristic of the poem, for Shelley elsewhere speaks of 'our living clay' (l. 351), 'the world's slow stain' (l. 356), and 'the dull dense world' (l. 382). Despite his observation about the anti-cosmic elements of *Adonais*, Barrell overlooked the possibility of any biblical basis for this dualism. Such a basis may lie in the undertones of the frequently pessimistic book of Ecclesiastes.[10] In that book, there is a clear distinction between what takes place 'under the sun' and the idea of transcendence. In Shelley's poem, this contrast is marked by the threshold beyond which the poem's spiritual guide Urania cannot go; for although she may be seen as a form of love—based on the notion of Uranian love in Plato's *Symposium*—the ultimate goal of that love is wisdom. As Diotima says (Shelley's translation): 'Wisdom is one of the most beautiful of all things; Love is that which thirsts for the beautiful, so that Love is of necessity a philosopher, philosophy being an intermediate state between ignorance and wisdom' (*Plat.* 443). Urania, then, is an impetus toward wisdom and away from the ignorance of weeping.[11]

[8] Cf. the similar depiction in Petrarch's 'The Triumph of Death' (beginning of second *capitolo*).

[9] See e.g. Rev. 6: 12–14.

[10] I do not minimize the more obvious influences on *Adonais* of Platonic philosophy, classical elegy, and Greek myth. However, my focus here is primarily with what may be seen as biblical elements in the poem.

[11] In *Paradise Lost*, Urania is identified either *with* or *as* the Holy Spirit, and is the sister of 'eternal Wisdom' (VII. 1–31). Lily Campbell discusses the conflation of Urania with the Holy Spirit during the Renaissance in 'The Christian Muse', *Huntington Library Bulletin*, no. 8 (1935), 29–70.

In *Adonais*, there is a transcending leap into the realm of spirit begin-
ning with stanza 38. However, here Urania is bound by time to the
lower realms of material existence. Earlier in the poem, she had
expressed her view of a threefold cosmic vision that reflected the per-
spective of Ecclesiastes, with its motif of hopelessness for the world
whose cycles go on 'under the sun' (4: 1):

> 'The sun comes forth, and many reptiles spawn;
> He sets, and each ephemeral insect then
> Is gathered into death without a dawn,
> And the immortal stars awake again;
> So is it in the world of living men:
> A godlike mind soars forth, in its delight
> Making earth bare and veiling heaven, and when
> It sinks, the swarms that dimmed or shared its light
> Leave to its kindred lamps the spirit's awful night.'
>
> (ll. 253–61)

Urania thus describes an anthropology strangely reminiscent of that of
the Gnostics, who classified humanity into three types: *sarkic* (fleshly)
man, *psychic* or natural (sensuous) man, and *pneumatic* (spiritual) man.[12]
In his critical reading of Shelley's poetry, Wasserman understands
Urania's classification to refer to the 'base and spiritless' (analogous to
insects), the 'lesser spirits' (likened to stars), and those of 'the godlike
mind' (similar to the sun) (p. 499). But from the perspective of the final
third of the poem, it is the stars who are identified with the apotheo-
sized Adonais, and not the sun. For Shelley ultimately identifies the sun
with the cyclical processes of nature, like the Preacher of Ecclesiastes,
who presents both the world under the sun, in which the spirits of ani-
mals return to the earth at death (3: 21), and the world of the sun itself,
which simply rises and sets (1: 5). Man's place in such a scheme is
uncertain. The Preacher ultimately says that after death 'the dust [shall]
return to the earth as it was: and the spirit shall return unto God who
gave it' (12: 7). But the thought does not represent an apocalyptic leap;
it simply occasions another lament on the vanity of all things (12: 8).
Shelley echoes this verse in writing 'Dust to the dust! but the pure spirit
shall flow / Back to the burning fountain whence it came' (ll. 338–9). It
is at this point that he transcends altogether the lower realms of time
and change, of Urania and the Preacher.

---

[12] This tripartite division of the human race may have been derived from misreadings
of St Paul (1 Cor. 2: 14–15, Rom. 7: 18–25, and Gal. 5: 16–26).

The poem shifts into the sphere of the heavens, the true οὐρανός of stars which Urania's world of flowers had dimly prefigured (ll. 173–4). Here at the pneumatic level Shelley describes a communion of poets who, like Keats, died young, and who now rise to greet his spirit:

> The inheritors of unfulfilled renown
> Rose from their thrones, built beyond mortal thought,
>
> .   .   .   .   .
>
> And many more, whose names on Earth are dark
> But whose transmitted effluence cannot die
> So long as fire outlives the parent spark,
> Rose, robed in dazzling immortality.
> 'Thou art become as one of us,' they cry . . .
>
>   (ll. 397–8, 406–10)

W. M. Rossetti long ago pointed out the affinity of these lines with those which anticipate the rebellion and fall of Lucifer: 'Hell from beneath is moved for thee to meet *thee* at thy coming . . . it hath raised up from their thrones all the kings of the nations. All they shall speak and say unto thee, Art thou also become weak as we?' (Isa. 14: 9–10).[13] Shelley's diabolical application is characteristic; he links poets with fallen angels here, an irony compounded by the apocalyptic picture of select spirits clothed in white garments standing before the angels (Rev. 3: 4–5). The élite brotherhood of Chatterton, Sidney, Lucan, and Keats (and others) have their thrones 'beyond mortal thought' (l. 398).

There are several biblical analogues in *Adonais* which amplify this idea of the eternal communion of the elect that constitutes poetic tradition. The brotherhood of poets is first of all a fellowship of the wise. As Daniel was a wise man among other court advisers, poets are conceived of as 'wise' men in *Adonais* (l. 312). And Wisdom is a protecting shield, a portion of the righteous man's spiritual armour which Urania claims that the youthful Keats lacked (l. 240).[14] Poetic tradition is dependent on scribal sagacity. Shelley writes in the *Defence* that

Even in modern times, no living poet ever arrived at the fulness of his fame; the jury which sits in judgement upon a poet, belonging as he does to all time, must be composed of his peers: it must be impanelled by Time from the selectest of the wise of many generations. (*SPP*, 486)

Secondly, this Shelleyan communion of saints is a fraternity of prophets. The sacred poets Milton and Dante are characterized by the

---

[13] *Adonais*, 2nd edn., rev. A. O. Prickard (London, 1918), 146.
[14] The idea of spiritual armour is explained in Isa. 59: 17, Wisd. 5: 17–21, 2 Cor. 6: 7, and Eph. 6: 13–17.

'mask and the mantle' of their religious beliefs in the *Defence* (*SPP*, 498). When seen in connection with Shelley's equation of poets with prophets in the preceding chapter, this passage may help to gloss a passage in *Adonais* which frankly stumped Rossetti (p. 132): '. . . the mountain shepherds came / Their garlands sere, their magic mantles rent' (ll. 262–3). The mantles themselves suggest both prophetic tradition, an implication Shelley might have seen in the similarity of the word μάντις (prophet) to 'mantle', and the prophet's call itself. The Old Testament says of Elisha that 'Elijah passed by him, and cast his mantle upon him' (1 Kgs. 19: 19). The symbolic gesture prompted the younger man to kill his oxen, leave his field, and follow Elijah. The vocational significance of the mantle is elsewhere reflected in *Hellas*, where Shelley speaks of the 'prophet's robe' of truth (l. 44). The fact that Shelley's shepherd-poets (Byron, Moore, himself, and Hunt) have rent mantles may simply indicate their grief at Keats's death. When Eliphaz, Bildad, and Zophar saw Job stricken with boils, they 'rent every one his mantle' in sympathy (Job 2: 12).

Thirdly, the poet is distinguished by his separateness from the masses as an outcast, or martyr. In the preface to *Adonais*, Keats's reviewers are equated with both the Roman soldiers who crucified Christ and the religious leaders with whom he disputed. Shelley writes that 'these wretched men know not what they do . . . . What gnat did they strain at here, after having swallowed all those camels? Against what woman taken in adultery, dares the foremost of these literary prostitutes to cast his opprobrious stone?' (*SPP*, 391).[15] Correspondingly, Shelley identifies himself with both Cain and Christ, fellow aliens stigmatized (like Shelley here) by the marked forehead (ll. 305–6). The allusion to Cain may be related to Byron's work of that name, a project which was completed by 10 September 1821, three months after the writing of *Adonais*.[16] Shelley's judgement in the following year was that 'Cain is apocalyptic—it is a revelation not before communicated to man'.[17] And he later indicated that he felt flattered to have been thought an influence on the work.[18] This admiration for Byron's play brings to mind the Gnostic idealization of the alienated hero; for Cain, like Prometheus, was a type of 'spiritual' man in Gnostic lore. Both defy all

[15] See Luke 23: 34, Matt. 23: 24, and John 8: 7.
[16] Letter to John Murray, 10 Sept. 1821, in *Byron's Letters and Journals*, ed. L. Marchand (12 vols.; Cambridge, Mass., 1973–82), viii. 205.
[17] Letter to John Gisborne, 26 Jan. 1822, *Letters*, ii. 388.
[18] Letter to Horace Smith, 11 Apr. 1822, *Letters*, ii. 412.

odds in the revolt against the orthodox God.[19] In his seminal study of the Gnostic element in Romanticism, Paul Cantor has demonstrated that Byron's *Cain* is an 'attack on human ignorance', on the state of innocence which is ordained by God in Eden. Thus the work reflects a disdain for 'blind reliance on divine revelation' (p. 137). Byron's Lucifer, as a messenger from the world of spirit, rationalizes the consequences of eating the forbidden fruit: 'It may be death leads to the highest knowledge' (II. ii. 164).[20] It is this sort of overturning of the orthodox view that typified the 'Gnostic' understanding of the Scriptures by Shelley's Assassins. And it seems to be present in the elegy on Keats, particularly in the Christological resonance of the final section, which revises the significance of Christ's resurrection (a triumph of life) by its counter-assertion of Keats's 'resurrection' of death. Shelley writes that 'He lives, he wakes—'tis Death is dead, not he' (l. 361), as if to rephrase St Paul's statement: 'Knowing that Christ being raised from the dead dieth no more; death hath no more dominion over him' (Rom. 6: 9). But what Shelley actually expresses is the triumph of (not over) death. His statement 'No more let Life divide what Death can join together' (l. 477) is clearly modelled on Jesus's teaching about marriage (Matt. 19: 6). And it reflects not only Shelley's mature view that earthly life is a form of death, but also the Luciferic view of death expressed in Byron's *Cain*.

The predominant apocalyptic theme of *Adonais* is that of the abandonment of redemptive processes that operate within time and the dissolution of earthly existence altogether (l. 464). The emblem of this earthly life, which reveals the ravages of Time, is the city of Rome, which emerges in the final stanzas of the poem as a vast sepulchre which attempts in vain to represent some form of permanence in this world. At the Protestant cemetery in Rome, site of the graves of both Shelley's son William and Keats, there stands a memorial pyramid to the tribune Caius Cestius, whose dust ironically coexists with the structure which was meant to immortalize him.[21] Since Rome stands for 'time's decay' in the poem, it is opposed to the realm of the timeless One which is Keats's true eternal dwelling-place. Similarly, the harlot of Babylon in the New Testament (Rev. 17: 3–5)—historically inter-

[19] See Jonas, *Gnostic Religion*, 95–7.

[20] *Lord Byron's Cain*, ed. T. G. Steffan (Austin, Tex., and London, 1968), 212.

[21] Cf. Byron's reference in *Don Juan* to the pyramid of Cheops, the greatness of which is ironic since 'not a pinch of dust remains of Cheops' (I. ccxix. 8). See *The Complete Poetical Works*, ed. J. McGann (5 vols. to date; Oxford, 1980–6), v. 79.

preted as Rome—stands as the apocalyptic contrary to the eternal new Jerusalem, city of the elect (Rev. 21: 2).

The apocalyptic dualism of the corrupted temporal realm and the anticipated realm of perfection is reflected in the antithetical states of material and spiritual life lamented and celebrated in *Adonais*. Nevertheless, there exists the compelling force of the One to redeem the world. What unites the fallen world of substance with the transcendent state of Mind which is the eschatological goal of the poem is the divine spark of 'thought'. While apocalyptic man (the speaker in the poem), who bears the spark, is an alien in the world, he is capable of transcending it by nurturing the spark and entering into the life of the mind. The rejection of all that is not subsumed in this expanding νοῦς is therefore the basis for the poem's occasional hostility to things material. Hence the dualism is overlaid on a vertically inclined monism. In the poem, Shelley, echoing Job, speaks of salvation from the 'world's slow stain' (l. 356).[22] His spiritual coterie is comprised of 'kings of thought' who have transcended the desolation of mundane existence. These are the élite whom Shelley has in mind when writing 'The soul of Adonais, like a star, / Beacons from the abode where the Eternal are' (ll. 494–5). The apocalyptic book of Daniel ends on a similar note by extolling the destiny of the wise: 'And they that be wise shall shine as the brightness of the firmament; and they that turn many to righteousness as the stars for ever and ever' (12: 3). It is this Old Testament book of vision, one of the two canonical apocalyptic books of the Bible, which, more than any other biblical source, colours Shelley's final lyrical drama *Hellas*.

There are three sources that one might profitably bear in mind when approaching *Hellas*. The first is Shelley's acknowledged model of Aeschylus's drama *The Persians*, which features the device of a troubled royal figure's symbolic dream coupled with that of a vision in which a previous leader returns from the dead to give advice—both of which Shelley employs. The second is Byron's *Sardanapalus*, written under the partial inspiration of William Mitford's *The History of Greece* and completed by 28 May 1821.[23] Here a sybaritic monarch, the last ruler of the Assyrian dynasty, witnesses—frequently with a Byronic detachment— the collapse of his empire. The third is the book of Daniel, which, with

---

[22] Job 3: 5. The foregoing remarks on monism and dualism are based on the discussion of Kurt Rudolf, *Gnosis*, trans. P. W. Coxon and F. H. Kuhn, ed. R. McLachlan Wilson (Edinburgh, 1983), 57–8, 86.

[23] See journal entries for 5, 6, and 13 Jan. 1821 and Byron's letter to John Murray, 28 May 1821, in *Byron's Letters and Journals*, viii. 13, 14, 26, 127.

its panoramic vision, relates the transfer of power through a succession
of world empires. In all these works, Greece is seen through Middle
Eastern eyes. Aeschylus's Persian chorus tells the queen Atossa that the
Greeks are not slaves.[24] The underlying motif of Greece in Byron's play
is relayed through the Ionian slave girl Myrrha, Sardanapalus's mistress,
who proclaims that as a Greek she was 'born a foe to monarchs' (I. ii.
499). And from an apocalyptic standpoint above history, the book of
Daniel presents Greece as the rival and successor of the Persian empire
(8: 21, 10: 20). While all these works thus reflect political developments
of which Greece (or its ideal of freedom) is a part, it is the book of
Daniel which allows the fullest scope for the historical imagination and
for the idea that Shelley had relished since writing *Queen Mab*, that
world empires are transitory.

    The overview of history in Daniel is suggested in chapter 2 by the
dream of the Babylonian king Nebuchadnezzar, who envisions the suc-
cession of empires in the image of a man whose body is comprised of
gold, silver, brass, and iron. In chapter 7, Daniel himself sees the four
empires as beasts of prey (lion, bear, leopard, and a beast with ten horns).
Since modern scholars generally regard the book of Daniel as an apoca-
lyptic work written during the Maccabean period (168–165 BC), they
identify the four empires as those of Babylon, Media, Persia, and Greece
(although there seems to have been no Median empire in history).[25]
However, in Shelley's time, Daniel was regarded as a prophet, and the
four world dominions were identified as Babylonian, Medo-Persian,
Greek, and Roman.[26] The millennarian fervour generated by the French
Revolution led to a reinterpretation of Daniel, and consequently to fresh
identities for the four beasts. The self-proclaimed prophet Richard
Brothers, for example, held that they stood for the kingdoms of Russia,
France, Germany, and England.[27] One Christian Zionist further
identified the ominous 'king of the north' in Daniel 11: 40–5 with the
Turkish empire, and linked its fall with the restoration of Israel.[28]

    Such international concerns are increasingly evident in Shelley. In his
own Zionist fragment, he had written that the Jewish people were eco-
nomically and militarily capable of 'wresting Jerusalem and Judea from
the feeble oppression of the Turk' (p. 191). He states that 'Russia and

---

[24] See *The Persians* (l. 242), *Aeschylus*, trans. H. W. Smyth (2 vols.; London, 1922,
1926), i. 129.

[25] See G. B. Caird, *The Language and Imagery of the Bible* (London, 1980), 228, 228 n.

[26] See *An Illustration of the Holy Scriptures*, ii. 1649, 1650.

[27] *A Revealed Knowledge* (2 pts.; London, 1794), ii. 7–12.

[28] J. Bicheno, *The Restoration of the Jews* (London, 1800), 53.

Persia would see with pleasure a division made to the Ottoman posses-
sions which the one watches as an [sic] contingent conquest and the
other as an overwhelming enemy; an [sic] rebel Bey of Egypt and the
Pasha of Syria would rejoice in a power which diverted their master
from the enforcing of his claims' (p. 191). This is essentially the tone of
both the preface to *Hellas* and the opening section of *A Philosophical
View of Reform*, where Shelley, like the Christian Zionist, linked the
return of the Jews to Palestine with the collapse of the Ottoman empire
(*SHC*, vi. 988–9). Shelley was viewing with an apocalyptist's eyes the
'Kingdoms of the earth' (*SHC*, vi. 983) and with an apocalyptist's antic-
ipation the coming of a new spiritual order. Poets can 'prophesy' such
developments because they discern the recurrent cycles of history. As
Wasserman has pointed out, the political ideal of peace and freedom
symbolized by Greece may be embodied in a variety of actual states (p.
375). Athens therefore ultimately emerges as the focal point not only of
the great new age of Hellas (l. 1084), but of the world as well (l. 1060).
It is Shelley's version of the new Jerusalem which descends from
heaven at the conclusion of the New Testament (Rev. 21: 2).

The book of Daniel offers at least a superficial structural parallel to
Hellas. Both works present a monarch troubled by dreams or visions.
Nebuchadnezzar summons the Chaldean soothsayers to find out what
these mean (Dan. 2: 1–13); in *Hellas*, Mahmud says to his adviser
Hassan that 'Thrice has a gloomy vision hunted me' (l. 128). Arioch,
captain of the royal guard in Daniel, tells Nebuchadnezzar that he has
found a Jew to interpret the king's dream (Dan. 2: 25). Likewise,
Mahmud reminds Hassan:

> . . . thou didst say thou knewest
> A Jew, whose spirit is a chronicle
> Of strange and secret and forgotten things.
> I bade thee summon him—'tis said his tribe
> Dream, and are wise interpreters of dreams.
>
> (ll. 132–6)

Daniel too is presented before rulers to interpret dreams and other phe-
nomena (Dan. 2: 25, 4: 8, and 5: 12). The fact that he survives the tran-
sition from one empire to another and from one king to another itself
suggests the eternity of wisdom, which is paralleled by the agelessness of
Ahasuerus.[29]

---

[29] Daniel was a court figure from the reign of Nebuchadnezzar (605–562 BC) to that of
Darius the Mede (521–485 BC). The name or title 'Ahasuerus', mentioned in Daniel (9:
1), came to be ascribed to the Wandering Jew of folklore.

The outward resemblance between Daniel's situation and that of Ahasuerus must not obscure the very real difference between them. Unlike Daniel, Ahasuerus does not actually interpret dreams (ll. 757–8). And unlike the biblical apocalypse in general, *Hellas* presents no over-ruling God superintending the revolutionary process. Both Shelley's drama and the book of Daniel see monarchies as impermanent. Daniel says that God 'removeth kings, and setteth up kings' (2: 21), and Mahmud acknowledges that 'Kings are like stars—they rise and set . . .' (l. 195). However, Shelley does not see a divine Providence in this; such occurrences are simply events in the cycle which dooms monarchs. Shelley echoes the apocalyptic invitation of the heavenly fowls to eat the flesh of fallen kings and their armies (ll. 434–5, 515–19, 1025; Rev. 19: 17–18). And he employs the device of the heavenly portents which accompany the biblical day of divine judgement—the sun turning black, the moon becoming blood-red, and the falling of the stars to earth (Rev. 6: 12–13)—signs which in *Hellas* are reconstructed as the red cross seen stamped on the sun, the raining down of blood from heaven, and the Islamic symbol of the crescent moon fading in the light shed by the star of Venus which heralds the new age (ll. 337–47, 603–4). But in all these images, there is the stamp of Shelley's loathing of monarchy on principle, a sentiment quite foreign to the Bible.

The significance of the Old Testament apocalypse for *Hellas* lies chiefly in the Daniel-figure of Ahasuerus himself. For him, the material world is merely a vision:

> . . . Thought
> Alone, and its quick elements, Will, Passion,
> Reason, Imagination, cannot die;
>
> .   .   .   .   .
>
> Would'st thou behold the future?—ask and have!
> Knock and it shall be opened—look and lo!
> The coming age is shadowed on the past
> As on a glass.
>
> (ll. 795–7, 803–6)

Thought survives 'Empires and superstitions' (l. 801) because in its spiritual state of noetic perception, it does not stand within time. Ahasuerus, who has become God-like from contemplating God (l. 761), is therefore a manifestation of the immortal Mind. As such, he dissolves time into an 'eternal now'. Whereas Jesus used the phrase 'knock, and it shall be opened unto you' (Matt. 7: 7) to characterize the relationship between earthly man and his heavenly Father, Ahasuerus uses it to obliterate the distinctions between temporal and eternal, past and present (l. 804). All that is exists in the eternal present of the One Mind and the attainment of the spiritual/intellectual perception which allows the enlightened one to participate in it.

Because of its setting in Constantinople and its concern with rebellion against the Ottoman empire, *Hellas* invites comparison with *The Revolt of Islam*, written four years earlier. The previous work was grounded in the apocalyptic dualism of earthly conflict below operating in tandem with a parallel spiritual universe. In *Hellas*, there is no divorce of symbol from event. Greece is simply struggling to attain its ideal identity as Hellas, the symbol of freedom. It thus corresponds with the final monarchy of Daniel, which is also eternal (2: 44). Shelley views this struggle amid the flow of successive kingdoms and empires, and his apocalyptic perspective brings to mind the overview of history presented in the book of Daniel. Both Daniel and Ahasuerus are wise men; but whereas the former views earthly events from a supramundane perspective, the latter sees the cosmos contained in thought. Shelley's Jew proclaims the one abiding reality to be the eternal Mind and its workings. And it is through this apotheosis of 'thought' that the poet is able to envision the new Athens, a seat of wisdom (l. 734), as a new 'Jerusalem' and to see history as it were from above, from an 'angelic' perspective.

In apocalyptic literature, angels are actively involved in spiritual conflict. Daniel, for example, speaks of an angelic ruler of Persia who opposes his heavenly visitant (10: 13). But the interest in angels does not end with their role in the metaphysical war between the forces of darkness and those of light. A characteristic feature of apocalyptic is conversation with a heavenly guide in the form of an *angelus interpres* who exists within the vision and who interprets it for the benefit of the visionary (as in Dan. 8: 16–26 and Rev. 17: 1–18). The angelic interpreter sometimes appears in the book of Revelation as a casual bystander who offers to reveal even greater truths to the apocalyptist (e.g. Rev. 21: 9). What is significant is that the voice of the Lord speaking directly in prophecy yields to the intermediary revelation of angelic beings in apocalyptic. For all practical purposes, the *angelus interpres* does not necessarily have to be an angel, as the apocalyptic Christophany of Revelation 1: 10–3: 22 and the conversation with the visionary elder seated near the heavenly throne (Rev. 5: 5) serve essentially the same purpose. But the growth of apocalyptic is very much associated with the functions of angels, and is a major step towards the development of a speculative angelology that would allow for human imagination.

Since the angelic interpreter both exists within the vision and explains it to the visionary, he is the vital liaison between two worlds. Such a link exists in 'The Triumph of Life' as well, for the majority of the poem's lines are delivered through the lips of the interpreting angel Rousseau.[30] The apocalyptic character of Shelley's poem is evident when one observes the operation of the interpreting angel in the Bible. The visions of the four beasts and of the heavenly throne-world in the book of Daniel are a model instance:

I beheld till the thrones were cast down, and the Ancient of days did sit, whose garment *was* white as snow, and the hair of his head like the pure wool: his throne *was like* the fiery flame, *and* his wheels *as* burning fire.

A fiery stream issued and came forth from before him: thousand thousands ministered unto him, and ten thousand times ten thousand stood before him: the judgment was set, and the books were opened . . . .

I Daniel was grieved in my spirit in the midst of *my* body, and the visions of my head troubled me.

I came near unto one of them that stood by, and asked him the truth of all this. So he told me, and made me know the interpretation of the things. (Dan. 7: 9–10, 15–16)

The essential features of this passage are as follows: first, the vision of a multitude of people standing before the throne of judgement, which is perceived as a chariot;[31] second, the perplexity of the visionary as to the meaning of the phenomena; third, the formulation of a question; and fourth, the explanation offered by the angelic being. The corresponding pattern in 'The Triumph of Life' may be seen in the speaker's response to the vision of the 'captive multitude' driven by the chariot bearing the mysterious shape: [32]

> Struck to the heart by this sad pageantry,
> Half to myself I said, 'And what is this?
> Whose shape is that within the car? & why' —

[30] My reading of 'The Triumph of Life' has appeared in a slightly different form as an article, 'The Interpreting Angel in "The Triumph of Life"', *Review of English Studies*, NS 39/155 (1988), 386–99.

[31] The *Illustration of the Holy Scriptures* provides the following explanation: 'The Thrones of the Kings in the Eastern Countries sometimes were carried from Place to Place, and therefore they had Wheels to them; and so GOD's Throne is here described in the Nature of a triumphal Chariot' (ii. 1664).

[32] My reading of the poem owes much to Lloyd Abbey, *Destroyer and Preserver* (Lincoln, Nebr., and London, 1979), 127–43.

I would have added—'is all here amiss?'
  But a voice answered. . 'Life' . . . I turned and knew
(O Heaven have mercy on such wretchedness!)

  That what I thought was an old root which grew
To strange distortion out of the hill side
  Was indeed one of that deluded crew,

And that the grass which methought hung so wide
  And white, was but his thin discoloured hair,
And that the holes it vainly sought to hide

  Were or had been eyes.—'If thou canst forbear
To join the dance, which I had well forborne,'
  Said the grim Feature, of my thought aware,

'I will tell all that which to this deep scorn
  Led me and my companions, and relate
The progress of the pageant since the morn . . .'

                                          (ll. 176–93)

It seems clear in this sequence of events that although Shelley presents
an apocalyptic pattern, he is inverting the biblical model. In the apoca-
lypses of Scripture, the seer ascends in spirit into the heavens (as in Rev.
4: 2). In Shelley's poem, however, 'spirit' is described as descending
from heaven only to be trapped in the material world (ll. 201–4). This is
a pattern that could apply equally to the speaker and his guide. Lloyd
Abbey therefore seems quite correct in describing the poem as 'a
reversed apocalypse in which static images of eternity are submerged
one by one in the natural cycle they should either encompass or super-
sede' (p. 128). To turn the apocalyptic experience back upon the self
would amount to a 'Gnostic' reversal, for the typical apocalypse dis-
closes a divine reality beyond the self. Abbey does not develop his dis-
cussion in this way, although he establishes a rationale that could be
used to describe the occluded mystical experience of Gnosticism. The
promotion of self-knowledge (l. 212) indicates a general movement in
the opposite direction to that of biblical apocalyptic, for to know the
self in the Shelleyan sense is to know the self as divine.

  Several of the poem's commentators have noticed the close relation-
ship between the poem's speaker and his visionary interpreter. G. M.
Matthews has stated that Rousseau's visionary experience parallels that of
the spectator. Both are situated on a lawn (ll. 36, 355) near musical water
(ll. 7, 314–20).[33] David Quint believes that Rousseau is a manifestation

---

[33] 'On Shelley's "The Triumph of Life"', *Studia Neophilologica*, 34 (1962), 107.

of the speaker's 'visionary imagination', a prototype whose errors are apparently repeated by the poet.[34] Donald Reiman previously took this view further in seeing Rousseau as a projection from within the poet of the need for a response to the questions asked and of an acknowledgement that lost vision is the consequence of an immersion in the phenomenal world of mortality.[35] Although he specifically rejects a view of Rousseau as the poet's 'mirror-image' (p. 58), Reiman understands the visionary guide in such a way as to imply that he is a second self, perhaps in the same way that Gil-Martin is young Robert's darker side in James Hogg's novel *The Private Memoirs and Confessions of a Justified Sinner* (1824). To view the *angelus interpres* as an alternate self, speaking with the authority that comes from either experience or deeper insight, would simply underscore the fact that Shelley's apocalypse is inverted, and discloses a reality that is ultimately self-referential.

The apocalyptic features of 'The Triumph of Life' are a foreshadowing that the poem will be a revelation. The providential scope of the book of Revelation is subsumed in the Alpha and Omega 'which is, and which was, and which is to come' (Rev. 1: 8). However, the blindness of Shelley's charioteer Life precludes the unveiling of 'all that is, has been, or will be done' (l. 104). Harold Bloom has perceptively analysed the description of Shelley's charioteer, whose four faces have eyes that are banded (l. 100), with reference to the vision which introduces the book of Ezekiel.[36] The tradition of the cherubic eyes in Ezekiel's vision, Bloom asserts, is reversed in Shelley's poem (p. 240). Blindness succeeds vision as fleshliness and mortality are the legacy of the spirit's corruption (ll. 201–5). The spectator eventually asks, 'Whence camest thou . . .?' (l. 296), the question God asks Satan in the prologue to the book of Job (1: 7). The implication is that, like Satan, Rousseau is spiritually a lord of this world, and is bound by its hylic constraints. The ascent of the spirit to the opened heavens in Revelation 4: 2 seems parodied by a descent of the spirit into the natural world in 'The Triumph of Life'. On the one hand, there is the freedom of visionary experience; on the other, the bondage of life lived according to natural impulses.

Related to the theme of lost vision in the speech of the poem's *angelus interpres* is the motif of the obscured sun. The visionary had wit-

---

[34] 'Representation and Ideology in *The Triumph of Life*', *Studies in English Literature, 1500–1900*, 18 (1978), 656.

[35] *Shelley's 'The Triumph of Life'* (1965; Urbana, Ill., 1966), 39.

[36] *Shelley's Mythmaking*, 232–42.

nessed the dissipation of the sun's light by the 'cold glare' of the chariot, just as the sunlight had caused the stars to 'disappear' (ll. 77–9). Correspondingly, there are two occasions when the sun, in this case emblematic of the ultimate reality of the νοῦς, is overshadowed. In the first instance it is eclipsed by papal intermediaries who usurped temporal authority (ll. 288–9); in the second it is fragmented by the seductive 'shape all light' (l. 352). Both of these are apocalyptic in character.

As priestcraft and tyranny had been inextricable in Shelley's mind from the time of *Queen Mab*, papal rulers are simply adjuncts of earthly monarchs in 'The Triumph of Life'. They join the procession of those chained to the chariot of Life:

> The Anarchs old whose force and murderous snares
>
>> Had founded many a sceptre bearing line
>> And spread the plague of blood and gold abroad,
>> And Gregory and John and men divine
>
> Who rose like shadows between Man and god
>> Till that eclipse, still hanging under Heaven,
>> Was worshipped by the world o'er which they strode
>
>> For the true Sun it quenched.—'Their power was given
>> But to destroy,' replied the leader . . .
>>> (ll. 285–93)

To those chained to the chariot, Shelley thus ascribes the character of the fourth horseman of the apocalypse, Death, who is followed by hell. The book of Revelation says, 'And power was given unto them over the fourth part of the earth, to kill with sword, and with hunger, and with death' (Rev. 6: 8). However, in the eighteenth century this coalition of spiritual and political tyranny was discussed in the light of the pouring out of the vials (Rev. 16) in the apocalyptic speculations of Robert Fleming, a Presbyterian clergyman whose anti-Catholic *Apocalyptical Key*, published in 1701, was reprinted in the years immediately following the French Revolution. According to Fleming, the papacy acquired temporal power during the time of Pepin the Short and Pope Paul I (*c*.758). Thus commenced the period of the Antichrist, in which political and spiritual sources of authority were conflated for the duration of a period of 1,260 'prophetic' years (based on Rev. 11: 3).[37] Fleming had seen in the pouring out of the seven vials a series of

[37] *Apocalyptical Key* (1701; London, 1809), 21–2. The prophetic calendar, with its 360-day year, is to be distinguished from the Julian system. Thus the 1,260-year period derived from Rev. 11: 3 is a time of 1,278 years in Western calendars.

epochs in modern history, culminating in the millennial reign of Christ. The present period, he said, was that of the pouring out of the fourth vial, a time lasting from approximately 1648 to 1794 on the prophetic calendar (or 1666 to 1812 by modern reckoning). The biblical text says that 'the fourth angel poured out his vial upon the sun; and power was given unto him to scorch men with fire' (Rev. 16: 8). Fleming here interprets the sun both as a sign of 'the papal kingdom' and as 'the emblem of princes and kingdoms' (p. 39). The two are to be considered together: 'Therefore the pouring out of this vial on the sun must denote the humiliation of some eminent potentates of the Romish interest, whose influences and countenances cherish and support the papal cause' (p. 39). The verse thus comes to refer to the ascendancy and chastisement of the House of Bourbon. Writing during the reign of the sun-king Louis XIV, Fleming prophesies on the basis of his apocalyptic arithmetic the downfall of the French monarch around the time of the prophetic year 1794:

I cannot but hope that some new mortification of the *chief supporters of antichrist will then happen; and perhaps the French monarchy may begin to be considerably humbled about that time: that whereas the present French king takes the sun for his emblem, and this for his motto*: Nec pluribus impar, *he may at length, or rather his successors, and the monarchy itself (at least before the year 1794), be forced to acknowledge, that (in respect to the neighbouring potentates) he is even* singulis impar. (p. 41)

Thus the Gallic corruption of the sun as a symbol is judged for its alliance with tyranny. Earlier in the book of Revelation, the sun was seen clothing the woman wearing a crown of twelve stars who appears in the heavens persecuted by a seven-headed red dragon (12: 1–4). Fleming identifies her as the Church, and thus views the sun as a symbol of the kingdom which stands in antithesis to 'the Beast's unstable kingdom of night and darkness' (p. 14). Its adoption as an emblem by the Bourbon monarch is thus all the more opprobrious for its linking earthly empire with the eternal new Jerusalem, where the glory of God is the sun (Rev. 21: 23).

The second apocalyptic falsification of the sun as a symbol occurs in the speech of Rousseau, who recounts his spiritual history for the speaker (ll. 308–543). Although this section of the poem is usually discussed with reference to Wordsworth's 'Intimations' ode, in which the vision of immortality attending infancy 'fade[s] into the light of common day', the epiphany of the 'shape all light' suggests by its imagery a derivation from the New Testament Apocalypse:

'And as I looked the bright omnipresence
   Of morning through the orient cavern flowed,
And the Sun's image radiantly intense

   'Burned on the waters of the well that glowed
Like gold, and threaded all the forest maze
   With winding paths of emerald fire—there stood

'Amid the sun, as he amid the blaze
   Of his own glory, on the vibrating
Floor of the fountain, paved with flashing rays,

   'A shape all light, which with one hand did fling
Dew on the earth, as if she were the Dawn
   Whose invisible rain forever seemed to sing

'A silver music on the mossy lawn,
   And still before her on the dusky grass
Iris her many coloured scarf had drawn.—

   'In her right hand she bore a chrystal glass
Mantling with bright Nepenthe . . . .

   .   .   .   .   .

'"Arise and quench thy thirst," was her reply.
And as a shut lily, stricken by the wand
   Of dewy morning's vital alchemy,

'I rose; and, bending at her sweet command,
   Touched with faint lips the cup she raised,
And suddenly my brain became as sand.'

                (ll. 343–59, 400–5)

Partly on the basis of a corrected text, recent commentators on the poem have drawn a clear distinction between the 'shape all light' and Iris, the rainbow.[38] However, as the editors of the Norton edition of Shelley have indicated, the two are closely associated in that the 'shape all light (352) assumes the shape of a rainbow' (*SPP*, 465 n. 7). This language recalls that of the incarnation of Christ in St Paul's account of his kenosis (Phil. 2: 5–8). But the assumption of an immanent form in Shelley is an atomistic phenomenon. As the shape stands for the dispelling of the light of the sun, Iris in turn becomes the means by which the shape is dissipated.

   Contemporary mythographers were fond of playing the sun against Iris as the diffusion of the one into the many. They were unanimous in

[38] See Reiman, *Shelley's 'The Triumph of Life'*, 63; Dawson, *Unacknowledged Legislator*, 274; and P. H. Butter, 'Sun and Shape in Shelley's *The Triumph of Life*', *Review of English Studies*, NS 13 (1962), 46 n.

pointing out that she was to be identified as the rainbow.[39] But Jacob Bryant took the matter further by distorting the image of the rainbow into that of Cupid's bow (ii. 345), and consequently the name Iris into Eros, stating his opinion that they were 'originally the same term' (ii. 346). In Orphic tradition, Bryant continued, 'the reflected colours of the Iris . . . arise from their opposition to the Sun' (ii. 354). In this, he followed the contrast presented by Thomas Blackwell, who had compared allegory, the 'Semblance of Truth', with Iris and opposed it to 'the resplendent *Sun* of *simple* TRUTH' (p. 287). The rainbow could thus suggest the idea of eroticism while standing in antithesis to the primary symbol of unity, the sun, which Shelley used in *Prometheus Unbound* to express the realization of the Promethean mind, the integrated self (I. 430–1, II. iv. 127). Iris is a chief obstacle to this form of unity, for she is the emblem of the mortal passions and of the many. She stands for the enticement of the phenomenal world and for the obliteration of the eternal realm of νοῦς.

The demolition of the mind takes place as the shape tramples its thoughts 'into the dust of death' (l. 388). In the messianic twenty-second Psalm, the speaker laments that he too is brought 'into the dust of death' (Ps. 22: 15). But for him there exists a hope of deliverance in the everlasting God (Ps. 22: 19). 'The Triumph of Life' can offer no such consolation. As in *Hellas*, it is thought that is eternal, at least for the pneumatic Ahasuerus (ll. 784, 795–7). Rousseau, however, resembles the sarkic man whom St Paul contrasts with the man walking in the Spirit (Rom. 8: 8–10). Shelley's shape simply extinguishes that which had already failed to ascend beyond the hylic stage of mortal thought. When Rousseau drinks of her cup, his brain becomes 'as sand' (l. 405), thereby preparing him for his ultimate destiny of following the sensual crowd.[40] If the seductiveness of Eros/Iris is seen together with the shape and her proffered cup, a consistent apocalyptic portrait emerges. This picture could be related to the theophany of St John, in which '*there was* a rainbow round about the throne, in sight like unto an emerald' (Rev. 4: 3). The imagery of an 'emerald fire' and of a rainbow attends the shape (ll. 348, 357). However, a more extensive analysis will

---

[39] Bryant, *New System*, ii. 343; Blackwell, *Letters concerning Mythology*, 287; Godwin, *Pantheon*, 52; and Edward Moor, *The Hindu Pantheon* (London, 1810), 260.

[40] G. M. Matthews is wrong, I believe, in stating that it does not matter whether Rousseau actually drinks of the cup or merely takes it to his lips (p. 116). Since the act is a perversion of the sacrament, the implication of the scene is that Rousseau partakes moderately.

reveal a far greater affinity with the harlot of Babylon, the MYSTERY of the Apocalypse:

AND there came one of the seven angels which had the seven vials, and talked with me, saying unto me, Come hither; I will shew unto thee the judgment of the great whore that sitteth upon many waters:

With whom the kings of the earth have committed fornication, and the inhabitants of the earth have been made drunk with the wine of her fornication.

So he carried me away in the spirit into the wilderness: and I saw a woman sit upon a scarlet coloured beast, full of names of blasphemy, having seven heads and ten horns.

And the woman was arrayed in purple and scarlet colour, and decked with gold and precious stones and pearls, having a golden cup in her hand full of abominations and filthiness of her fornication:

And upon her forehead was a name written, MYSTERY, BABYLON THE GREAT, THE MOTHER OF HARLOTS AND ABOMINATIONS OF THE EARTH. (Rev. 17: 1–5)

This passage, which immediately follows the pouring out of the vials, sheds light on the nature of Shelley's shape. The great whore rests upon the waters, as does the shape in the poem. She is clothed in colourful garments, and holds in her hand the cup of fornications. To drink of this cup incurs the wrath of divine judgement on those 'kings of the earth' who commit fornication with the woman (Rev. 18: 3). In Shelley's poem, drinking of the cup functions as the initiation into the Bacchanal in which kings appear as those in thrall to that other spectre, Life. Thus the substitution of the shape for the sun in the testimony of Rousseau links his destiny with those who attempted to eclipse the sun, the kings and popes discussed earlier.

Partaking of a sacramental cup of sorrow is not a new image in Shelley. However, in this particular case, the cup offered by the shape is consonant with that of the apocalyptic whore of Babylon. One eighteenth-century commentator on the enticements of the woman sitting upon the beast (Rev. 17: 4) emphasized the aphrodisiac quality of her cup:

the *Golden Cup* in her Hand is an allusion to Harlots, who with their Philters, or Inchanted Cups, do allure and provoke Men to sensual Satisfaction; in like manner doth *Rome* by her outward Splendor allure, and by other specious Pretences and Means draw Persons to her Idolatries and Superstitions.[41]

[41] William Burkitt, *Expository Notes, with Practical Observations, on the New Testament of our Lord and Saviour Jesus Christ*, 11th edn. (London, 1739), n. p.

Drinking of the cup is therefore linked with abandonment of rational faculties in favour of sensual ones. As the same commentator says concerning Revelation 13: 1, the seven heads of the beast—which the apocalyptist says are seven mountains (Rev. 17: 9)—suggest that the great whore is Rome, the city which rests on seven hills. The reference of St John, he continues, could be either to pagan Rome or to 'Papal' Rome. What is important for an understanding of the biblical text in relation to Shelley's poem is that the true light of the common sun (l. 338) has been distorted, as the apocalyptic woman clothed with the sun (Rev. 12: 1) gives way to the woman clothed in purple and scarlet (Rev. 17).

Critics of 'The Triumph of Life' have curiously avoided making the connection between the shape and the MYSTERY of Babylon in the Bible. Carlos Baker draws attention to the triumphal procession of Lucifera depicted in *The Faerie Queene* with a dragon at her feet (I. iv. 10), but without pursuing the image to its apocalyptic source.[42] Likewise, Bloom suggests a kinship between the shape and Blake's Rahab, the great whore of Revelation as she is interpreted in *Milton*, *The Four Zoas*, and *Jerusalem*, but does not refer to the apocalypse of St John.[43] P. H. Butter, on the other hand, protests against Bloom's suggestion that the shape may derive from Rahab or the Blakean harlot of Babylon, for he feels that her movements are exquisite and beautiful, even if potentially dangerous (p. 47). The biblical response to this would be that outward beauty can be deceptive; St Paul cautions that 'Satan himself is transformed into an angel of light' (2 Cor. 11: 14).

That Shelley may have been drawing on the book of Revelation indirectly is a possibility. In 1817, Coleridge published his second lay sermon, which featured in its introduction the 'Allegoric Vision', a brief narrative which shares with 'The Triumph of Life' an orientation in the apocalyptic imagery of St John.[44] The vision of the valley of Life in the earlier work answers in several respects to Shelley's poem about the triumph of Life. Like Shelley (l. 26), Coleridge sets his visionary experience in the Apennines.[45] The vision itself is related by Coleridge's travelling companion, a fellow pilgrim. The topography is as follows: 'I found myself in a vast plain, which I immediately knew to be the

[42] *Shelley's Major Poetry*, 260 n., 261 n.   [43] *Shelley's Mythmaking*, 271.

[44] See *A Lay Sermon*, in *Lay Sermons*, 115–230. The first lay sermon, *A Statesman's Manual* (1816), was read by Shelley in January 1817 (*JMS*, i. 98).

[45] Ibid. 132. The more obvious analogue is of course Petrarch's 'The Triumph of Death'.

VALLEY OF LIFE' (p. 134). At the entrance to the valley there is a huge building:

Every part of the building was crowded with tawdry ornaments and fantastic deformity. On every window was pourtrayed, in glaring and inelegant colors, some horrible tale, or preternatural incident, so that not a ray of light could enter, untinged by the medium through which it passed. The body of the building was full of people, some of them dancing, in and out, in unintelligible figures, with strange ceremonies and antic merriment, while others seemed convulsed with horror, or pining in mad melancholy. Intermingled with these, I observed a number of men, clothed in ceremonial robes, who appeared now to marshal the various groups . . . .

I stood for a while lost in wonder, what these things might mean; when lo! one of the Directors came up to me . . . . (p. 134)

The elements to note in this passage are the mass of figures (dancing, mourning, or convulsed), the perplexity of the visionary as to the meaning of the spectacle, and the emergence of the 'Director'. This attendant, who functions as the apocalyptic *angelus interpres*, is best understood in the light of Revelation 17. Here the angel explains to St John the significance of the woman clothed in different colours whose name is MYSTERY. Likewise, Coleridge's guide leads the visionary into a large hall, which he claims is the residence of the goddess Religion. Here he says, 'Read and believe: these are MYSTERIES!' (p. 135). Coleridge is unquestionably summoning up the apocalyptic MYSTERY that Englishmen from the time of Spenser had identified as the Roman Church. For him, the mysteries are a corollary of superstition (p. 135), who, like the blind charioteer in Shelley's poem (l. 94), is 'Janus-headed' (p. 137). In the cave of Superstition, an old man myopically scrutinizes the torso of Nature. However, just as the matronly form of true Religion provides an 'optic glass' by which to see beyond the valley of Life, so blindness is the condition of those in the cave. This failure of vision, the inability to see beyond the natural world, is equally a theme of 'The Triumph of Life'.

In Shelley's time, the interpreting angel was a familiar character in the writings of the apocalyptist Richard Brothers. Informed by God of the impending destruction of London (commercial Babylon) in 1791, Brothers is privileged with a series of visions which are explained by an 'attending Angel'.[46] Shelley too employs this device in 'The Triumph of Life', though not in the literal sense that Brothers does. Shelley's

[46] *A Revealed Knowledge*, i. 42–3; see also ii. 70. Cf. Dante's Virgil.

visionary interpreter Rousseau is already fictionalized in so far as he is
derived from the protagonist Saint-Preux of *Julie, ou la nouvelle
Héloïse.*[47] Saint-Preux is the tormented lover of an unobtainable woman
who increasingly attains the status of an ideal. In *Epipsychidion*, Shelley
also expresses the futility of the attempt to realize that ideal in earthly
life. Shelley's Rousseau is therefore best understood as an aspect of the
poem's speaker, a second self existing in a parallel universe entered
through visionary experience. Like Dante's Virgil, he is a literary ances-
tor. The interpreting angel in this case becomes a projection of the dic-
tum 'Know thyself'. As Henry Corbin has said of the Persian tradition
of the enlightened man: 'By the same inversion and reciprocity which
in Sufism makes the "heavenly Witness" simultaneously the one
Contemplated and the Contemplator, the man of light appears both as
the one guided and the guide.'[48] Such a reversal in 'The Triumph of
Life' marks Shelley's final poem as an inverted apocalypse.

Adonais, Hellas, and 'The Triumph of Life' all express the primacy of
thought as an eternally noetic perception, a perception that is attained
through self-knowledge. The result of this new insight is not so much a
reconciliation of subject and object as the subject's assimilating in itself
all objectivity. What Paul Hamilton says of sublimation in discussing
the relation of Coleridge to German thought seems equally relevant to
a consideration of this mature Shelley:

Immediacy of perception is sacrificed in the interests of a higher state of mental
organization. The poet, expressing this kind of experience, finds that the world
he is describing disappears as the mechanism of sublimation goes into action.
Wordsworth is a poet who constantly tries to retain a vivid sense of the natural
world which has inspired in him experiences which seem to reach beyond it.
These experiences demand a personal rhetoric, expressing an egotistical sub-
lime—the language of the expanding self.[49]

The discovery of the new personal identity as a divine afflatus, itself a
revelation, establishes the basis for reinterpreting with authority that
other 'definitive' revelation of the canonical Scriptures. Shelley's
'Gnostic' Assassins are exemplars of this revisionist impulse which sees
the conventional interpretation of the Bible and of Christ's teachings to
be flawed. Living as 'disembodied spirits', Shelley's Assassins have an
affinity both with the apocalyptists and with the Gnostics, two groups

---

[47] See Reiman, *Shelley's 'The Triumph of Life'*, 58–61.
[48] *The Man of Light in Iranian Sufism*, trans. N. Pearson (1971; Boulder, Colo., and
London, 1978), 15.
[49] *Coleridge's Poetics* (Oxford, 1983), 55.

whose rather striking resemblance to each other has been analysed in Kurt Rudolf's *Gnosis* (pp. 279–80). Although the Jewish apocalyptists did not denigrate the created world, as did the Gnostics, both proclaimed salvation to lie outside the world and history. The apocalyptist, however, ascended into the heavens, whereas the Gnostic ascended into the self. The one confessed his vision to come from God; the other professed his vision of the self *as* God, and went about the task of recreating the world according to the perception of the pneumatic Mind. Thus the *angelus interpres* of Shelley's vision is ultimately his own spiritual Self, his *fravashi*.[50] Biblical materials, like the material of the cosmos, are thus reformed, and their reinterpretation finds expression in the new revelation which is the corpus of Shelley's poetry.

---

[50] Guardian spirit, or *Doppelgänger* in Zoroastrian myth. See Curran, *Shelley's Annus Mirabilis*, 73–4.

Appendix: A Biblical Reference Guide
to Shelley's Poetry

The following list is not intended to be a compilation of biblical echoes and allusions, but rather a simple checklist of biblical glosses intended to illuminate in some way the Shelleyan literary corpus. In some instances, the affinity with the corresponding biblical gloss is essentially one of verbal resemblance; in others, Shelley is clearly inverting the sense of the biblical passage. Others still may be seen as quotations, paraphrases, allusions, or echoes, depending on how one defines these terms. I do not pretend to have produced an exhaustive list. And some of the associations I have indicated may be disputed. My intention has been to provide students of Shelley's poetry with a suggestive, rather than a definitive, listing of biblical references. For the sake of convenience, the text for all of the poems is that of *SPW* unless otherwise indicated. The text for the 'Esdaile' poems which appear in *SPW* is that of the Longman edition (*PS*). Shelley's poetry is here divided into three categories: (i) juvenilia, (ii) shorter poems, arranged chronologically by year, and (iii) longer poems, arranged alphabetically.

I. JUVENILIA

POEMS IN THE 'ESDAILE' NOTEBOOK *(PS):*

'The Crisis': (15) Isa. 9: 2; (19–20) Mal. 4: 2, 2 Pet. 1: 19.
'Passion: To the [Woody Nightshade]': (13–14) Matt. 10: 28.
'Falsehood and Vice: A Dialogue': (99–101) Mic. 3: 11, Zeph. 3: 4.
'On Leaving London for Wales': (61–2) Isa. 25: 4, Ps. 69: 33.
'To Liberty': (41) Jer. 51: 44; (42) Isa. 14: 5; (50) 2 Pet. 1: 19.
'On Robert Emmet's Tomb': (25) 2 Pet. 1: 19.
'A Tale of Society as it is: from facts, 1811': (8–9) Mark 12: 42; (34) 2 Tim. 4: 1; (36–7) Luke 2: 14; (60) 1 Sam. 8: 11–12.
'To the Republicans of North America': (20) Isa. 61: 1; (41)Mal. 4: 2, 2 Pet. 1: 19.
'Written at Cwm Elan': (6) 2 Pet. 1: 19.
'To Death': (1, 5) 1 Cor. 15: 55; (24) Rev. 6: 8.
'Death-spurning rocks!': (28) 2 Pet. 1: 19.
'To Harriet' ('It is not blasphemy to hope that Heaven'): (10) Rev. 10: 6; (22) Deut. 22: 9.

'Sonnet: To a Balloon, Laden with *Knowledge*': (9) Job 20: 19.

'Sonnet: On Waiting for a Wind': (1–2) Acts 2: 2.

'A Retrospect of Times of Old': (21) 1 Cor. 15: 54; (72–3) Exod. 32: 26–8, Num. 31: 17.

'The Voyage': (37) 2 Pet. 1: 19; (291) Ps. 101: 1; (292–5) Matt. 19: 16–24; (295) Matt. 4: 10; (298) Job 31: 6.

'A Dialogue': (26) John 14: 2.

'How eloquent are eyes!': (19) Rev. 10: 6; (22) Deut. 28: 49.

'To Mary'—I': (13) Luke 22: 42.

'Dares the llama': (3–4) Ps. 18: 33; (21) Rev. 7: 17; (35) Isa. 13: 13–14; (36) Job 2: 9.

'I will kneel at thine altar': (33–6) Isa. 14: 5, 12, 16.

'On an Icicle that clung to the grass of a grave': (15–17) 2 Pet. 1: 19.

'Henry and Louisa': (60–1) 2 Pet. 1: 19; (79) Eph. 6: 16, 17; (82) Eph. 6: 16; (95) Phil. 3: 14; (96) Jude 25; (164–5) Rev. 19: 17–18.

'A Translation of the Marseillaise Hymn': (11) Mal. 4: 2.

'Zeinab and Kathema': (37–8) John 14: 26; (40) Eph. 5: 6; (114) Ps. 91: 6.

'The Retrospect: Cwm Elan 1812': (3) Dan. 7: 9; (72) Job 13: 12; (73) Ps. 139: 9; (136–7) Job 24: 20; (164) Matt. 27: 29.

'The Wandering Jew's Soliloquy': (2) Ezek. 1: 15–21, Dan. 7: 9; (16) Ps. 91: 6; (18–20) 2 Kgs. 19: 35; (21–2) Num. 16: 32–3; (23–4) Gen. 3: 24; (26) Rom. 8: 29; (29) Luke 22: 42.

'Full many a mind with radiant genius fraught': (7) Matt. 7: 7.

'Margaret Nicholson' POEMS *(SPW, 861–8):*

'War': (17) Ps. 25: 1; (46) Isa. 2: 4; (61) Isa. 14: 5; (81–2) Isa. 1: 23.

'Despair': (8) John 14: 2.

'Fragment': (3) Job 13: 12.

'The Spectral Horseman': (27–8) Rev. 6: 2; (36) Rev. 12: 7; (47–52) Jude 6, Rev. 20: 10.

MISCELLANEOUS JUVENILE POEMS *(SPW, 868–83):*

'Love': (3) John 10: 28; (11–12) 2 Pet. 1: 19.

'To Ireland': (17) Rev. 6: 2.

'The Devil's Walk': (87) Gen. 4: 1–15; (104) Lev. 11: 7.

'Fragment from *The Wandering Jew*': (4) Jude 23.

Queen Mab (SPW, 762–800):

Canto I: (45) Ezek. 3: 12–13, Acts 2: 2; (59) Dan. 7: 9; (122–3) Luke 1: 30; (123–5) Rev. 3: 21; (145–56) Eccles. 12: 7; (167–9) Matt. 13: 11; (180–1) Matt. 27: 51; (215) Dan. 7: 9; (272–3) Job 24: 20, Isa. 14: 11.

Canto II: (38) Rev. 21: 21; (110) Isa. 34: 13; (129) Jer. 51: 44, 58; (130) Matt. 24: 2; (135–6) Isa. 13: 20; (141) Isa. 1: 17; (149–52) Num. 31: 14–18; (199–203) Ezek. 27: 27; (204) Ps. 62: 10; (227–9) Jas. 1: 11; (252–4) Matt. 4: 5, Luke 4: 9.

Canto III: (27–9) Job 29: 11–12; (30–3) 1 Sam. 8: 10–18; (39) Eccles. 2: 1; (44) Eccles. 2: 3; (46) Eccles. 2: 8; (71) Eccles. 2: 4; (89–90) Matt. 27: 29, Ezek. 19: 11; (118–22) 1 Sam. 8: 10–18; (122) Matt. 6: 11; (150) Job 24: 20; (169) Matt. 24: 35; (177–8) 1 Sam. 15: 22; (193–5) Eccles. 1: 4–5; (229) Mal. 3: 6.

Canto IV: (32–6) Rev. 6: 12–13; (46) Rev. 6: 8; (82–3) Matt. 3: 10; (88–9) Gen. 2; (117–18) Rom. 5: 12–13; (188–90) Ps. 91: 6; (196–9) Zeph. 3: 3, Mic. 7: 3; (214) Luke 16: 24–6; (215) Isa. 16: 24, Mark 9: 44–8; (227–8) Eccles. 1: 4; (237–9) Zeph. 3: 3–4; (260–1) Prov. 1: 12.

Canto V: (1–2) Eccles. 1: 4; (53–7) Job 36: 19, Ps. 62: 10; (60) Isa. 3: 15; (90) 1 John 2: 16; (166–9) 2 Pet. 1: 3–5; (235) Deut. 25: 15; (256–7) Isa. 2: 4.

Canto VI: (56–7) Rev. 3: 5; (61) 1 Cor. 15: 55; (80) Rom. 1: 21; (83–7) Rom. 1: 21–5; (111–13) Isa. 13: 10; (118–19) Num. 31: 14–18; (203) Jas. 1: 17; (216) Acts 10: 34.

Canto VII: (12–13) Ps. 14: 1; (28) Rom. 1: 25; (34) Job 3: 5; (43) Rom. 8: 22; (44–8) Hos. 6: 8–9; (60–1) Matt. 13: 11; (66) John 11: 43; (66–75) 1 Sam. 28: 14; (100–1) Exod. 2: 12; (106–11) Gen. 1–3; (117–19) Num. 31: 14–18; (134) Acts 2: 38; (135–6) Isa. 53: 4; (136–9) Matt. 27: 35–50; (141) Rom. 9: 21, 2 Tim. 2: 21; (148) Luke 16: 24–6; (156) Matt. 22: 14; (163–5) Phil. 2: 6–8; (165) Isa. 53: 3; (215–16) Matt. 10: 21, 35; (218) Rev. 19: 15; (234) Gen. 9: 13–17.

Canto VIII: (12) Matt. 27: 51; (22–3) John 3: 7–8, Rom. 11: 15; (48–9) Matt. 13: 11; (70–5) Isa. 35: 1; (79) Isa. 11: 6; (84–7) Isa. 11: 8; (124–6) Isa. 11: 6; (131) Isa. 25: 8; (231) Gal. 5: 17.

Canto IX: (112–13) Job 19: 26; (146) 2 Tim. 4: 7; (152–3) Ezek. 1: 14–16, Dan. 7: 9; (164) 1 Cor. 16: 13; (216) Dan. 7: 9.

St Irvyne POEMS *(SPW, 857–60):*

'Victoria': (10) Ps. 42: 6; (14) 1 Kgs. 19: 12.
'Sister Rosa': (74) Rom. 10: 13.

Victor and Cazire POEMS *(SPW, 843–56):*

'IV. Song': (9–10) 1 John 2: 16–17.
'V. Song': (21–4) 1 Tim. 6: 17.
'VI. Song': (12) Isa. 28: 4.
'St Edmond's Eve': (24) Matt. 3: 2–3; (88) John 17: 1; (112) Isa. 26: 19.
'Ghasta': (5–6) Joel 2: 10; (94) Mal. 4: 5.
'Fragment': (10) Ps. 42: 6; (14) 1 Kgs. 19: 12.

The Wandering Jew (PS, i. 38–83):

(274) Rev. 20: 7; (575) 1 Cor. 15: 52; (580) Matt. 27: 35; (592) Luke 24: 40,
John 20: 27; (594) John 19: 34; (598) Luke 23: 34; (599) Matt. 27: 45; (608)
Matt. 27: 51; (609) Matt. 27: 52; (641) Matt. 28: 6; (643) Matt. 27: 29; (644)
Luke 22: 44; (714) Ezek. 33: 28; (715) Ezek. 26: 4; (778) 2 Pet. 3: 10; (799)
Rev. 10: 6; (831) Rev. 19: 17–18; (943) Gen. 3: 1; (1049) Ps. 8: 4; (1444)
Gen. 4: 15; (1448) Jer. 8: 22.

II. SHORTER POEMS

EARLY POEMS *(SPW, 524–5):*

'A Summer Evening Churchyard': (19–21) Ps. 143: 3.
'OH! there are spirits of the air': (19–20) Matt. 7: 26.

POEMS WRITTEN IN 1816 *(SPW, 528–36):*

'Hymn to Intellectual Beauty': (1) Ps. 91: 1; (37) 1 Cor. 13: 13; (49) 1 Cor. 13:
11; (59–60) 1 Sam. 10: 6, Ezek. 11: 5; (61–2) Ps. 61: 5.
'Mont Blanc': (16–17) Rev. 22: 1, Job 38: 25, 29; (16–19) Isa. 64: 1, 3, 66: 1;
(41) Mark 5: 9; (52) Ps. 121: 1; (53) Acts 17: 23; (58–9) Job 7: 9; (67–74) Isa.
13: 20–2, Joel 2: 3; (85–6) Gen. 1: 28; (86–7) 1 Kgs. 19: 11–12, Rev. 8: 5;
(94–5) Eccles. 1: 4, 8, 3: 2; (114–15) Jer. 51: 37; (117–19) Jas. 4: 14, Ps. 103:
15–16; (120) Job 7: 10.
'Mont Blanc: Unadopted Passage': (1–2) Isa. 40: 3, Matt. 3: 3.

POEMS WRITTEN IN 1817 *(SPW, 536–52):*

'Marianne's Dream': (51–3) Jer. 49: 16, Obad. 4; (71–7) Gen. 19: 24–5; (81)
Gen. 6–9.
'To Constantia Singing': (14) Isa. 64: 1; (22) Ps. 17: 8.
'To the Lord Chancellor': (1–8) Mic. 3: 11, Zeph. 3: 3–5; (44) Matt. 7: 26;
(46–7) Mic. 3: 11; (64) Deut. 23: 5.
'To William Shelley': (25–6) Zeph. 1: 4; (31) Isa. 14: 5.
'Death': (1) Job 7: 9–10, 10: 21, Prov. 2: 18–19.
'Fragment: Satan Broken Loose': (1) Job 1: 6; (2) Rev. 20: 11–12; (6) Rev. 12: 7;
(7) Rev. 20: 7; (12) Ezek. 3: 13; (14–15) Rev. 4: 5.
'Fragment: *Igniculus Desiderii*': (1) Isa. 29: 8.
'Fragment: *Amor Aeternus*': (1–5) Matt. 6: 19–20.
'Lines to a Critic': (5–6) Matt. 6: 7.
'Ozymandias': (10–11) Exod. 1: 8–11, Rev. 17: 14; (12) Isa. 5: 14, 14: 11–17,
Ezek. 30: 18, 32: 12, 33: 28.

POEMS WRITTEN IN 1818 *(SPW, 552–71)*

'To the Nile': (12–14) Gen. 2: 17, Eccles. 1: 18.

'On a Faded Violet': (3) Isa. 40: 7, 8.

'Lines Written among the Euganean Hills': (26) Job 14: 13, 17: 13; (127) Isa. 23: 2, 6; (134–7) Isa. 19: 8; (142–6) Isa. 30: 25, 32: 14, 33: 18, Ezek. 26: 4; (174–8) Isa. 16: 2; (215) Isa. 16: 6, Jer. 48: 29; (227–30) Matt. 13: 30; (231) Gal. 6: 7; (232) Ezek. 35: 5–6; (238) Rom. 5: 12, 6: 23, Jas. 1: 15; (317) Gen. 27: 28.

'Song for "Tasso" ': (4) 1 Cor. 13: 11.

'Invocation to Misery': (41–2) Job 17: 13; (48–9) Jas. 4: 14.

'Marenghi': (3) Rom. 12: 17, 21, 1 Pet. 3: 9; (15–17) Matt. 26: 26–9, 1 Cor. 11: 17–34; (30) Jer. 51: 64; (135) Prov. 23: 7; (136–7) Matt. 3: 4.

'Sonnet: "Lift not the painted veil" ': (13–14) Eccles. 12: 10.

POEMS WRITTEN IN 1819 *(SPW, 571–88)*

'Song to the Men of England': (17) Lev. 26: 16, Mic. 6: 15; (18) Lam. 5: 2, Prov. 5: 10, Ps. 49: 10; (21) Lev. 26: 16, Mic. 6: 15; (22) Prov. 5: 10.

'Fragment: To the People of England': (2) Matt. 25: 26; (5) Deut. 28: 30.

'Fragment: "What Men Gain Fairly" ': (1) Prov. 28: 10; (2–3) Prov. 13: 22; (5–7) Ezek. 22: 12–13, Prov. 28: 8.

'A New National Anthem': (22–3) Ps. 9: 16, 10: 2, 141: 10; (36) Isa. 6: 5–7; (40–1) 1 Cor. 15: 52, 1 Thess. 4: 16.

'Sonnet: England in 1819': (1–6) Ezek. 22: 27; (7) Ezek. 7: 15; (9) Ps. 149: 6, Prov. 5: 4; (11) Isa. 29: 11, Rev. 5: 1; (13–14) Matt. 28: 6.

'An Ode: Omitted Stanza': (7) Matt. 10: 16.

'Ode to Heaven': (33–6) Rom. 8: 18, 1 Cor. 2: 9.

'Ode to the West Wind': (1) Ps. 61: 1; (1–7) Ps. 104: 3; (4–7) Zech. 6: 1–8; (10) 1 Cor. 15: 52; (11) Job 38: 27; (16–18) Job 36: 29, 37: 11; (28) Rev. 8: 7; (38) Gen. 8: 1, Exod. 14: 21, Job 38: 24–7; (51) Gen. 32: 24–30; (54) Job 10: 9, Ps. 22: 14, Matt. 27: 29; (58) Ps. 1: 3, Jer. 17: 8; (63–4) Ps. 1: 3–4, Isa. 1: 30; (64) Ps. 71: 20, John 3: 3; (67) Ezek. 2: 7; (68–9) Isa. 6: 7, 58: 1; (70) S. of S. 2: 11–13.

'The Indian Serenade': (1) S. of S. 3: 1–2; (19) S. of S. 1: 2.

'To Sophia': (1) S. of S. 1: 15–16, 4: 1, 7; (7) S. of S. 1: 15.

'To William Shelley' [second version]: (4) Job 24: 20.

'Fragment: Wedded Souls': (1–3) Ps. 139: 1–2.

'Fragment: Sufficient unto the Day': (1–2) Matt. 6: 34.

'Fragment: A Roman's Chamber': (9) Rev. 18: 2.

'Fragment: Rome and Nature': (1) Isa. 21: 9, Jer. 51: 8, Rev. 14: 8.

'A Ballad: [Young Parson Richards]', in William McTaggart, *England in 1819*, 9–10: (43–4) Matt. 15: 21–8; (47–8) Luke 16: 19–31.

POEMS WRITTEN IN 1820 *(SPW, 589–636)*

'The Sensitive Plant': (I. 9–11) Ps. 42: 1; (I. 21) S. of S. 2: 1; (I. 86) Isa. 18: 4;
(I. 94) Heb. 1: 13–14; (II. 2) Gen. 2–3; (II. 4) Ps. 147: 4; (II. 52) Matt. 4: 11,
Heb. 1: 13–14; (II. 54) 1 Cor. 15: 12; (III. 17) Gen. 3: 17; (III. 92–5) Dan. 7:
9; (III. 113) 1 Cor. 15: 52, 1 Thess. 4: 16.

'A Vision of the Sea': (4) Gen. 6–9; (52) Gen. 1: 5; (57–8) Exod. 16: 4; (113–14)
Matt. 24: 2.

'The Cloud': (5) Prov. 3: 20; (5–12) Job 38: 25–7, Ps. 77: 17–18; (68) Ps. 148: 8;
(69) Eph. 2: 2; (83–4) 1 Thess. 4: 16.

'To a Skylark': (15) Ps. 19: 5; (98–100) Prov. 3: 14, 8: 11; (101–2) Ps. 25: 5.

'Ode to Liberty': (5) Ps. 142: 7; (8) Prov. 23: 5; (11–12) Ezek. 1: 4, 15; (15)
Rev. 1: 10–19; (16–17) Gen. 1: 14–18; (21–5) Gen. 1: 2, Jer. 4: 23; (31–2)
Gen. 1: 26–8; (43–4) Ezek. 22: 26–7, Isa. 1: 18; (79) Mark 13: 31; (88–9)
Gen. 1: 2; (119) John 3: 14; (146) Mark 13: 31; (157) Rev. 6: 8; (204) Gen. 3;
(210) Isa. 32: 14; (225) Gen. 3: 15; (232–40) Rev. 20: 11–12; (233) Acts 17:
23; (241–3) Heb. 2: 9; (260) Ezek. 1: 4, Ps. 104: 3.

'The Two Spirits': (4) John 9: 4; (21–2) Matt. 16: 2–3.

'Ode to Naples': (21–2) Gen. 1: 2; (23) Acts 2: 2; (43) Isa. 1: 18; (50–1) 2 Pet. 1:
21; (71) 1 John 4: 8; (71–2) Eph. 6: 11–17, Rom. 13: 12; (112–13) Gen. 3: 15;
(122) Heb. 12: 1; (124) Phil. 3: 14; (137) Jer. 6: 1, 25: 26; (138) Gen. 1: 2;
(139) Jer. 5: 15; (149–51) Acts 17: 28.

'Death': (11) Gen. 3: 19, Ps. 103: 14.

'The Tower of Famine': (18–20) Isa. 3: 16–26.

'Sonnet: "Ye hasten to the grave!" ': (7) John 8:14; (12) Job 14: 13; (13–14)
Eccles. 9: 10.

'Fragment of a Satire on Satire': (3) Rev. 19: 20, 21: 8; (5) Rev. 20: 15; (6) Ps.
37: 11, Matt. 5: 5; (14) Matt. 3: 7; (37) Prov. 15: 1; (42–3) Jas. 3: 11.

'Orpheus': (118–19) Isa. 11: 6.

'Fragment: "The Viewless and Invisible Consequence" ': (1–2) Ps. 121: 8, Isa.
37: 28.

'Fragment: "*Pater Omnipotens*" ': (1–9) Rev. 4: 2–11.

'Fragment: "To the Mind of Man" ': (1) John 1: 4, 8: 12; (16–17) Gen. 2–9.

POEMS WRITTEN IN 1821 *(SPW, 636–64)*

'From the Arabic': (3) Ps. 42: 1; (12) Ps. 17: 8, 36: 7, 68: 13.

'Song: "RARELY, rarely. . ." ': (2–3) Ps. 51: 11–12; (5–6) Ps. 6: 6, 42: 3, 88: 1;
(10) Ps. 25: 18; (15) Ps. 116: 3–4; (16–17) Ps. 79: 11–12; (18) Ps. 119: 22; (25)
Ps. 139: 21; (38–9) Ps. 1: 1; (46) Ps. 18: 1; (47–8) Ps. 69: 18.

'Mutability': (1–2) Job 14: 2, Isa. 40: 7–8, 1 Pet. 1: 24, Jas. 1: 10, 11.

'Lines . . . Napoleon': (5) Isa. 14: 12.

'Sonnet: Political Greatness': (8–9) Rom. 1: 23.

'To Edward Williams' ('The Serpent is Shut Out from Paradise'): (1) Gen. 3: 14; (2) Isa. 13: 14–15, Prov. 6: 5; (16) Isa. 5: 20, Rom. 12: 21; (23) Isa. 13: 15; (31–2) Ps. 69: 20, Ezek. 7: 25; (42) Matt. 8: 20.

'Epithalamium': (25) S. of S. 2: 7.

'Fragment: Written for *Hellas*': (18–20) Rev. 8: 10; (31–2) Matt. 28: 2–6.

'Ginevra': (16–27) Isa. 3: 16–21; (161–2) Amos 8: 10.

'Music': (1–2) Ps. 42: 1.

'Sonnet to Byron': (5–6) Gen. 1: 1–2; (13–14) Ps. 148: 7–13.

'To-morrow': (1–6) Matt. 6: 34.

'Fragment: "I faint. . ."': (4) Ps. 22: 14.

'Fragment: The Lady of the South': (1) 2 Chr. 9: 1–20, 1 Kgs. 10: 1–13, 17, 21.

'Fragment: "When Soft Winds and Sunny Skies"': (4–7) Isa. 13: 14–15, Prov. 6: 5, Lam. 1: 6.

'Fragment: "Great Spirit"': (1) Ps. 104: 25.

'Fragment: "O Thou Immortal Deity"': (1–2) Ps. 45: 6.

'Fragment: The False Laurel and the True': (13) Job 14: 2, Isa. 40: 7–8, 1 Pet. 1: 24, Jas. 1: 10–11.

'Fragment: "I Stood. . ."': (1–2) Matt. 4: 5; (3–5) Ps. 22: 15, 143: 4.

POEMS WRITTEN IN 1822 *(SPW, 664–80)*

'The Magnetic Lady': (43–5) John 16: 16.

'Lines: "When the Lamp is Shattered"': (29–31) Obad. 4.

'To Jane: The Invitation': (40) Matt. 6: 34.

'To Jane: The Recollection': (57) Gen. 1: 6–9; (85) S. of S. 1: 15, 16, 4: 1, 7.

'The Pine Forest . . .': (23) S. of S. 4: 9–12; (24) S. of S. 2: 13.

'With a Guitar, to Jane': (38–9) Rom. 7: 24.

'Lines . . . Lerici': (33–5) Ps. 68: 17.

'Fragment: To the Moon': (4) 1 John 2: 15.

III. LONGER POEMS

Adonais (SPW, 430–45):

Section I (st. i–xvii): (11–12) Ps. 91: 5; (34–6) Acts 2: 30–1; (147–9) Ps. 103: 5; (151) Gen. 4: 12.

Section II (st. xviii–xxxviii): (154) Jer. 4: 31, 10: 19; (154–9) S. of S. 2: 11–13; (166–7) Gen. 1: 2; (178–9) Jer. 14: 12, Heb. 4: 12; (184) Job 7: 17, 18; (188–9) Eccles. 1: 4, 18; (238) Jer. 9: 11, 10: 22; (244–7) Isa. 34: 8–17; (253–5) Eccles. 1: 4, 5, 3: 21; (263) 1 Kgs. 19: 19, Job 2: 12; (305–6) Gen. 4: 15, Matt. 27: 29; (316–17) Ps. 58: 4–5; (318) Mark 14: 36; (331–3) Gen. 4: 12–15; (338) Eccles. 12: 7.

Section III (st. xxxix–lv): (356) Job 3: 5; (361) Rom. 6: 9; (397–414) Isa. 14: 9–10; (406–9) Rev. 3: 4–5; (410) Gen. 3: 22; (460) Mal. 3: 6, Jas. 1: 17; (477) Matt. 19: 6; (478–9) Acts 17: 28; (494–5) Dan. 12: 3.

Fragments: (5) Ezek. 3: 13; (29–33) Dan. 7: 9, Rev. 4: 2, 5.

Alastor (SPW, 14–31)

(110–11) Jer. 51: 58, Rev. 18: 2; (227–8) Rev. 12: 14; (280–1) Matt. 8: 20; (675–7) Matt. 26: 39, Luke 22: 42; (678) Rom. 9: 22.

The Cenci (SPW, 274–337)

Act I: (i. 36–7) 2 Cor. 5: 20; (i. 112) Rom. 8: 26; (i. 113) Luke 22: 44; (i. 114–15) Matt. 10: 28; (ii. 84–7) Ps. 139: 2; (iii. 12) Rom. 5: 12, 6: 1–2; (iii. 115–19) Ps. 6: 6.

Act II: (i. 4–5) Ps. 4: 8, 62: 2; (i. 46–8) 1 Tim. 2: 5; (i. 135) Rev. 18: 10; (i. 181) John 3: 19; (i. 183) Isa. 24: 23.

Act III: (i. 13) Lev. 16: 15; (i. 48) Jude 7; (i. 78) Rom. 6: 7; (i. 95) Lev. 17: 14; (i. 97) Deut. 12: 16; (i. 98) Rev. 1: 5; (i. 124–5) Matt. 7: 14, 27: 29; (i. 129) 1 Cor. 6: 19; (i. 158–60) Deut. 28: 37, 1 Kgs. 9: 7–8; (i. 215) Lev. 8: 34, Rom. 5: 11; (i. 234) Job 25: 6; (i. 283) Matt. 10: 35; (i. 286) Rom. 1: 26–30; (i. 319–20) Luke 15: 13; (i. 331–4) Lev. 16: 6; (i. 387–90) Rom. 12: 9–10; (ii. 1–2) Job 25: 4–6; (ii. 24) Rev. 20: 11–12; (ii. 92) Job 3: 3.

Act IV: (i. 91) 2 Kgs. 9: 10; (i. 98–9) Luke 16: 26; (i. 121) John 1: 9; (i. 143–4) Gen. 1: 28; (i. 151) 2 Pet. 3: 18; (i. 161–2) Acts 17: 31; (i. 173–4) Prov. 17: 12; (i. 185–6) Luke 15: 7; (i. 186–7) Luke 2: 14; (iii. 40–2) 1 Cor. 15: 54; (iii. 42) John 1: 4, John 8: 12; (iii. 58) 1 Cor. 15: 52; (iv. 21–4) Heb. 9: 27, Rev. 20: 11–12; (iv. 126) Jer. 12: 12; (iv. 142) John 1: 4, 8: 12; (iv. 160–2) Job 22: 29–30, Ps. 132: 15–16.

Act V: (ii. 67–8) 2 Cor. 4: 4, Heb. 1: 3; (iii. 32–3) Deut. 28: 37; (iii. 56) Heb. 9: 27; (iii. 66–7) Rom. 8: 26; (iii. 94–5) Matt. 10: 28; (iv. 37) Isa. 9: 4; (iv. 76–7) Luke 23: 43; (iv. 87–9) Ps. 118: 8; (iv. 106) Ps. 91: 6; (iv. 109) Gen. 4: 8; (iv. 134) John 8: 12; (iv. 148–9) Isa. 53: 12, Mark 15: 28; (iv. 151–2) Gen. 4: 15, Mark 15: 17.

Charles the First (SPW, 488–507)

Scene I: (12–14) Exod. 22: 22–3; (44) Matt. 7: 13; (56) Matt. 26: 47–9; (62–3) Rev. 17: 1–6; (64–5) Rev. 18: 3–6; (69) Rev. 2: 20; (69–70) 2 Kgs. 9: 36; (80) Lam. 2: 10; (93) Gen. 1: 26; (105) 2 Sam. 2: 23; (108) Exod. 2: 23; (114) Eph. 2: 3; (126) Prov. 12: 5; (131) Lev. 13: 45; (153) Gen. 41: 20, Ezek. 39: 4; (156–7) Matt. 6: 28–9.

Scene II: (5) Mark 15: 17; (75–6) Matt. 5: 26; (101) Ps. 64: 3; (127) Mark 14: 44–5; (130) Matt. 4: 5–6; (188) Rom. 15: 18; (221–2) Acts 1: 8; (223) Matt. 16: 19; (242) Matt. 5: 39; (245) 1 John 2: 2; (252–3) Matt. 10: 34; (254–5) Luke 22: 36; (326) Acts 3: 6; (351) Rom. 3: 15, Prov. 1: 16; (365) Isa. 14: 12–14; (408–9) Gen. 9: 14–15; (439–41) Matt. 21: 1–11; (465) Isa. 7: 14, Matt. 1: 21–3; (466) Isa. 9: 6–7, Rev. 19: 16.

Scene III: (26–7) Matt. 24: 9; (28) Rev. 21: 10; (31–2) Rom. 13: 1.

The Daemon of the World (SPW, 1–14)

Part I: (48) Acts 2: 2; (84) Luke 1: 30; (126) Dan. 7: 9; (184–5) Isa. 14: 11, Job 24: 20; (238) Rev. 21: 21; (239–41) Matt. 4: 8; (287–8) Matt. 4: 5; (291) Jas. 1: 17.

Part II: (306–8) John 16: 11, Jer. 28: 8; (339–40) Matt. 28: 18; (381–3) Isa. 11: 8; (536–7) Ezek. 1: 15–19, Dan. 7: 9; (547–8) Job 38: 17, Ps. 9: 13; (600) Dan. 7: 9.

Epipsychidion (SPW, 411–30)

(45) S. of S. 8: 1; (72–84) Prov. 5: 3–5, 7: 6–27; (123) Isa. 6: 5; (124–5) 1 Sam. 26: 10; (130) S. of S. 4: 9–12; (139–40) S. of S. 8: 6; (147) Prov. 8–9; (156–9) Eccles. 12: 5; (186–9) Isa. 35: 1, 51: 3; (199) 2 Cor. 4: 17; (200) Luke 9: 32, John 1: 14; (226) Dan. 7: 9–10, Rev. 4: 2, 5; (230–1) Luke 16: 26; (269) Prov. 31: 30; (270) Prov. 16: 24; (387) Gen. 2: 9, Ezek. 31: 9, 18; (393) Isa. 62: 5, Rev. 21: 2; (394) John 12: 23, 2 Pet. 1: 19; (397–402) S. of S. 8: 6; (405–6) Isa. 61: 1–2; (407) Isa. 26: 19; (459) Isa. 14: 12; (465) Ps. 77: 17–18; (491) S. of S. 1: 17; (492) S. of S. 4: 9; (496) 1 Pet. 2: 4; (539) Gen. 2: 7; (573–4) Gen. 2: 24, Matt. 19: 5–6; (583) Matt. 5: 18; (587–90) Isa. 6: 5; (596–7) Luke 6: 35; (599–604) Rom. 16; (602) 1 John 5: 2; (603) 2 Pet. 3: 17.

Fragments: (13–16) Eccles. 12: 5; (34–5) Matt. 5: 43–6; (65) Gen. 1: 2; (116) Prov. 9: 17; (117) Prov. 16: 21–2; (134–5) 1 Cor. 6: 19; (140–1) Rev. 6: 8; (179) Rom. 8: 38–9.

Fragments of an Unfinished Drama (SPW, 482–8)

(33) S. of S. 5: 1; (54–5) S. of S. 2: 3; (203) S. of S. 2: 1; (230–2) Gen. 1: 7.

Hellas (SPW, 446–82)

Prologue: (1–2) Job 1: 6; (43) Jer. 6: 1; (52–3) Matt. 27: 51; (68–9) Rev. 9: 9; (87–8) Luke 24: 39; (89) Matt. 27: 29; (107) Gen. 3: 15; (112–16) Gen. 1: 2; (119) Gen. 2: 7; (122–3) Mark 15: 17–19; (126–7) Job 1: 7, Eph. 2: 2; (138)

Isa. 43: 19; (138–9) Jer. 25: 24–6; (151–2) Luke 15: 7; (152) Job 38: 17; (154)
Isa. 14: 5; (160) Zech. 3: 2; (162) Isa. 14: 12–17; (163) John 16: 11; (174–5)
John 1: 1.

Drama: (46–8) Gen. 1: 2; (59) Isa. 40: 31; (80–1) Deut. 32: 11; (102–5) Ps. 139:
8; (111–13) S. of S. 2: 7; (128–9) Gen. 41: 8, Dan. 2: 3; (132–4) Gen. 41: 12,
Dan. 5: 10–12; (149–53) Matt. 16: 14; (160) Dan. 2: 22; (195–6) Dan. 2: 21;
(211) Acts 17: 23; (231) Matt. 2: 9; (237) Exod. 7: 20, Rev. 11: 6; (252–3) 2
Kgs. 20: 17; (257) Prov. 16: 16; (262) Isa. 18: 1; (264–5) Exod. 21: 17, Matt.
15: 4; (270) Jer. 25: 15, Rev. 16: 19; (287) Deut. 32: 42; (333) Eph. 4: 4–6;
(344–5) Matt. 2: 2–10; (355) Gen. 4: 10; (356) Ps. 37: 11; (434–5) Rev. 19:
17–18; (515–19) Rev. 19: 17–18; (598–9) Matt. 24: 30, 26: 64; (600–1) Acts
17: 28; (601–4) Joel 2: 10, Matt. 24: 29; (673) Job 38: 35; (682) Gen. 1: 3;
(720) Acts 2: 2; (728) 1 Kgs. 19: 12; (735) Acts 17: 23; (738–40) Matt. 26:
63–4, Acts 14: 15; (757) Gen. 41: 15, Dan. 5: 12, 16; (768) Mal. 3: 6, Jas. 1:
17; (772) Gen. 1: 6–8; (801–2) Matt. 6: 27; (803–4) Matt. 7: 7; (805) 1 Cor.
13: 12; (856) Heb. 12: 1, Jas. 1: 12; (939) Isa. 22: 13, 1 Cor. 15: 32; (1025)
Rev. 19: 17–18; (1029) Matt. 2: 9; (1057–8) Isa. 61: 1; (1084) Rev. 21: 2;
(1092) Mark 16: 6.

Julian and Maddalo (SPW, 189–204)

(7–9) Ezek. 26: 14, 47: 10; (81) Rev. 19: 20; (116–17) John 10: 12–14; (174–5)
Phil. 4: 8; (306) Acts 17: 28; (315–16) Job 14: 13; (341) Rom. 8: 26; (369) Job
14: 13; (436–8) Luke 22: 42; (472–3) Isa. 36: 5, Eph. 5: 6; (506–7) Job 7: 5,
Isa. 14: 11.

Fragment: (618) Job 13: 12.

Letter to Maria Gisborne (SPW, 363–70)

(1–2) Prov. 30: 28; (5) Job 25: 6; (28–9) Rom. 8: 12; (49–51) Gen. 4: 22; (174)
John 4: 14; (178–9) Isa. 14: 5; (180) Mark 5: 9; (200) Rev. 20: 11; (210) Matt.
5: 13.

The Mask of Anarchy (SPW, 338–45)

(2–4) Dan. 7: 2; (22) Rom. 13: 12; (30–3) Rev. 6: 8, 19: 13; (34) Rev. 6: 2;
(36–7) Rev. 19: 16; (42) Rev. 19: 14; (48–9) Rev. 18: 3; (61) Rev. 19: 16;
(62–3) 1 Cor. 1: 7; (71) Rev. 19: 16; (95) Ps. 22: 15; (165) Isa. 2: 4, Joel 3: 10;
(173–4) Luke 16: 19–21; (195–6) Matt. 5: 39–40; (197–200) Matt. 8: 20;
(203–4) Matt. 8: 20; (246–7) Luke 7: 45; (247–8) Matt. 19: 21; (258) Gal. 5:
22; (260) Jas. 1: 22–3, 1 John 3: 18; (282) Matt. 13: 25; (307–16) Ezek. 26:
9–11; (309–14) Nahum 3: 2–3; (319–20) Matt. 5: 39; (341–3) Matt. 5: 39.

Oedipus Tyrannus; or Swellfoot the Tyrant (SPW, 389–410)

Act I: (i. 33–6) Mic. 3: 2–3; (i. 55–6) Mark 5: 13; (i. 104) Matt. 6: 24; (i. 152–5) Isa. 7: 18; (i. 269–70) Matt. 16: 23, Mark 9: 44.
Act II: (i. 79) Isa. 40: 6; (ii. 9–10) Gen. 1: 11; (ii. 65) Acts 17: 23.

Peter Bell the Third (SPW, 346–63)

Prologue: (36) Jer. 18: 6, Rom. 9: 21; (38) Gen. 2–3.
Parts 1–7: (12) Job 2: 7; (16) Job 2: 11; (20) Rom. 8: 29–30, Eph. 1: 5, 11; (40) Job 3: 3; (47) Job 16: 9, Ps. 112: 10; (48) Job 4: 14–16; (61) Job 38: 1; (79) John 4: 24; (86) 1 Thess. 5: 2; (182) Isa. 3: 16; (314) Matt. 19: 12; (315) Matt. 9: 20, 14: 36; (390–1) John 3: 8; (392) Prov. 3: 20; (444) Jer. 18: 6; (458–9) Job 31: 35; (672) Luke 10: 7; (716) Col. 1: 5; (749) Gen. 1: 20–3.

Prince Athanase (SPW, 158–66)

(40–2) Luke 12: 42; (110) Col. 2: 8; (139) Prov. 23: 7; (195–7) Job 9: 9.

Prometheus Unbound (SPW, 204–74)

Act I: (20) Matt. 27: 35; (24–30) Matt. 27: 46; (31–3) John 19: 34; (36) Matt. 27: 39–40; (38–43) Isa. 29: 6, Matt. 27: 51; (49–51) Ps. 2: 12; (78–9) Exod. 7: 20–1, Rev. 8: 10–11; (102) Exod. 10: 21–3, Joel 2: 31, Matt. 27: 45, Acts 2: 20, Rev. 6: 12; (113–18) John 19: 26; (170) Exod. 8: 3; (172–3) Exod. 9: 3, 9, Rev. 18: 8; (179) Exod. 12: 29; (229–30) S. of S. 2: 7, John 19: 25; (276–7) Gen. 1: 2; (289–90) Matt. 27: 28–9; (303) Isa. 36: 5, Eph. 5: 6; (305) Deut. 23: 5; (310) Num. 16: 48, Rom. 14: 9; (345) Matt. 13: 42, 50; (378) Prov. 18: 12; (380–1) Isa. 5: 20; (430) Isa. 26: 3; (450) Prov. 23: 7; (474) Luke 22: 42; (539) Matt. 27: 51; (563) Matt. 8: 20, 27: 29; (564–5) Luke 22: 44; (574) Rom. 5: 21; (584–5) Matt. 27: 33–56; (598–9) Mark 15: 17, John 19: 2; (631) Luke 23: 34; (634) 1 John 4: 18, Jas. 4: 7; (638–40) Job 3: 21–2, 14: 13; (646–7) Rev. 9: 12; (652) Acts 2: 2; (691) Rev. 1: 11; (694–751) Rev. 8: 2–13; (708) Rev. 10: 1; (711) Rev. 6: 2; (716) Rev. 8: 9; (721–2) John 15: 13; (782) Rev. 6: 8; (787) Rev. 6: 8; (810) 1 Cor. 11: 25, Eph. 5: 23.
Act II: (i. 118) Job 4: 15; (i. 135) Jer. 1: 11–12; (ii. 28) S. of S. 2: 5; (ii. 37) Ezek. 3: 13; (ii. 93–5) Jude 6, Rev. 20: 3; (iii. 79) Mark 12: 32, Jas. 2: 19; (iii. 94) 2 Cor. 12: 9; (iii. 97) Rev. 12: 9; (iv. 9–10) Col. 1: 16–17; (iv. 32) Gen. 1: 1; (iv. 78–9) Matt. 14: 26; (iv. 87–90) Job 9: 7–9; (iv. 94–5) Gen. 4: 17, 10: 12; (iv. 112) Matt. 26: 64; (iv. 126–7) Rev. 21: 23, 22: 16; (iv. 160) S. of S. 1: 15; (v. 48) John 1: 4, 8: 12; (v. 110) Matt. 14: 26.
Act III: (i. 3) Rev. 19: 6; (i. 18–20) Ps. 2: 7; (i. 25–6) Rev. 14: 10; (i. 47–8) Dan. 7: 9; (i. 62) Jude 6; (i. 72) Rev. 12: 14; (i. 74–6) Rev. 19: 20, 20: 2–3; (ii.

38–9) Rev. 2: 28; (iii. 6) John 1: 4, 8: 12; (iii. 45) S. of S. 2: 14; (iii. 46) S. of S. 1: 15, 4: 1; (iii. 62) Matt. 27: 51; (iii. 80) 1 Thess. 4: 16; (iii. 105–7) 1 Cor. 15: 26; (iii. 113) Matt. 27: 51; (iv. 69–77) Eph. 4: 22–4; (iv. 95) Matt. 25: 7; (iv. 101) Rom. 12: 2; (iv. 117) Exod. 24: 4, Rev. 21: 14; (iv. 166) Isa. 14: 5; (iv. 190–2) Matt. 27: 51.

Act IV: (14) Rev. 10: 6; (133) Isa. 17: 12–13; (164–5) Rev. 21: 1; (171) 1 John 4: 18; (182–4) Job 36: 27–8; (219–28) Dan. 7: 9, Rev. 1: 14; (230–3) Ezek. 1: 19–21; (243) Ezek. 1: 16; (273) Rev. 21: 1; (274) Ezek. 1: 15–16; (276) Rev. 4: 5; (310) Job 40: 15–16; (313) Gen. 1: 28; (315–18) Gen. 1: 1, 7: 10; (350) Isa. 14: 12; (356–7) Job 37: 6, Isa. 55: 10, Rev. 7: 17; (406–11) Eph. 2: 3–6; (418) Ps. 135: 7; (436) Rev. 21: 20; (451) S. of S. 1: 2; (453) S. of S. 2: 3; (463) Rev. 21: 11; (466) S. of S. 1: 15, 4: 9; (467–8) S. of S. 2: 5; (471) S. of S. 5: 10–16; (476–80) S. of S. 8: 1–3; (489) Rev. 21: 20; (503) 1 Pet. 3: 21; (523) S. of S. 5: 2; (529–30) Col. 1: 16; (553) Matt. 24: 35; (554) Rev. 20: 1–3; (556) Ps. 68: 18; (557–62) Gal. 5: 22–3; (570–4) Rom. 5: 3–5, Gal. 5: 22–3; (572) 1 Sam. 15: 22; (573–4) Prov. 23: 7.

Fragments: (I. 221 ff. [cancelled stage direction]) Dan. 7: 9, Rev. 4: 2, 5; (I. 718) Isa. 14: 5, 61: 1; (II. iv. 29) Rom. 8: 26; (II. iv. 30) Luke 22: 44.

The Revolt of Islam (SPW, 31–158); Laon and Cythna (Jul. i. 239–408)

Dedication: (41) Eph. 6: 11–13; (76) Rom. 12: 17.

Canto I: (i. 8) Isa. 24: 18; (iii. 1) Acts 2: 2; (viii. 4) Rev. 12: 14; (xvi. 1) Rev. 12: 1–2; (xviii. 6) Rev. 12: 1–2; (xxvi. 5–6) Rev. 12: 7; (xxvi. 9) Rev. 8: 10; Gen. 4: 8; (xxvii. 8) Luke 10: 18; (xxvii. 9) Gen. 3: 1, 14; (xxviii. 4–6) Gen. 4: 14; (xxix. 1) Mark 5: 9; (xxix. 9) Rom. 14: 9; (xxxi. 2–6) Rev. 12: 7–17; (xxxiv. 6–9) Rev. 12: 12; (xxxv. 3) Luke 24: 39; (xli. 7–8) 2 Pet. 1: 19; (xliii. 1) Luke 1: 28; (xliv. 5) Dan. 6: 22.

Canto II: (xiii. 5–7) Ps. 72: 4; (xvii. 6–7) Eph. 4: 6; (xxxvi. 7–8) Matt. 15: 26; (xxxvi. 8–9) Mark 5: 5; (xlii. 1) Isa. 25: 11–12; (xlii. 6) Isa. 61: 1; (xlv. 1) Acts 17: 31; (xlv. 7) Gen. 22: 17.

Canto III: (v. 6) Mark 5: 9.

Canto IV: (xvi. 7–9) Isa. 62: 1–2; (xix. 9) Matt. 10: 16.

Canto V: (vi. 7–8) 2 Kgs. 19: 35; (viii. 1–2) 2 Kgs. 7: 7; (ix. 1) John 19: 34; (x. 8) John 8: 32; (xv. 4–6) Matt. 21: 9; (xix. 2) Heb. 7: 3; (xxiii. 1–6) Eccles. 4:13; (xxviii. 2) Isa. 14: 5; (xxxii. 1–2) Matt. 7: 2; (xxxii. 2) Gen. 4: 10; (xxxiii. 9) John 3: 3; (xxxiv. 1–2) John 8: 7; (xxxiv. 3) Prov. 20: 9; (xxxviii. 4) Rev. 11: 8; (xxxviii. 7–8) Matt. 27: 51; (xliv. 9) Exod. 34: 30–5; (xlix. 6–8) Isa. 9: 6, 14: 5; (l. 1–3) Isa. 11: 8; (l. 7–8) Gen. 3: 15; (li. [st. 2] 3) John 8: 12; (lvi. 9) Rev. 22: 1.

Canto VI: (vi. 9) Ezek. 28: 23; (viii. 1–2) Rev. 19: 17–18; (xii. 6–8) Josh. 10: 12–13; (xix. 3–4) Rev. 6: 5; (xix. 6) Rev. 19: 11–16; (xxx. 1) Titus 1: 15; (xlii. 1–2) Rev. 1: 15; (xlix. 1) Ezek. 6: 11; (l. 8) Jer. 27: 13; (lii. 2–3) Isa. 22: 13.

Canto VII: (iv. 6–9) 1 Sam. 19: 9; (xxxviii. 4) Gen. 6–9; (xl. 1) Gen. 1: 2.

Canto VIII: (vi. 1–5) Acts 17: 22–9; (vi. 4) Rom. 1: 23; (vii. 7–8) 1 Cor. 15: 56; (viii. 1) Acts 17: 31; (viii. 3–4) Isa. 66: 24; (x. 3–4) Gal. 5: 19–21; (xii. 7–9) 1 Cor. 13: 13; (xiii. 1–2) Eph. 6: 1; (xiii. 3) Eph. 4: 6; (xiv. 1–2) Job 31: 24, 28; (xviii. 6–8) Isa. 1: 15–18; (xxi–xxii) Prov. 10: 12; (xxviii. 1–9) Matt. 27: 45, 51–2.

Canto IX: (v. 6–7) Mal. 4: 1, 2 Pet. 3: 12; (viii. 1–3) John 10: 20, Matt. 28: 6; (viii. 7) Matt. 18: 11; (viii. 8–9) Isa. 53: 6; (xiv. 1) Matt. 26: 60; (xv. 1) Rom. 3: 13; (xv. 9) John 16: 33; (xvii. 1) Lam. 4: 1; (xxvi. 4–5) Luke 17: 21; (xxvii. 1) Eph. 1: 14; (xxvii. 4) Matt. 3: 11; (xxx. 3) Acts 17: 28; (xxxvi. 6) Acts 1: 11.

Canto X: (iv. 6) Rev. 19: 19; (x. 3–4) Rev. 6: 2, 5; (xi. 7–8) Ezek. 28: 23; (xiii. 8–9) Jer. 8: 2, Ezek. 39: 11–12; (xv. 1–5) Hos. 4: 3; (xx. 3–4) Ezek. 28: 23; (xxvi. 4–5) Rev. 9: 6; (xxvi. 5) Luke 6: 39; (xxvii. 1–2) Jer. 49: 16; (xxvii. 5–6) Gen. 3: 19; (xxx. 2) Rom. 1: 25; (xxxv. 1–3) Joel 2: 1, Matt. 12: 36; (xxxvi. 2, 5) Ps. 91: 6; (xxxvi. 8) Job 38: 17; (xl. 4–6) Rev. 4: 1–5.

Canto XI: (xvii. 1–2) Prov. 3: 13–14; (xxiii. 7) Gen. 22: 17.

Canto XII: (ix. 1–2) Matt. 13: 41–2; (xii. 5–6) Rev. 20: 11–12; (xv. 6–7) Matt. 27: 51; (xv. 7) Rom. 14: 9; (xxix. 9) 2 Pet. 1: 19; (xxxi. 1–3) Rev. 20: 11–12; (xxxviii. 4–6) Rev. 21: 1, 23.

Rosalind and Helen (SPW, 167–89)

(284) Ps. 19: 2; (285) John 1: 4, Acts 17: 25; (443) Matt. 15: 26; (553–4) Phil. 4: 8; (656) Mic. 6: 15; (657–8) Matt. 19: 22–4; (690) Matt. 5: 44; (727) Prov. 13: 12; (775–7) Ezek. 27: 31; (834) Job 41: 21; (900–1) Isa. 14: 5; (1129–30) Matt. 26: 39, Luke 22: 42; (1187) 1 Kgs. 19: 4, Job 7: 15.

The Triumph of Life (SPP, 455–70)

(1–3) Ps. 19; (19–20) Gen. 3: 19; (27–30) Rev. 4: 1–2; (43–5) Matt. 13: 3–23; (86–7) Ezek. 1: 4, 3: 13; (96–7) Ezek. 1: 13–14; (98) Ezek. 1: 24; (99) Ezek. 1: 6; (100) Ezek. 1: 18; (104) Rev. 1: 8; (132–3) Ezek. 21: 26; (173) Gen. 3: 19; (179–80) Rev. 5: 2; (289) 1 Tim. 2: 5; (292–3) Rev. 6: 8; (296) Job 1: 7; (357) Rev. 17: 4–5; (358) Rev. 4: 6, 17: 4; (372) Rev. 21: 20; (388) Ps. 22: 15; (472–4) Eph. 4: 9–10; (476) 1 Cor. 13: 8; (489) Exod. 19: 4; (525–6) Hos. 13: 8; (542–4) Jas. 4: 14.

The Witch of Atlas (SPW, 371–89)

(87–8) John 12: 32, Matt. 2: 11; (89–104) Gen. 2: 19–20; (93) Isa. 11: 6–9; (170) Gen. 2: 9; (237) Heb. 12: 1; (314–15) Gen. 2: 7; (325–6) Gen. 1: 27, 2: 7; (459–60) Matt. 26: 53, Heb. 1: 13–14, Rev. 19: 14; (511) Isa. 11: 6; (546–50) Matt. 8: 24–6; (570–1) 1 Sam. 16: 7, Ps. 44: 21; (606–8) Rev. 20: 14; (619) Isa. 40: 4; (645) Isa. 2: 4; (646) Isa. 61: 1; (661–4) Matt. 5: 22–4.

Bibliography

ABBEY, LLOYD, *Destroyer and Preserver: Shelley's Poetic Skepticism* (Lincoln, Nebr., and London: University of Nebraska Press, 1979).

ABRAMS, MEYER H., 'Apocalypse: Theme and Romantic Variations', in *The Correspondent Breeze: Essays on English Romanticism* (New York: Norton, 1984), 225–57.

—— 'The Correspondent Breeze: A Romantic Metaphor', *Kenyon Review*, 19 (1957), 113–30; rev. repr. in M. H. Abrams, ed., *English Romantic Poets: Modern Essays in Criticism* (1960; New York: Oxford University Press, 1973), 37–54.

—— 'English Romanticism: The Spirit of the Age', in Northrop Frye, ed., *Romanticism Reconsidered: Selected Papers from the English Institute* (New York: Columbia University Press, 1963), 26–72.

—— *The Mirror and the Lamp: Romantic Theory and the Critical Tradition* (1953; New York and Oxford: Oxford University Press, 1976).

—— *Natural Supernaturalism: Tradition and Revolution in Romantic Literature* (1971; New York: Norton, 1973).

Aeschylus, trans. H. W. Smyth (2 vols.; Loeb Classical Library; London: William Heinemann, 1922, 1926).

ALLSUP, JAMES O., *The Magic Circle: A Study of Shelley's Concept of Love* (Port Washington, NY: Kennikat, 1976).

ANDERSON, GEORGE K., 'Ahasuerus in the Romantic Heyday', in *The Legend of the Wandering Jew* (Providence, RI: Brown University Press, 1965), 174–211.

ANON., 'A Help to the Reading of the Holy Scriptures', in *The New Whole Duty of Man, containing the Faith as well as Practice of a Christian* (1741; London, c.1762), 521–61.

ARNOLD, MATTHEW, *The Complete Prose Works of Matthew Arnold*, ed. R. H. Super (11 vols.; Ann Arbor, Mich.: University of Michigan Press, 1960–77).

AUERBACH, ERICH, *Mimesis: The Representation of Reality in Western Literature* (1946), trans. Willard Trask (1953; Garden City, NY: Anchor, Doubleday, 1957).

AUGUSTINE, *St. Augustine's Confessions*, trans. William Watts (1631) (2 vols.; Loeb Classical Library, 1912; London: William Heinemann, 1977, 1979).

BACON, FRANCIS, *Of the Wisdom of the Ancients* (1609), trans. James Spedding, in *The Works of Francis Bacon*, ed. James Spedding, Robert Leslie Ellis, and Douglas Denon Heath (14 vols.; London: Longman, 1857–74), vi. 689–764.

BAKER, CARLOS, *Shelley's Major Poetry: The Fabric of a Vision* (1948; Princeton, NJ: Princeton University Press, 1973).

BARCUS, JAMES (ed.), *Shelley: The Critical Heritage* (London: Routledge and Kegan Paul, 1975).

BARNARD, ELLSWORTH, *Shelley's Religion* (Minneapolis, Minn.: University of Minnesota Press, 1937).

BARRELL, JOSEPH, *Shelley and the Thought of his Time: A Study in the History of Ideas* (New Haven, Conn.: Yale University Press, 1947).

BARRUEL, ABBÉ AUGUSTIN, *Memoirs Illustrating the History of Jacobinism*, trans. anon. [R. Clifford] (4 vols.; London, 1797–8).

BATE, WALTER JACKSON, *The Burden of the Past and the English Poet* (London: Chatto and Windus, 1971).

—— *From Classic to Romantic: Premises of Taste in Eighteenth-Century England* (1946; New York: Harper and Row, 1961).

BECKER, CARL, *The Heavenly City of the Eighteenth-Century Philosophers* (1932; New Haven, Conn.: Yale University Press, 1967).

BICHENO, J., *The Restoration of the Jews, the Crisis of all Nations; or, An Arrangement of the Scripture Prophecies, which Relate to the Restoration of the Jews* (London, 1800).

BLACKWELL, THOMAS, *Letters concerning Mythology* (London, 1748).

BLAIR, HUGH, 'The Poetry of the Hebrews', in *Lectures on Rhetoric and Belles Lettres* (2 vols.; London, 1783), ii. 385–405.

BLAKE, WILLIAM, *Blake: Complete Writings*, ed. Geoffrey Keynes (1966; London: Oxford University Press, 1971).

BLOOM, HAROLD, *Agon: Towards a Theory of Revisionism* (1982; New York and Oxford: Oxford University Press, 1983).

—— *The Anxiety of Influence: A Theory of Poetry* (New York: Oxford University Press, 1973).

—— '*Coleridge*: The Anxiety of Influence', in *Figures of Capable Imagination* (New York: Seabury Press, 1976), 1–17.

—— *Kabbalah and Criticism* (New York: Continuum, Seabury Press, 1975).

—— *A Map of Misreading* (1975; New York and Oxford: Oxford University Press, 1980).

—— 'Percy Bysshe Shelley', in *The Visionary Company: A Reading of English Romantic Poetry*, rev. edn. (1961; Ithaca, NY: Cornell University Press, 1971), 282–362.

—— *Poetry and Repression: Revisionism from Blake to Stevens* (New Haven, Conn., and London: Yale University Press, 1976).

—— *Shelley's Mythmaking* (1959; Ithaca, NY: Cornell University Press, 1969).

BODKIN, MAUD, *Archetypal Patterns in Poetry: Psychological Studies of Imagination* (1934; London: Oxford University Press, 1963).

The Book of Common Prayer (London, 1638, 1811).

BRADLAUGH, CHARLES, *Jesus, Shelley, and Malthus; or Pious Poverty and Heterodox Happiness* (London, 1878).

BRAILSFORD, HENRY NOEL, *Shelley, Godwin, and their Circle* (1913; London: Oxford University Press, 1942).

BRANDT, HEINZ, 'Der Protest Shelleys in den Symbolen', in *Das protestierende Element in der Dichtung Shelleys* (Wrocław: Verlag Priebatch's Buchhandlung, 1934), 43–51.

BRAUN, HERBERT, '*ποιέω*', in *Theological Dictionary of the New Testament*, ed. Gerhard Kittel and Gerhard Friedrich, trans. G. W. Bromiley (10 vols.; Grand Rapids, Mich.: Eerdmans, 1964–76), vi. 458–84.

BREW, CLAUDE, 'A New Shelley Text: Essay on Miracles and Christian Doctrine', *K–SMB*, no. 28 (1977), 10–28.

BRISMAN, LESLIE, 'Mysterious Tongue: Shelley and the Language of Christianity', *Texas Studies in Literature and Language*, 23/3 (1981), 389–417.

BROMBERT, VICTOR, 'The Happy Prison: A Recurring Romantic Metaphor', in David Thorburn and Geoffrey Hartman, eds., *Romanticism: Vistas, Instances, Continuities* (Ithaca, NY: Cornell University Press, 1973), 62–79.

BROTHERS, RICHARD, *A Revealed Knowledge, of the Prophecies and Times* (2 pts.; London, 1794).

BROWNELL, MORRIS, '"Struck" and "Stricken Deer": An Image in Pope and Cowper', *Notes and Queries*, NS 25 (1978), 62–4.

BROWNING, ROBERT, 'Essay on Shelley' (1852), ed. Donald Smalley, in *The Complete Works of Robert Browning*, ed. Roma King and Jack Herring (8 vols.; Athens, Oh., and Waco, Tex.: Ohio University Press and Baylor University, 1969–89), v. 135–51.

BRYANT, JACOB, *A New System, or, An Analysis of Ancient Mythology: Wherein an Attempt is Made to Divest Tradition of Fable; and to Reduce the Truth to its Original Purity*, 2nd edn. (3 vols.; London, 1775–6).

—— *Observations upon the Plagues Inflicted upon the Egyptians, in which is Shown the Peculiarity of those Judgments, and their Correspondence with the Rites and Idolatry of that People* (London, 1794).

BULTMANN, RUDOLF, *Gnosis* (1933), trans. J. R. Coates (London: A. and C. Black, 1952).

BURKITT, WILLIAM, *Expository Notes, with Practical Observations, on The New Testament of our Lord and Saviour Jesus Christ*, 11th edn. (London, 1739).

BURTON, E. H., and POLLEN, J. H. (eds.), 'Venerable Edward Shelley, Layman', in *Lives of the English Martyrs*, 2nd ser. (London: Longman, 1914), i. 416–21.

BURWICK, FREDERICK, 'The Language of Causality in *Prometheus Unbound*', *K–SJ*, 31 (1982), 136–58.

BUTLER, JOSEPH, *The Analogy of Religion, Natural and Revealed* (1736; London: Dent, 1906).

BUTLER, MARILYN, 'The Cult of the South: The Shelley Circle, its Creed and its Influence', in *Romantics, Rebels, and Reactionaries: English Literature and its Background, 1760–1830* (Oxford: Oxford University Press, 1981), 113–37.

—— 'Myth and Mythmaking in the Shelley Circle', *Journal of English Literary History*, 49 (1982), 50–72.

BUTTER, PETER H., *Shelley's Idols of the Cave* (Edinburgh: Edinburgh University Press, 1954).

BUTTER, PETER H., 'Sun and Shape in Shelley's *The Triumph of Life*', *Review of English Studies*, NS 13 (1962), 40–51.

BYRON, LORD, *Byron's Letters and Journals*, ed. Leslie Marchand (12 vols.; Cambridge, Mass.: Belknap, Harvard University Press, 1973–82).

—— *Lord Byron: The Complete Poetical Works*, ed. Jerome J. McGann (5 vols. to date; Oxford: Clarendon Press, 1980–6).

—— *Lord Byron's Cain*, ed. Truman Guy Steffan (Austin, Tex., and London: University of Texas Press, 1968).

CAIRD, G. B., *The Language and Imagery of the Bible* (London: Duckworth, 1980).

CALDERÓN DE LA BARCA, PEDRO, *El Magico Prodigioso* (1635), 2nd edn. (Zaragoza: Biblioteca Clasica Ebro, 1966).

CALVIN, JOHN, *Institutes of the Christian Religion* (1536), trans. F. L. Battles, ed. J. T. McNeill (2 vols.; Philadelphia: Westminster Press, 1960).

CAMERON, KENNETH NEIL (ed.), *The Esdaile Notebook: A Volume of Early Poems by Percy Bysshe Shelley* (London: Faber and Faber, 1964).

—— 'A Major Source of *The Revolt of Islam*', *PMLA*, 56 (1941), 175–206.

—— 'The Planet-Tempest Passage in *Epipsychidion*', *PMLA*, 63 (1948), 950–72; repr. in *SPP*, 637–58.

—— 'The Political Symbolism of *Prometheus Unbound*', *PMLA*, 58 (1943), 728–53.

—— Review of *Il pensiero religioso di Shelley, con particolare riferimento alla 'Necessity of Atheism' et al 'Triumph of Life'*, Bice Chiapelli, *Modern Philology*, 55 (1957), 62–3.

—— 'Shelley and *Ahrimanes*', *Modern Language Quarterly*, 3 (1942), 287–95.

—— *The Young Shelley: Genesis of a Radical* (London: Victor Gollancz, 1951).

CAMPBELL, GEORGE, 'Proper Terms', in *The Philosophy of Rhetoric* (2 vols.; London, 1776), ii. 159–75.

CAMPBELL, LILY, 'The Christian Muse', *Huntington Library Bulletin*, no. 8 (1935), 29–70.

CANTOR, PAUL, *Creature and Creator: Myth-Making and English Romanticism* (Cambridge: Cambridge University Press, 1984).

CHERNAIK, JUDITH, *The Lyrics of Shelley* (Cleveland: Case Western Reserve University Press, 1972).

—— and BURNETT, TIMOTHY, 'The Byron and Shelley Notebooks in the Scrope Davies Find', *Review of English Studies*, NS 29/113 (1978), 36–49.

Choice Emblems, Natural, Historical, Fabulous, Moral, and Divine (London, 1788).

CLARK, DAVID LEE, 'Shelley's Biblical Extracts', *Modern Language Notes*, 66 (1951), 435–41.

CLARK, TIMOTHY, *Embodying Revolution: The Figure of the Poet in Shelley* (Oxford: Clarendon Press, 1989).

CLEMENTS, R. E., *Prophecy and Tradition* (1975; Oxford: Basil Blackwell, 1978).

CLUBBE, JOHN, and LOVELL, ERNEST, jun., 'Shelley: The Growth of a Moral Vision', in *English Romanticism: The Grounds of Belief* (London: Macmillan, 1983), 115–30.

COHN, NORMAN, *The Pursuit of the Millennium: Revolutionary Millennarians and Mystical Anarchists of the Middle Ages* (1957; London: Paladin, 1972).

COLERIDGE, JOHN TAYLOR, Review of *Laon and Cythna* and *The Revolt of Islam*, Percy Bysshe Shelley, *Quarterly Review*, 21 (1819), 460–71.

COLERIDGE, SAMUEL TAYLOR, *Biographia Literaria; or Biographical Sketches of My Literary Life and Opinions* (1817), ed. James Engell and Walter Jackson Bate (2 vols.; 1983; Princeton, NJ, and London: Princeton University Press and Routledge and Kegan Paul, 1984); *The Collected Works of Samuel Taylor Coleridge*, vol. vii, ed. Kathleen Coburn.

—— *Confessions of an Inquiring Spirit*, ed. Henry Nelson Coleridge (London, 1840).

—— *Lay Sermons* (1816–17), ed. R. J. White (Princeton, NJ, and London: Princeton University Press and Routledge and Kegan Paul, 1972); *The Collected Works of Samuel Taylor Coleridge*, vol. vi, ed. Kathleen Coburn.

—— *The Poetical Works of Samuel Taylor Coleridge*, ed. E. H. Coleridge (London: Oxford University Press, 1912).

COLLINS, JOHN J., 'Apocalyptic Eschatology as the Transcendence of Death', *Catholic Biblical Quarterly*, 36 (1974), 21–43; repr. in Paul D. Hanson, ed., *Visionaries and their Apocalypses* (London: SPCK, 1983), 61–84.

COLPE, CARSTEN, 'The Challenge of Gnostic Thought for Philosophy, Alchemy, and Literature', in Bentley Layton, ed., *The Rediscovery of Gnosticism: The School of Valentinus* (Leiden: Brill, 1980), 32–56.

CONDORCET, JEAN ANTOINE NICOLAS DE CARITAT, MARQUIS DE, *Outlines of an Historical View of the Progress of the Human Mind*, trans. anon. (London, 1795).

CORBIN, HENRY, *The Man of Light in Iranian Sufism*, trans. Nancy Pearson (1971; Boulder, Colo., and London: Shambhala, 1978).

CORNELIUS, R. M., *Christopher Marlowe's Use of the Bible* (New York: Lang, 1984).

COWPER, WILLIAM, *Cowper: Poetical Works*, ed. H. S. Milford, 4th edn., rev. N. Russell (1934; London: Oxford University Press, 1967).

CRONIN, RICHARD, *Shelley's Poetic Thoughts* (London: Macmillan, 1981).

CURRAN, STUART, 'Percy Bysshe Shelley', in Frank Jordan, ed., *The English Romantic Poets: A Review of Research and Criticism*, 4th edn. (New York: Modern Language Association, 1985), 593–663.

—— *Shelley's Annus Mirabilis: The Maturing of an Epic Vision* (San Marino, Calif.: Huntington Library, 1975).

—— *Shelley's Cenci: Scorpions Ringed with Fire* (Princeton, NJ: Princeton University Press, 1970).

'Current Bibliography', *K–SJ*, 1952– .

CURTIUS, ERNST ROBERT, 'Poetry and Theology', in Willard Trask, trans., *European Literature and the Latin Middle Ages* (1948) (1953; New York: Harper and Row, 1963), 214–27.

DAICHES, DAVID, *The King James Version of the English Bible; an Account of the Development and Sources of the English Bible of 1611 with Special Reference to the Hebrew Tradition* (Chicago: University of Chicago Press, 1941).

DANTE ALIGHIERI, *Dante's* Vita Nuova, trans. Mark Musa (Bloomington, Ind.: Indiana University Press, 1973).

DARWIN, ERASMUS, *The Temple of Nature; or The Origin of Society: A Poem with Philosophical Notes* (London, 1803).

DAWSON, P. M. S., *The Unacknowledged Legislator: Shelley and Politics* (Oxford: Clarendon Press, 1980).

DIXON, RICHARD WATSON, *History of the Church of England from the Abolition of the Roman Jurisdiction* (6 vols.; Oxford: Clarendon Press, 1902).

DODD, C. H., *The Authority of the Bible* (1929; Glasgow: Fount, Collins, 1978).

—— *The Parables of the Kingdom*, rev. edn. (1961; Glasgow: Fount, Collins, 1980).

DONOVAN, JOHN, 'Incest in *Laon and Cythna*: Nature, Custom, Desire', *K–SR*, no. 2 (1987), 45–90.

DROOP, ADOLF, 'Die Bibel', in *Die Belesenheit Percy Bysshe Shelley's nach den direkten Zeugnissen und den bisherigen Forschungen* (Weimar: R. Wagner Sohn, 1906), 7–12.

DRUMMOND, SIR WILLIAM, *Academical Questions* (London, 1805).

—— *The Oedipus Judaicus* (London, 1811).

DUFFY, EDWARD, 'Shelley, the Trinity, and the Enlightenment', *English Language Notes*, 19 (1981), 41–4.

DUNBAR, CLEMENT, *A Bibliography of Shelley Studies: 1823–1950* (New York: Garland, 1976).

EATON, DANIEL ISAAC (ed.), *Trial of Mr Daniel Isaac Eaton, for Publishing the Third and Last Part of Paine's* Age of Reason; *before Lord Ellenborough in the Court of the King's Bench, Guildhall, March 6, 1812* (London, 1812).

EIGELDINGER, MARC, 'L'Amour et le pays des chimères', in *Jean-Jacques Rousseau et la réalité de l'imaginaire* (Neuchâtel: Baconnière, 1962), 85–108.

ELIADE, MIRCEA, *Images and Symbols: Studies in Religious Symbolism* (1952), trans. Philip Mairet (London: Harvill, 1961).

—— *The Myth of the Eternal Return, or Cosmos and History* (1949), trans. Willard R. Trask (1954; Princeton, NJ: Princeton University Press, 1974).

ELLIS, F. S., *A Lexical Concordance to the Poetical Works of Percy Bysshe Shelley* (London, 1892).

ENGELL, JAMES, *The Creative Imagination: Enlightenment to Romanticism* (Cambridge, Mass.: Harvard University Press, 1981).

ERKELENZ, MICHAEL, 'Shelley's Draft of "Mont Blanc" and the Conflict of "Faith"', *Review of English Studies*, NS 40 (1989), 100–3.

EVANS, FRANK B. III, 'Shelley, Godwin, Hume, and the Doctrine of Necessity', *Studies in Philology*, 37 (1940), 632–40.

The Examiner, ed. Leigh Hunt (London, 1808–21).

FALCONET M., 'Dissertation sur les Assassins, peuple d'Asie', *Mémoires de littérature tirés des registres de l'Académie royale des inscriptions et belles-lettres*, 17 (1751), 127–70.

FERGUSON, GEORGE, *Signs and Symbols in Christian Art* (1954; Oxford: Oxford University Press, 1980).

FILORAMO, GIOVANNI, *A History of Gnosticism*, trans. Anthony Alcock (Oxford: Basil Blackwell, 1990).

FLEMING, ROBERT, *Apocalyptical Key: An Extraordinary Discourse on the Rise and Fall of Papacy; or the Pouring out of the Vials, in the Revelation of St. John, chap. XVI* (1701; London, 1809).

FOGLE, RICHARD H., *The Imagery of Keats and Shelley: A Comparative Study* (Chapel Hill, NC: University of North Carolina Press, 1949).

FOOT, PAUL, *Red Shelley* (London: Sidgwick and Jackson, 1980).

FREIMARCK, VINCENT, 'The Bible and Neo-Classical Views of Style', *Journal of English and Germanic Philology*, 51 (1952), 507–26.

—— 'The Bible in Eighteenth-Century English Criticism' (Ph. D. diss., Cornell University, 1950).

FRYE, NORTHROP, *Fearful Symmetry: A Study of William Blake* (1947; Princeton, NJ: Princeton University Press, 1974).

—— *The Great Code: The Bible and Literature* (1981; London: Routledge and Kegan Paul, 1982).

—— 'History and Myth in the Bible', in Angus Fletcher, ed., *The Literature of Fact* (New York: Columbia University Press, 1976), 1–19.

—— *A Study of English Romanticism* (Brighton: Harvester Press, 1968).

GAY, PETER, *The Enlightenment: An Interpretation*, i. *The Rise of Modern Paganism* (New York: Random House, 1966).

GIBBON, EDWARD, *Gibbon on Christianity* [Chapters 15 and 16 of *The Decline and Fall of the Roman Empire*, 1776–88], ed. J. M. Robertson (London: Watts, 1930).

GILFILLAN, GEORGE, 'Percy Bysshe Shelley', in *A Gallery of Literary Portraits*, 1st ser. (Edinburgh, 1845), 71–105.

GINGERICH, SOLOMON F., 'Shelley's Doctrine of Necessity *versus* Christianity', *PMLA*, 33 (1918), 444–73.

GISBORNE, MARIA, and WILLIAMS, EDWARD, *Maria Gisborne and Edward Williams: Shelley's Friends, their Journals and Letters*, ed. Frederick L. Jones (Norman, Okla.: University of Oklahoma Press, 1951).

GODWIN, WILLIAM, *Enquiry concerning Political Justice and its Influence on Morals and Happiness* (1798), 3rd edn., ed. F. E. L. Priestley (3 vols.; facs. repr. Toronto: University of Toronto Press, 1946).

—— [Edward Baldwin], *The Pantheon: or, Ancient History of the Gods of Greece and Rome* (London, 1806).

GOETHE, JOHANN WOLFGANG VON, *Goethe's Faust*, trans. and ed. Walter Kaufmann (1961; Garden City, NY: Anchor, Doubleday, 1963).

GUTTELING, JOHANNA F. C., 'Demogorgon in Shelley's *Prometheus Unbound*', *Neophilologus*, 9 (1924), 283–5.

HALL, SPENCER, 'Power and the Poet: Religious Mythmaking in Shelley's "Hymn to Intellectual Beauty"', *K–SJ*, 32 (1983), 123–49.

HAMILTON, PAUL, *Coleridge's Poetics* (Oxford: Basil Blackwell, 1983).

HANSON, PAUL, 'The Phenomenon of Apocalyptic in Israel: Its Background and Setting', in *The Dawn of Apocalyptic: The Historical and Sociological Roots of Jewish Apocalyptic Eschatology* (1975; Philadelphia: Fortress Press, 1979), 1–31.

HARDING, ANTHONY JOHN, *Coleridge and the Inspired Word* (Kingston and Montreal: McGill–Queens University Press, 1985).

HARRISON, J. F. C., *The Second Coming: Popular Millenarianism, 1780–1850* (London: Routledge and Kegan Paul, 1979).

HARTLEY, DAVID, *Observations on Man, his Frame, his Duty, and his Expectations* (2 vols.; 1749), ed. T. L. Huguelet (facs. repr. Gainesville, Fla.: Scholar's Facsimiles and Reprints, 1966).

HAZLITT, WILLIAM, *The Complete Works of William Hazlitt*, ed. P. P. Howe (21 vols.; London: Dent, 1930–4).

HENDRIX, RICHARD, 'The Necessity of Response: How Shelley's Radical Poetry Works', *K–SJ*, 27 (1978), 45–69.

HENN, T. R., *The Bible as Literature* (London: Lutterworth, 1970).

HERMES TRISMEGISTUS, *The Divine Pymander*, trans. John Everard (1650; London, 1657).

HERVEY, JAMES, 'Reflections on a Flower Garden', in *Meditations and Contemplations* (1748; Edinburgh, 1802), 119–92.

HICKS, ARTHUR C., 'The Place of Christianity in Shelley's Thought' (Ph. D. diss., Stanford University, 1932).

HILDEBRAND. WILLIAM H., 'Naming-Day in Asia's Vale', *K–SJ*, 32 (1983), 190–203.

HIPPOLYTUS, *The Refutation of all Heresies*, trans. J. H. MacMahon, *The Ante-Nicene Fathers: Translations of the Writings of the Fathers down to A.D. 325*, ed. Alexander Roberts and James Donaldson, rev. A. C. Coxe (10 vols., 1885–96; Grand Rapids, Mich.: Eerdmans, 1971–8), v. 9–153.

HOAGWOOD, TERENCE A., *Prophecy and the Philosophy of Mind: Traditions of Blake and Shelley* (Tuscaloosa, Ala.: University of Alabama Press, 1985).

HOBBES, THOMAS, *Leviathan; or the Matter, Form, and Power of a Commonwealth, Ecclesiastical and Civil* (1651), *The English Works of Thomas Hobbes*, vol. 3, ed. William Molesworth (11 vols.; 1839–45; London: Scientia Aalen, 1962).

HOGG, JAMES, *The Private Memoirs and Confessions of a Justified Sinner* (1824), ed. John Carey (London: Oxford University Press, 1969).

HOGG, THOMAS JEFFERSON, *The Life of Percy Bysshe Shelley* (1858), in *The Life of Percy Bysshe Shelley*, ed. Humbert Wolfe (2 vols.; London: Dent, 1933), i–ii. 158.

HOGLE, JERROLD, *Shelley's Process: Radical Transference and the Development of His Major Works* (New York and Oxford: Oxford University Press, 1988).

HOLBACH, BARON PAUL HENRI DIETRICH D', *Le Christianisme dévoilé, ou, Examen des principes et des effets de la religion chrétienne* (London, 1767).

—— *Histoire critique de Jésus-Christ, ou, Analysis raisonnée des Evangiles* (Amsterdam, c.1770).

—— *Système de la nature, ou Des lois du monde physique et du monde moral* (2 pts.; London [pirated in Amsterdam], 1770).

HOLMES, RICHARD, *Shelley: The Pursuit* (1974; London: Quartet Books, 1976).

The Holy Bible Conteyning the Old Testament and the New (Authorized Version; London, 1639).

The Holy Bible (Authorized Version; New York: Oxford University Press, 1945).

HUGHES, A. M. D., 'The Theology of Shelley' [Warton Lecture on English Poetry], *Proceedings of the British Academy*, 24 (1938), 191–203 (repr. London: Oxford University Press, 1939).

HUME, DAVID, *Enquiries concerning Human Understanding and concerning the Principles of Morals* (1777), ed. L. A. Selby-Bigge, 3rd edn. (1975; Oxford: Clarendon Press, 1979).

—— *The Natural History of Religion* and *Dialogues concerning Natural Religion* (1757, 1779), ed. Wayne Colver and J. V. Price (Oxford: Clarendon Press, 1976).

—— *A Treatise of Human Nature: Being an Attempt to Introduce the Experimental Method of Reasoning into Moral Subjects* (1739–40), ed. L. A. Selby-Bigge, 2nd edn., rev. P. H. Nidditch (1978; Oxford: Clarendon Press, 1981).

HUNT, LEIGH, 'Mr Shelley', in *Lord Byron and Some of his Contemporaries: With Recollections of the Author's Life and of his Visit to Italy*, 2nd edn. (2 vols.; London, 1828), i. 294–406.

—— *The Religion of the Heart; A Manual of Faith and Study* (London, 1853).

An Illustration of the Holy Scriptures, by Notes and Explications on the Old and New Testament, 6th edn. (London, 1759).

IRENAEUS, *Irenaeus against Heresies*, trans. Alexander Roberts and W. H. Rambaut, in *The Ante-Nicene Fathers: Translations of the Writings of the Fathers down to A.D. 325*, ed. Alexander Roberts and James Donaldson, rev. A. C. Coxe (10 vols., 1885–96; Grand Rapids, Mich.: Eerdmans, 1971–8), i. 315–567.

ISER, WOLFGANG, *The Act of Reading: A Theory of Aesthetic Response* (1976), trans. David Wilson (London: Routledge and Kegan Paul, 1978).

JEFFREY, LLOYD N., 'Shelley's "Plumèd Insects Swift and Free"', *K–SJ*, 25 (1976), 103–21.

JENYNS, SOAME, *A View of the Internal Evidence of the Christian Religion* (London, 1776).

JONAS, HANS, *The Gnostic Religion: The Message of the Alien God and the Beginnings of Christianity*, 2nd edn. (1963; Boston: Beacon, 1970).

—— 'The Soul in Gnosticism and Plotinus', in *Philosophical Essays: From Ancient Creed to Technological Man* (Englewood Cliffs, NJ: Prentice-Hall, 1974), 324–34.

JONES, CLAUDE, 'Christ a Fury?', *Modern Language Notes*, 50 (1935), 41.

JONES, FREDERICK L., 'Shelley and Milton', *Studies in Philology*, 49 (1952), 488–519.

JONES, SIR WILLIAM, 'The Palace of Fortune', in *The Poetical Works of Sir William Jones* (2 vols.; London, 1810), ii. 147–66.

KANT, IMMANUEL, *Immanuel Kant's Critique of Pure Reason* (1781, 1787), trans. N. K. Smith (1929; London: Macmillan, 1982).

KAPSTEIN, ISRAEL, 'The Meaning of Shelley's "Mont Blanc"', *PMLA*, 62 (1947), 1046–60.

KEATS, JOHN, *The Letters of John Keats: 1814–21*, ed. Hyder Rollins (2 vols.; Cambridge, Mass.: Harvard University Press, 1958).

KELLEY, THERESA, 'Proteus and Romantic Allegory', *Journal of English Literary History*, 49 (1982), 623–52.

KERMODE, FRANK, *The Genesis of Secrecy: On the Interpretation of Narrative* (Cambridge, Mass.: Harvard University Press, 1979).

KERNAHAN, COULSON, 'The Cross Leads Generations On', *London Quarterly and Holborn Review*, 6th ser., 6/162 (1937), 456–76.

KINNAIRD, JOHN, ' "But for such faith": A Controversial Phrase in Shelley's "Mont Blanc" ', *Notes and Queries*, NS 15 (1968), 332–34.

KNIGHT, G. WILSON, *The Christian Renaissance*, rev. edn. (London: Methuen, 1962).

—— 'The Naked Seraph: An Essay on Shelley', in *The Starlit Dome: Studies in the Poetry of Vision* (1941; London: Methuen, 1959), 179–257.

KORSHIN, PAUL J., *Typologies in England, 1650–1820* (Princeton, NJ: Princeton University Press, 1982).

KOSZUL, A. H. (ed.), *Shelley's Prose in the Bodleian Manuscripts* (London: Henry Frowde, 1910).

KUHN, ALBERT, 'English Deism and the Development of Romantic Mythological Syncretism', *PMLA*, 71 (1956), 1094–1116.

LANDY, FRANCIS, 'The Song of Songs', in Robert Alter and Frank Kermode, eds., *The Literary Guide to the Bible* (Cambridge, Mass.: Belknap, Harvard University Press, 1987), 305–19.

LESLIE, CHARLES, *A Short and Easy Method with the Deists; Wherein the Certainty of the Christian Religion is Demonstrated by Infallible Proof, from Four Rules, which are Incompatible to any Imposture that ever has been, or can possibly be* (1698; London, 1799).

LEWIS, C. S., 'The Literary Impact of the Authorised Version', in *They Asked for a Paper: Papers and Addresses* (London: Geoffrey Bles, 1962), 26–50.

—— *A Preface to* Paradise Lost*: Being the Ballard Matthews Lectures* (1942; Oxford: Oxford University Press, 1979).

—— 'Shelley, Dryden, and Mr. Eliot', in *Rehabilitations: And Other Essays* (London: Oxford University Press, 1939), 1–34.

LEWIS, MATTHEW G., *The Monk: A Romance* (3 vols.; London, 1796).

LIDDELL, H. G., and SCOTT, ROBERT, *A Greek–English Lexicon*, 9th edn., rev. H. S. Jones (1940; Oxford: Clarendon Press, 1953).

LOCKE, JOHN, *An Essay concerning Human Understanding*, 4th edn. (1700), ed. P. H. Nidditch (Oxford: Clarendon Press, 1979).

LOOPER, TRAVIS, *Byron and the Bible: A Compendium of Biblical Usage in the Poetry of Lord Byron* (Metuchen, NJ: Scarecrow Press, 1978).

LOWER, MARK A., 'The Shelleys', in *The Worthies of Sussex* (Lewes, Sussex, 1865), 128–31.

LOWTH, ROBERT, *Lectures on the Sacred Poetry of the Hebrews* (1753), trans. G. Gregory (2 vols.; London, 1787).

Luca, V. A. de, 'The Style of Millennial Announcement in *Prometheus Unbound*', *K–SJ*, 28 (1979), 78–101.

McGann, Jerome J., 'The Secrets of an Elder Day: Shelley after *Hellas*', *K–SJ*, 15 (1966), 25–41; repr. in R. B. Woodings, ed., *Shelley: Modern Judgements* (Nashville, Tenn.: Aurora, 1970), 253–71.

—— 'Shelley's Veils: A Thousand Images of Loveliness', in W. Paul Elledge and Richard L. Hoffman, eds., *Romantic and Victorian: Studies in Memory of William H. Marshall* (Cranbury, NJ: Associated University Presses, 1971), 198–218.

McNiece, Gerald, *Shelley and the Revolutionary Idea* (Cambridge, Mass.: Harvard University Press, 1969).

McTaggart, William, *England in 1819: Church, State and Poverty; a Study Textual and Historical of 'A Ballad', by Shelley* (London: Keats–Shelley Memorial Association, 1970).

Man, Paul de, 'Shelley Disfigured', in Harold Bloom, Paul de Man, Jacques Derrida, Geoffrey Hartman, and J. Hillis Miller, *Deconstruction and Criticism* (London: Routledge and Kegan Paul, 1979), 39–73.

Manning, Roger, 'Richard Shelley of Worminghurst and the English Catholic Petition for Toleration of 1585', *Recusant History*, 6/5 (1962), 265–74.

Mason, John, *Self-Knowledge: A Treatise Showing the Nature and Benefit of that Important Science, and the Way to Attain it* (1745; London, 1810).

Matthews, G. M., 'On Shelley's "The Triumph of Life"', *Studia Neophilologica*, 34 (1962), 104–34.

—— 'Percy Bysshe Shelley', in George Watson, ed., *The New Cambridge Bibliography of English Literature* (5 vols.; Cambridge: Cambridge University Press, 1969–77), iii. 309–43.

Medwin, Thomas, *The Life of Percy Bysshe Shelley* (1847), ed. H. B. Forman, rev. edn. (London: Oxford University Press, 1913).

Milton, John, *The Poems of John Milton*, ed. John Carey and Alistair Fowler (1968; London and New York: Longman, 1980).

Moor, Edward, *The Hindu Pantheon* (London, 1810).

Morgan, Lady [Sydney Owenson], *The Missionary: An Indian Tale*, 3rd edn. (3 vols.; London, 1811).

Morse, David, 'From Protestantism to Romanticism', in *Perspectives on Romanticism: A Transformational Analysis* (London: Macmillan, 1981), 102–78.

Mosheim, John Lawrence, *An Ecclesiastical History, Antient and Modern* (c.1755), trans. Archibald MacLaine (6 vols.; c.1765; London, 1803).

Murray, E. B., 'The Dating and Composition of Shelley's *The Assassins*', *K–SJ*, 34 (1985), 14–17.

—— 'Gnashing and Wailing in *Prometheus Unbound*', *K–SJ*, 24 (1975), 17–20.

The Nag Hammadi Library, trans. Members of the Coptic Gnostic Library Project of the Institute for Antiquity and Christianity, ed. James Robinson, 3rd edn. (San Francisco: Harper and Row, 1988).

NEWLYN, LUCY, *Coleridge, Wordsworth, and the Language of Allusion* (Oxford: Clarendon Press, 1986).

NEWTON, JOHN FRANK, *The Return to Nature, or, A Defence of the Vegetable Regimen* (London, 1811).

NOTOPOULOS, JAMES A., *The Platonism of Shelley: A Study of Platonism and the Poetic Mind* (Durham, NC: Duke University Press, 1949).

NYGREN, ANDERS, *Agape and Eros*, trans. Philip S. Watson (1932, 1939; London: SPCK, 1982).

The Old Testament Pseudepigrapha, ed. James H. Charlesworth (2 vols.; Garden City, NY: Doubleday, 1983, 1985).

O'NEILL, MICHAEL, 'Fictions, Visionary Rhyme and Human Interest: A Reading of Shelley's "The Witch of Atlas"', *K–SR*, no. 2 (1987), 105–33.

ORSINI, G. N. G., *Coleridge and German Idealism: A Study in the History of Philosophy with Unpublished Materials from Coleridge's Manuscripts* (Carbondale, Ill.: Southern Illinois University Press, 1969).

OWEN, J. H., 'The Stricken Deer and the Emblem Tradition', *Bulletin of the New York Public Library*, 75 (1971), 66–78.

PAINE, THOMAS, *The Complete Writings of Thomas Paine*, ed. Philip S. Foner (2 vols.; New York: Citadel Press, 1945).

PALEY, WILLIAM, *Natural Theology: or, Evidences of the Existence and Attributes of the Deity, Collected from the Appearances of Nature* (1802; London, 1803).

—— *A View of the Evidences of Christianity* (2 vols.; 1794; London, 1807).

PARACELSUS [PHILIPPUS AUREOLUS THEOPHRASTUS], *Of the Nature of Things* (*c.*1537), trans. J. French (London, 1650).

PARK, ROY, *Hazlitt and the Spirit of the Age: Abstraction and Critical Theory* (Oxford: Clarendon Press, 1971).

PARKER, A. A., *The Theology of the Devil in the Drama of Calderón* (London: Blackfriars, 1958).

PARSONS, COLEMAN, 'Shelley's Prayer to the West Wind', *K–SJ*, 11 (1962), 31–7.

PEACOCK, THOMAS LOVE, *Memoirs of Shelley* (1875), in *The Life of Percy Bysshe Shelley*, ed. Humbert Wolfe (2 vols.; London: Dent, 1933), ii. 303–463.

—— *The Works of Thomas Love Peacock*, ed. H. F. B. Brett-Smith and C. E. Jones (10 vols.; London: Constable, 1924–34).

PECK, WALTER EDWIN, *Shelley: His Life and Work* (2 vols.; London: Benn, 1927).

PERRIN, NORMAN, *The Kingdom of God in the Teaching of Jesus* (London: SCM Press, 1963).

PETRARCA, FRANCESCO, 'To his brother Gherardo', 2 Dec. 1348, in *Petrarch: The First Modern Scholar and Man of Letters*, trans. and ed. J. H. Robinson and H. W. Rolfe (New York: 1898), 261–75.

—— *Tryumphes of Fraunces Petrarcke*, trans. Lord Morley (*c.*1553), ed. D. D. Carnicelli (Cambridge, Mass.: Harvard University Press, 1971).

PLATIZKY, ROGER, 'Shelley's "Mont Blanc"', *Explicator*, 48 (1990), 183–5.

POTTLE, FREDERICK, 'The Case of Shelley', *PMLA*, 67 (1952), 589–608; repr. in

Meyer H. Abrams, ed., *English Romantic Poets: Modern Essays in Criticism* (1960; New York and Oxford: Oxford University Press, 1973), 289–306.

—— 'Wordsworth in the Present Day', in David Thorburn and Geoffrey Hartman, eds., *Romanticism: Vistas, Instances, Continuities* (Ithaca, NY: Cornell University Press, 1973), 115–33.

PRICE, RICHARD, 'On Providence', in *Four Dissertations* (London, 1768), 3–194.

PRICKETT, STEPHEN (ed.), 'The Religious Context', in *The Romantics* (London: Methuen, 1981), 115–63.

PRIESTLEY, JOSEPH, *The Doctrine of Philosophical Necessity Illustrated; Being an Appendix to the* Disquisitions Relating to Matter and Spirit (London, 1777).

—— and PRICE, RICHARD, 'Of the Doctrine of Necessity', in *A Free Discussion of the Doctrines of Materialism and Philosophical Necessity; in A Correspondence between Dr. Price and Dr. Priestley* (London, 1778), 127–417.

PULOS, CHRISTOS, *The Deep Truth: A Study of Shelley's Scepticism* (Lincoln, Nebr.: University of Nebraska Press, 1954).

QUATREMÈRE, ETIENNE-MARC, 'Notice historique sur les Ismaëliens', *Mines de l'Orient*, 4 (1814), 339–76.

QUELL, GOTTFRIED, '*ἀγαπάω*', in *Theological Dictionary of the New Testament*, ed. Gerhard Kittel and Gerhard Friedrich, trans. G. W. Bromiley (10 vols.; Grand Rapids, Mich.: Eerdmans, 1964–76), i. 21–35.

QUILLER-COUCH, SIR ARTHUR, 'On Reading the Bible', in *Cambridge Lectures* (1943; London: Dent, 1948), 59–90.

QUINT, DAVID, 'Representation and Ideology in *The Triumph of Life*', *Studies in English Literature, 1500–1900*, 18 (1978), 639–57.

RABEN, JOSEPH, 'A Computer-Aided Study of Literary Influence: Milton to Shelley', in J. B. Bessinger, jun., Stephen Parrish, and Harry Arader, eds., *Literary Data Processing Conference Proceedings* (New York: IBM, 1964), 230–74.

RAD, GERHARD VON, *The Message of the Prophets* (1957, 1960), trans. D. M. G. Stalker (London: SCM Press, 1968).

READ, HERBERT, 'In Defence of Shelley', in *In Defence of Shelley and Other Essays* (London: William Heinemann, 1936), 3–86; rev. repr. in *The True Voice of Feeling: Studies in English Romantic Poetry* (London: Faber and Faber, 1968), 212–87.

REDPATH, THEODORE, 'Percy Bysshe Shelley', in *The Young Romantics and Critical Opinion, 1807–1824: Poetry of Byron, Shelley, and Keats as Seen by their Contemporary Critics* (London: Harrap, 1973), 304–417.

REIMAN, DONALD H., *Intervals of Inspiration: The Skeptical Tradition and the Psychology of Romanticism* (Greenwood, Fla.: Penkevill, 1988).

—— *Percy Bysshe Shelley* (New York: St Martin's Press, 1969).

—— *Romantic Texts and Contexts* (Columbia, Mo.: University of Missouri Press, 1987).

—— *Shelley's 'The Triumph of Life': A Critical Study* (1965; Urbana, Ill.: University of Illinois Press, 1966).

—— 'Structure, Symbol, and Theme in "Lines Written among the Euganean Hills"', *PMLA*, 77 (1962), 404–13; repr. in *SPP*, 579–96.

RIEGER, JAMES, *The Mutiny Within: The Heresies of Percy Bysshe Shelley* (New York: George Braziller, 1967).

ROBINSON, AUDREY M., *Shelley: His Links with Horsham and Warnham* (Horsham, Sussex: The Horsham Society, 1983).

ROGERS, NEVILLE, *Shelley at Work: A Critical Inquiry*, 2nd edn. (Oxford: Clarendon Press, 1967).

ROSSETTI, WILLIAM M., ed., *Adonais*, 2nd edn., rev. A. O. Prickard (London: Oxford University Press, 1918).

ROSTON, MURRAY, *Prophet and Poet: The Bible and the Growth of Romanticism* (London: Faber and Faber, 1965).

ROUSSEAU, JEAN-JACQUES, *Julie, ou la nouvelle Héloïse* (1761), in *Œuvres complètes de Jean-Jacques Rousseau*, ed. Bernard Gagnebin and Marcel Raymond (4 vols.; Paris: Gallimard, 1959–69), ii. 1–793.

RUDOLF, KURT, *Gnosis: The Nature and History of an Ancient Religion* (1977), trans. P. W. Coxon and K. H. Kuhn, ed. R. McLachlan Wilson (Edinburgh: T. and T. Clark, 1983).

RYKEN, LELAND, *How to Read the Bible as Literature* (Grand Rapids, Mich.: Academie Books, 1984).

SCHMIDT, KARL, '$\beta\alpha\sigma\iota\lambda\epsilon\acute{\iota}\alpha$', in *Theological Dictionary of the New Testament*, ed. Gerhard Kittel and Gerhard Friedrich, trans. G. W. Bromiley (10 vols.; Grand Rapids, Mich.: Eerdmans, 1964–76), i. 579–93.

SCHULZE, EARL J., *Shelley's Theory of Poetry: A Reappraisal* (The Hague: Mouton, 1966).

SEWELL, JAMES, 'Registrum Custodum, Sociorum, et Scholarium, Collegii Nov.', Archives of New College, Oxford, 1850–8.

SHAKESPEARE, WILLIAM, *The Complete Works of Shakespeare*, ed. Hardin Craig (1951; Glenview, Ill.: Scott, Foresman and Co., 1961).

SHAW, GEORGE BERNARD, 'Shaming the Devil about Shelley', *Albemarle*, 2/3 (1892), 91–8.

SHELLEY, BRYAN, 'The Interpreting Angel: Shelley and Scripture' (D. Phil. thesis, Oxford University, 1986).

—— 'The Interpreting Angel in "The Triumph of Life"', *Review of English Studies*, NS 39/155 (1988), 386–99.

—— Review of *Against the Protestant Gnostics*, by Philip J. Lee, *World*, 3/12 (1988), 14.

—— 'The Synthetic Imagination: Shelley and Associationism', *The Wordsworth Circle*, 14/1 (1983), 68–73.

SHELLEY, MARY, *The Journals of Mary Shelley: 1814–1844*, ed. Paula R. Feldman and Diana Scott-Kilvert (2 vols.; Oxford: Clarendon Press, 1987).

SHELLEY, PERCY BYSSHE, Bodleian MS Shelley e. 4.

—— Bodleian MS Shelley adds. c. 4.

—— Bodleian MS Shelley adds. e. 8.

—— Bodleian MS Shelley adds. e. 14.

—— Bodleian MS Shelley adds. e. 9.

—— Bodleian MS Shelley adds. e. 19.

—— *The Bodleian Shelley Manuscripts*, gen. ed. Donald H. Reiman (13 vols. to date; New York and London: Garland, 1986–92).

—— *The Complete Poetical Works of Percy Bysshe Shelley*, ed. Neville Rogers (2 of 4 projected volumes; Oxford: Clarendon Press, 1972, 1975).

—— *The Complete Works of Percy Bysshe Shelley* [The Julian Edition], ed. Roger Ingpen and Walter E. Peck (10 vols.; London: Benn, 1926–30).

—— *The Esdaile Notebook: A Facsimile of the Holograph Copybook*, ed. Donald H. Reiman; *Manuscripts of the Younger Romantics: Shelley*, vol. 1 (New York: Garland, 1985).

—— *The Harvard Shelley Poetic Manuscripts*, ed. Donald H. Reiman; *The Manuscripts of the Younger Romantics: Shelley*, vol. 5 (New York: Garland, 1991).

—— *The Letters of Percy Bysshe Shelley*, ed. Frederick L. Jones (2 vols.; Oxford: Clarendon Press, 1964).

—— *The Mask of Anarchy Draft Notebook: A Facsimile of Huntington MS. HM 2177*, ed. Mary A. Quinn; *The Manuscripts of the Younger Romantics: Shelley*, vol. 4 (New York: Garland, 1990).

—— *The Poems of Shelley*, ed. Geoffrey Matthews and Kelvin Everest (1 vol. to date; London and New York: Longman, 1989).

—— *The Prose Works of Percy Bysshe Shelley*, ed. E. B. Murray (1 vol. to date; Oxford: Oxford University Press, 1993).

—— *Shelley: Poetical Works*, ed. Thomas Hutchinson, 2nd edn. rev. G. M. Matthews (Oxford: Oxford University Press, 1970).

—— *Shelley and his Circle, 1773–1822* [The Carl H. Pforzheimer Library], ed. Kenneth Neill Cameron (vols. 1–4) and Donald H. Reiman (vols. 5–8) (8 vols. to date; Cambridge, Mass.: Harvard University Press, 1961–86).

—— *Shelley's Poetry and Prose*, ed. Donald H. Reiman and Sharon B. Powers (New York: Norton, 1977).

—— *Shelley's Prose, or The Trumpet of a Prophecy*, ed. David Lee Clark (1954; Albuquerque, N. Mex.: University of New Mexico Press, 1966).

—— 'Untitled Fragment on Zionism', in *The Shelley Memorial Volume*, ed. the English Club at the Imperial University of Tokyo (Tokyo: University of Tokyo, 1922), 188–91.

SIDNEY, PHILIP, *A Defence of Poetry* (*c.*1580), in *Miscellaneous Prose of Sir Philip Sidney*, ed. Katherine Duncan-Jones and Jan van Dorsten (Oxford: Clarendon Press, 1973), 59–121.

SIEPER, ERNST, 'Spuren ophitisch-gnostischer Einflüsse in den Dichtungen Shelleys', *Archiv für das Studium der neueren Sprachen und Literaturen* [*Herrigs Archiv*], 62 (1908), 315–31.

SIMS, JAMES, *The Bible in Milton's Epics* (Gainesville, Fla.: University of Florida Press, 1962).

SISMONDI, J. C. L. SIMONDE DE, 'Conquête de Pise par les Florentins', *Histoire des républiques italiennes du Moyen Âge* (16 vols.; Paris, 1809–18), viii. 137–88.

SMITH, JOHN, 'The True Way or Method of Attaining to Divine Knowledge' (1660), in C. A. Patrides, ed., *The Cambridge Platonists* (Cambridge: Cambridge University Press, 1969), 128–44.

SMITH, JONATHAN Z., 'Wisdom and Apocalyptic', in B. A. Pearson, ed., *Religious Syncretism in Antiquity* (Missoula, Mont.: Scholars Press, 1975), 131–56; repr. in Paul, D. Hanson, ed., *Visionaries and their Apocalypses* (London: SPCK, 1983), 101–20.

SOUTHEY, ROBERT, *The Poems of Robert Southey*, ed. Maurice Fitzgerald (London: Oxford University Press, 1909).

SPENSER, EDMUND, *The Poetical Works of Edmund Spenser*, ed. J. C. Smith and E. de Selincourt (London: Oxford University Press, 1912).

SPERRY, STUART, 'Necessity and the Role of the Hero in Shelley's *Prometheus Unbound*', *PMLA*, 96 (1981), 242–54.

SPINOZA, BENEDICT DE, *A Theologico-Political Treatise* (1670), trans. R. H. M. Elwes (1883; New York: Dover, 1951).

STAUFFER, ETHELBERT, 'ἀγαπάω', in *Theological Dictionary of the New Testament*, ed. Gerhard Kittel and Gerhard Friedrich, trans. G. W. Bromiley (10 vols.; Grand Rapids, Mich.: Eerdmans, 1964–76), i. 35–55.

STEPHEN, LESLIE, *History of English Thought in the Eighteenth Century* (1876), 3rd edn. (2 vols.; 1902; London: Harbinger, Harcourt, 1962).

SUNSTEIN, EMILY, 'Shelley's Answer to Leslie's *Short and Easy Method with the Deists* and Mary Shelley's Answer, "The Necessity of a Belief in the Heathen Mythology to a Christian"', *K–SMB*, no. 32 (1981), 49–54.

TERTULLIAN, *The Prescription against Heretics*, trans. Peter Holmes, in *The Ante-Nicene Fathers: Translations of the Writings of the Fathers down to A.D. 325*, ed. Alexander Roberts and James Donaldson, rev. A. C. Coxe (10 vols., 1885–96; Grand Rapids, Mich.: Eerdmans, 1971–8), iii. 243–65.

TOKOO, TATSUO, *The Contents of Shelley's Notebooks in the Bodleian Library* (offprint of *Humanities: Bulletin of the Faculty of Letters*), Kyoto Prefectural University, 36 (1984).

—— *Index to the Contents of Shelley's Notebooks and Other Literary MSS, Mainly in the Bodleian Library* (offprint of *Humanities: Bulletin of the Faculty of Letters*), Kyoto Prefectural University, 34 (1982).

TRELAWNY, EDWARD, *Recollections of the Last Days of Shelley and Byron* (1858), in *The Life of Percy Bysshe Shelley*, ed. Humbert Wolfe (2 vols.; London: Dent, 1933), ii. 159–301.

TUVESON, ERNEST LEE, *The Avatars of Thrice Great Hermes: An Approach to Romanticism* (Lewisburg, Pa., London, and Toronto: Associated University Presses, 1982).

VOEGELIN, ERIC, *From Enlightenment to Revolution*, ed. John Hallowell (Durham, NC: Duke University Press, 1975).

—— *Science, Politics, and Gnosticism: Two Essays* (1959), trans. W. Fitzpatrick and E. Voegelin (Chicago: Gateway, Regnery, 1968).

VOISINE, JACQUES, 'Childe Harold et autres pèlerins', in *J.-J. Rousseau en Angleterre a l'époque romantique: Les Écrits autobiographiques et la légende* (Paris: Didier, 1956), 259–343.

VOLNEY, CONSTANTIN, COMTE DE, *The Ruins, or a Survey of the Revolutions of Empires* (1791), trans. anon., 5th edn. (London, 1811).

VOLTAIRE [FRANÇOIS MARIE AROUET], *La Bible enfin expliquée* (Geneva, 1776).

WALKER, CONSTANCE, 'The Urn of Bitter Prophecy: Antithetical Patterns in Hellas', *K–SMB*, no. 33 (1982), 36–48.

WASSERMAN, EARL REEVES, '"Mont Blanc"', in *The Subtler Language: Critical Readings of Neoclassic and Romantic Poems* (Baltimore: Johns Hopkins University Press, 1959), 189–240; repr. of pp. 198–240 in George Ridenour, ed., *Shelley: A Collection of Critical Essays* (Englewood Cliffs, NJ: Prentice-Hall, 1965), 69–102.

—— *Shelley: A Critical Reading* (1971; Baltimore: Johns Hopkins University Press, 1977).

WATSON, RICHARD, *An Apology for the Bible, in a Series of Letters Addressed to Thomas Paine* (Dublin, 1796).

WEAVER, BENNETT, 'Shelley's *Biblical Extracts*: A Lost Book', *Papers of the Michigan Academy of Sciences, Arts, and Letters*, 20 (1934), 523–38.

—— *Toward the Understanding of Shelley* (1932; New York: Octagon, 1966).

WEBB, TIMOTHY, '"The Avalanche of Ages": Shelley's Defence of Atheism and *Prometheus Unbound*', *K–SMB*, no. 35 (1984), 1–39.

—— *Shelley: A Voice not Understood* (Manchester: Manchester University Press, 1977).

—— (ed.), *Percy Bysshe Shelley: Selected Poems* (London: Dent, 1977).

WERBLOWSKY, R. J. Z., *Lucifer and Prometheus: A Study of Milton's Satan* (London: Routledge and Kegan Paul, 1952).

WHITE, NEWMAN IVEY, *Shelley* (2 vols.; 1940; New York: Knopf, 1947).

WILFORD, FRANCIS, 'On Mount Caucasus', *Asiatick Researches* [Calcutta edn.], 6 (1799), 455–534.

WILKIE, BRIAN, 'Shelley: "Holy and Heroic Verse"', in *Romantic Poets and Epic Tradition* (Madison and Milwaukee, Wis.: University of Wisconsin Press, 1965), 112–44.

WILLEY, BASIL, *The Eighteenth Century Background: Studies on the Idea of Nature in the Thought of the Period* (1940; London: Chatto and Windus, 1946).

WILLIAMS, JAMES, 'Proverbs and Ecclesiastes', in Robert Alter and Frank Kermode, eds., *The Literary Guide to the Bible* (Cambridge, Mass.: Belknap, Harvard University Press, 1987), 263–82.

WILSON, MILTON, *Shelley's Later Poetry: A Study of his Prophetic Imagination* (1957; New York: Columbia University Press, 1961).

WITTREICH, JOSEPH A., Jun., *The Romantics on Milton: Formal Essays and Critical Asides* (Cleveland: Press of Case Western Reserve University, 1970).

—— 'The "Satanism" of Blake and Shelley Reconsidered', *Studies in Philology*, 65 (1968), 816–33.

WOODMAN, ROSS GREIG, *The Apocalyptic Vision in the Poetry of Shelley* (Toronto: University of Toronto Press, 1964).

YEATS, WILLIAM BUTLER, 'The Philosophy of Shelley's Poetry' (1900), in *Essays and Introductions* (1961; New York: Collier, 1973), 65–95.

—— *'Prometheus Unbound'* (1932), in *Essays and Introductions* (1961; New York: Collier, 1973), 419–25.

Index